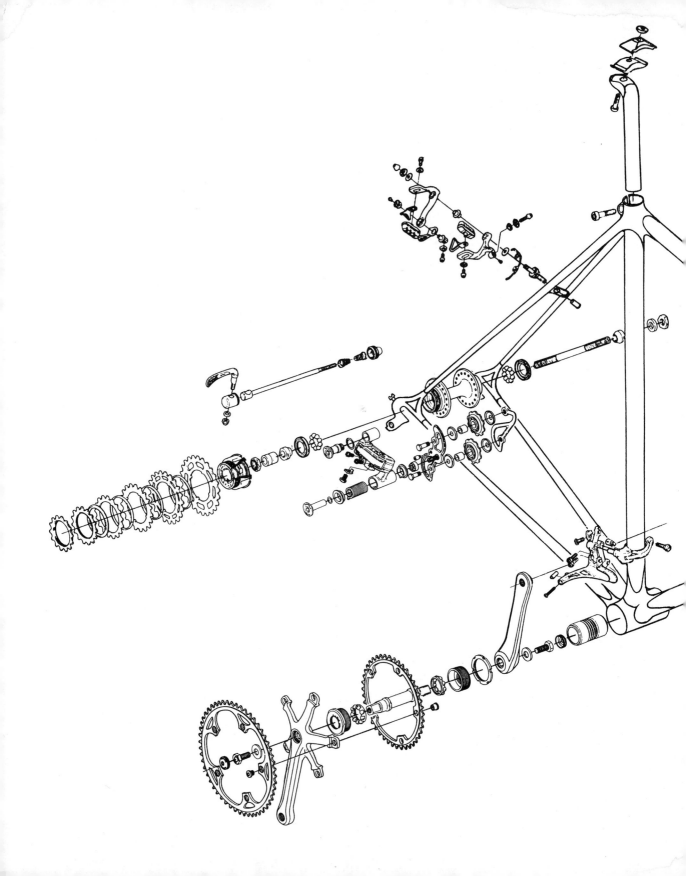

Bicycle
Technology

Understanding,
Selecting
and
Maintaining
the Modern
Bicycle
and its
Components

Rob Van der Plas

Illustrated by the author

Bicycle Books — San Francisco

Copyright _____ © Robert van der Plas, 1991

Printed in the United States of America

Publisher _____ Bicycle Books, Inc.
P.O. Box 2038
Mill Valley, CA 94941
USA

Book trade distributors _____ (USA) The Talman Company, New York, NY
(Canada) Raincoast Book Distribution, Vancouver, BC
(UK) Chris Lloyd Sales and Marketing Services, Poole, Dorset

This book appears simultaneously in the Dutch language
with Elmar bv, Rijswijk, The Netherlands.

Cover design _____ Pam van Vliet (Raster bv) and Rob van der Plas

Cover photograph _____ Ton van der Neut

Frontispiece illustration _____ Shimano

Cataloging in Publication Data_____ Van der Plas, Robert, 1938 —
Bicycle Technology, Understanding, selecting and maintaining the modern bicycle. Bibliography: p. Includes index.
1. Bicycles and bicycling — manuals, handbooks, etc.
2. Authorship.
I. Title.

Library of Congress Catalog Card Number 90-80064

ISBN 0-933201-30-3 (Softcover)

As is the case with all books published by Bicycle Books, *Bicycle Technology* is available both in the US and in other English-speaking countries. That makes sense in a market that has become truly international. Unfortunately, there is less unanimity about the English language. Current American usage is adhered to both for spelling and terminology in the book. Consequently, some confusion about the choice of words invariably arises.

Although, for example, most British readers have got used to seeing *centre, tyre, aluminium* and *pedalling* written the American way as *center, tire, aluminum* and *pedaling*, it is not always clear when words vary by more than the spelling alone. Thus, it may not be immediately clear that a *crankset* is the same as a *chainset*, that *drop-outs* are *fork-ends*, or that *gruppo* means *group-set*. On the other hand, I assume that using words like *wrench* instead of *spanner*, and *rag* instead of *cloth*, is clear enough.

Every effort has been made to explain, either by means of labels in the illustrations or otherwise, the terms used in such a way that they are readily understood. Thus, the book should be as useful to British and other readers as it is to the American public. If any serious discrepancies remain, I will be grateful to any reader who points them out, and the first reader to do so for any particular error will receive a free copy of the next (corrected) edition of the book. Address your comments to Bicycle Books, Inc. at the address shown on the copyright page.

Another detail that is particularly important in a technical text is the use of certain units and dimensions. Whereas even the presumably conservative British have converted to international scientific units, most people in the US still feel at ease only with feet and inches, pounds and miles. However, this is hard to keep up in a technical discourse, where less archaic measures must be used to express some of the other (interrelated) dimensions. For that reason, I have chosen to use scientific units throughout. For units that are in the everyday non-technical realm, US equivalents are usually given in parentheses.

The third point relating to the choice of words concerns the use of the masculine form when addressing the reader or when referring to others whose sex is not specified. I am aware that this offends some, and I have seriously considered other options, including repeated use of expressions like *he or she, his or her*, etc. as well as alternate use of the masculine and the feminine forms. However, after critically reading my own and other people's writings using these methods, both I and my (female) publisher have concluded that clarity and reading ease are greater when the masculine form is used consistently; so that is what I have done here — with my apologies to anyone whom it may offend.

Finally, I am aware that facts have a way of getting ahead of the written word. Consequently, some of the things you will read here may no longer be fully applicable by the time the book comes off the press. In other instances the information may even be incorrect — however much verifying and proofreading goes into a book. I will be indebted to anyone who takes the trouble to point out such inaccuracies to me (care of Bicycle Books, at the address shown on the copyright page). As an encouragement, the first person to point out any particular error will receive a complimentary copy of the next (corrected) printing of the book.

The Author

Rob Van der Plas is a professional engineer with a lifelong passion for the bicycle. In addition to being an avid cyclist, he has spent much of the last 15 years involved in bicycle technology and writing about the subject. His articles regularly appear in specialized periodicals on both sides of the Atlantic, and his books have been published in English, Dutch and German originals, as well as in Swedish, Spanish, Italian and Danish translations.

Bicycle Books has published many of his earlier works, including *The Mountain Bike Book*, *The Bicycle Repair Book*, *Mountain Bike Maintenance*, *The Bicycle Racing Guide*, *Roadside Bicycle Repairs* and *The Bicycle Touring Manual*. In the present book, Van der Plas explains the technical mysteries of the bicycle, its design, use and maintenance in terms that are technically correct, yet clear — not only to the experienced engineer or mechanic, but equally to readers without a technical background.

Table of Contents

Chapter 8 99
The Wheels

Chapter 9 121
The Drivetrain

Chapter 1
_ The Bicycle and its Development

The modern bicycle did not come falling out of the sky. A complex and interesting process of technical development has taken place since the German baron Karl Drais zu Sauerbronn (usually referred to as Von Drais) developed his walking machine — the first recognizable predecessor of today's bicycle. Understanding this process of development will help achieve a thorough understanding of the technical aspects that are relevant to today's bicycle.

Only with the knowledge of the historical development and the many systems and concepts that have been integrated in the process, will it be possible to fully appreciate and evaluate the technical developments of today. Conversely, it will facilitate a sober look at concepts that are presented as new, revolutionary improvements. Only too often, these represent non-solutions for problems that are incorrectly perceived. Or they may amount to nothing more than a new version

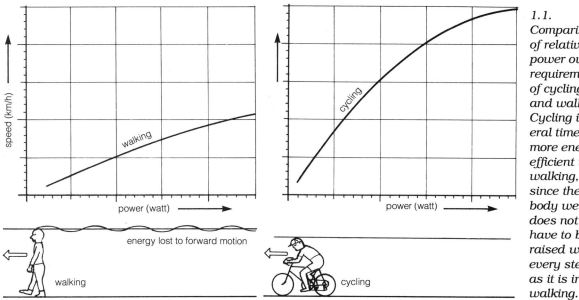

1.1. Comparison of relative power output requirements of cycling and walking. Cycling is several times more energy-efficient than walking, since the body weight does not have to be raised with every step, as it is in walking.

of an old idea that had failed before — usually for sound technical reasons. An informed bicycle rider is not easily fooled.

The laws of physics have not changed in the more than 170 years since the first bicycles appeared. And remarkably, much of what makes for the quality of a bicycle is simply a matter of applied physics. Phenomena ranging from the rolling resistance of the wheels to leverage of the cranks, from the power of the brakes to steering and maneuvering, are all simple mechanical matters that can be understood, calculated and influenced by rational methods. A sober view of these subjects can contribute significantly to guide future development in the right direction, lest we waste time and resources trying to solve problems that don't exist or that are fixed by the laws of nature.

The First Bicycle

The bicycle Von Drais introduced in the year 1817 was a wooden two-wheeled vehicle that weighed some 45 kg (100 lbs). It comprised a wooden beam structure, straddled by the rider, with a fixed wooden rear wheel and a steerable wheel in front, controlled over a tiller mechanism. It was propelled by pushing off with the legs, rolling along between these propulsive pushes.

Accounts according to which a certain De Sivrac was supposed to have invented a similar, though unsteerable, vehicle some 20 years earlier were proven to be fakes that were unfortunately copied from one book to the next. Even Leonardo da Vinci never built (or even drew) the vehicle in which some see a bicycle that was depicted on the back of an original manuscript page. In short, it is safe to say Von Drais was indeed the first person to perceive the idea of the bicycle — two-wheeled, human-powered, single-track propulsion.

Despite the technical and visual development the bicycle has undergone in the years since, the basic concept is clearly present in Von Drais' invention, and what is more, unlike so many other ideas, this one was actually built and used in practice. The essential principle was the transition from an intermittent (walking) to a continuous (rolling) movement, which greatly reduces energy consumption, as depicted in Fig. 1.1.

The most important principles of the modern bicycle were present in this machine: the idea of placing the two wheels in line and steering the front wheel. This allowed balancing the inherently unstable vehicle through a combination of the effect of the inertia of the rolling mass and the direction of the steered wheel. In Chapter 6, *The Steering System*, we will discuss this

1.2. Von Drais' original bicycle of 1817

principle in more detail.

Everything that has changed on the bicycle in the intervening years can be regarded as refinements on the basis of this basic principle, rather than as new developments or even revolutionary concepts. How ingenious it was should be clear from the dramatic improvements it has allowed since its early days, without changing the basic concept. The maximum speed has gone from 15 to 50 km/h (10 and 30 mph, respectively), its weight from 45 to 9 kg (100 and 20 lbs, respectively). These improvements were due to a more refined choice of materials, more precise manufacturing techniques, detail improvements ranging from the use of ball bearings and pneumatic tires, and better road surfaces. Thus the overall efficiency of the machine could be raised from perhaps 40% to something more like 90%, meaning that the modern bicycle transforms some 90 watts of every 100 watt input into propulsive power.

1.3. Michaux' velocipede (approx. 1860). This was the first commercially produced crank-driven bicycle.

Even during Von Drais' lifetime, several ingenious tinkerers attempted to improve on the basic design by introducing some form of continuous mechanical drivetrain to replace the stepping motion. Although Gavin Dalzell (or, according to unsubstantiated speculative interpretation, Kirkpatrick Macmillan) in Scotland built ingenious treadle-driven machines, others simply connected foot-driven cranks to the front wheel. The first commercial application of this method was one introduced and patented by father and son Pierre and Erneste Michaux in France.

The Crank-Driven Bicycle

The Michaux themselves, as well as others, worked continuously on refining the design and its mechanical details. This way, the total weight of a typical bicycle could be halved during the time from 1860 to 1870, due to the use of lighter, but structurally sounder construction techniques, and the rolling resistance could be dramatically reduced through the use of ball bearings.

But even this improved bicycle did not go much faster than its simpler predecessors as long as the wheel was driven directly. After all, the overall speed was determined by the pedaling speed and the circumference of the driven wheel. With a diameter of 70 cm (28"), the typical wheel had a circumference of 2.20 m (7'-4"). Even when pedaling at a rate of 80 rpm, the speed did not exceed 80 x 2.20 = 176m/min or 10.5km/h (6.5mph), and that is about the same speed Von Drais had achieved, even though the crank-driven bicycle required less effort.

1.4. Replica of Gavin Dalzell's treadle-driven machine, often attributed to Kirkpatrick Macmillan.

1.5. High-wheel, or ordinary, bicycle of around 1870.

The Indirectly Driven Bicycle

On the newer, more efficient machine, the rider noticed a distinct excess power, certainly under favorable conditions — level roads with a firm, smooth surface. To exploit this excess power, it would be necessary to improve the drivetrain by increasing the ratio between pedaling speed and riding speed. The easiest way to achieve this was through the use of a larger diameter driven wheel. Made twice as big in diameter, its circumference would also be doubled, allowing twice the speed, even if at the expense of more effort.

This development, as well as several other technical refinements of the bicycle, took place mainly in England, which had become the center of the bicycle industry around 1870, when the French were more preoccupied fighting a war against Germany. Besides increasing the wheel size, many refinements such as tension-spoked wheels, tubular steel frames, as well as brakes and lights were introduced during this time.

Although the *high-wheel* bicycle, with its big driven front wheel, dominated the scene for a period of some 20 years towards the end of the 19th century, it was clearly a dead-end development. Indirect drives were added to overcome the limitation of the wheel size to something compatible with the rider's leg size. But eventually it became clear that there were other methods of power transmission available that provided the same benefits without the cumbersome large diameter wheel, which had severe problems such as toppling the rider over the handlebars when it suddenly stopped — whether intentionally or accidentally.

Lawson had introduced the concept as early as 1873, be it without much initial response: a chain connecting

1.6. Probably the first bicycle driven by means of a chain to the rear wheel: Lawson's 1873 safety bicycle.

the cranks with the rear wheel. Such an indirect drive system connecting the cranks with the driven wheel (which no longer had to be the same one that was steered) allowed an almost infinite ratio between crank speed and wheel speed. Consequently, without making the wheel particularly big, it was possible to achieve quite sensational traveling speeds, as long as the cyclist's power was adequate and conditions were favorable.

Oddly enough, it took until 1885 before the concept of the chain-driven bicycle, as refined by John Kemp Starley on his Rover Safety Bicycle, from which our modern bicycle developed, began to catch on. The term *safety bicycle* referred to the use of small wheels, with the rider so far back that the risk of toppling over was minimized as compared to the conventional high-wheel bicycle. The term *ordinary*, often used to describe the high-wheel, dates from the period 1885 to 1890 — between the introduction of the safety bicycle and the ultimate decline of the high wheel.

Although the American introduction of solid rubber tires around 1870 had provided a significant improvement over the original iron-hooped wooden wheels, and were standard on all high-wheels, the comfort of the safety bicycle was distinctly inferior to that on the high wheel. With the reduced wheel diameter, the shocks to which the road surface irregularities subjected the rider were much greater. This led to poor control over the bike, fatigue and other physical complaints such as headaches.

In 1887, the Irish veterinary surgeon John Boyd Dunlop, in trying to eliminate the cause of headaches of which his son complained after riding his small-wheeled tricycle, essentially reinvented the pneumatic tire (although a patent had been issued to an English inventor some twenty years before, it had never been applied and Dunlop was unaware of it). This development combined light weight with an effective suspension at the most suitable point, namely as close to the contact point between road and vehicle as possible. The pneumatic tire not only increased comfort, it also improved the bicycle's overall efficiency on most road surfaces.

On a bike with solid tires, irregularities in the road surface were translated into vertical movement which was lost to forward motion. The pneumatic tire, by contrast, formed itself around the unevenness, absorbing much less of the propulsive force. Consequently, even bicycle racers, most of whom had disdainfully snubbed this

Fig. 1.7. Starley safety cycle, approx. 1885.

Pneumatic Tires and Other Novelties

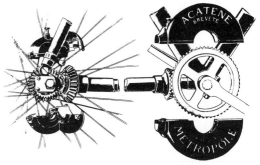

Fig. 1.8. Early high-tech drivetrain with shaft drive, dating back to 1885.

comfort that contradicted their macho image of the sport, soon converted their bikes to pneumatic tires. By 1890 the pneumatic tire was used almost universally on all bicycles.

The Modern Bicycle

1.9. Aerodynamic gadgets such as disk wheels are nothing new. These full and open disks were introduced as early as 1893.

During the last ten years of the 19th century and the first few years of the 20th, quite a number of other clever technical refinements were developed for the bicycle, ranging from low-resistance freewheels to effective braking systems, and from electric lighting to multiple speed gearing mechanisms. By and by, however, the industry's interest in bicycle technology began to decline. That was due largely to the development of the motor car and the airplane, which soon attracted most of the engineers who had formerly worked on the development of the bicycle.

Even so, there remained to be a great demand for the bicycle at a time when it was the only form of individual transportation available to large numbers of people. Consequently, the first 20 years of the 20th century were by no means devoid of technical progress. What declined most dramatically was the newsworthiness of these developments. Instead of presenting the latest in bicycle technology, newspapers started to pay more attention to the pioneering feats associated with motoring and aviation.

Both these new industries — if that is the word to use for what remained a backyard operation for at least ten years, while the bicycle was being produced by modern industrial methods — owed much to the bicycle and the engineers who had perfected it. Many of the parts that went into the first planes and cars were borrowed from the bicycle, and the men who were responsible for their development had gained their knowledge in the field of bicycle engineering.

Renaissance of Bicycle Technology

It is interesting to observe that with the present renaissance of bicycle technology, the younger industries are beginning to repay their debt to the bicycle. Thus, quite a number of the new materials and construction techniques used on state-of-the-art bicycles were first developed for aerospace use. Similarly, the testing equipment used in other branches of industry are slowly finding acceptance in the bicycle field. The development of the HPV (human powered vehicle), as well as of some of the aerodynamic bicycle components used on more conventional racing bikes, would be impossible without the airfoil designs and materials derived from aerospace applications.

But there is much more to the renewed interest in bicycle technology, which is largely centered in North America. Even though the industry seems to be more firmly than ever in the hands of a limited number of large, mainly Japanese, component manufacturers, who manage to dictate what will be fashionable in bike-tech matters, a surprising number of small American companies and individual designers are responsible for the real innovations, much of which is being absorbed by these large component makers.

There has been much progress in the last ten or fifteen years. Steel is slowly being supplanted by other materials for many purposes. We now have conventional tires that roll as lightly as the best tubular racing tires, brakes that require little force to stop reliably, and gears that predictably shift in defined steps. The same goes for the accessories: whereas a good luggage rack or light was virtually non-existent when I first started writing about the subject, there is now an abundance of good products in each of these areas.

1.10. Today's version of the aero-dynamic bicycle may look sleeker, the principles behind it remain the same.

Although the concept of the conventional bike is clear enough, there have been special machines ever since the bicycle was first developed. Von Drais already offered a tricycle, and in later times unusual machines of various types have often been available: tandems and trikes, recumbent bicycles and sociables (two-up bikes on which the riders sit side-by-side). From time to time, bicycles with fairings and completely enclosed machines, bikes with treadle drives and with shaft systems, indirectly driven ones and any number of oddities have been introduced.

Recently, there is also a renewed interest in even more unusual machines, including the HPV's that were mentioned above. These special designs are intended to prove how fast man can go on muscle power alone. Interesting though this is, it should not be forgotten that perhaps the main factor that makes the bicycle so fascinating is its practical application. Whereas other pieces of sports equipment are strictly limited in their use, the bicycle serves as a practical vehicle as well.

Special Bikes

1.11. The German Minister of Transportation inspecting a futuristic bicycle derivative at the biannual Cologne International Bicycle and Motorcycle Show.

It is interesting and entertaining to observe the development of the torpedo-shaped HPV's and other record machines, not to mention the flying bicycles with which such isolated feats as the crossing of the English Channel have been achieved. But even the most enthusiastic people involved in their development agree that they offer little in the way of practical applications for the bicycle as it is used today, or for the future of cycling. Prepare to see bikes that are very much like those of today for many years to come, even if the HPV and

1.12. High-tech frame by industrial designer Frans de la Haye, using a cross frame design and tension wires. It never went into production.

The Scientific Bicycle

1.13. Mountain Bike adaptation of the tension wire cross frame by California mountain bike pioneer Joe Breeze.

flying bike records continue to be broken on highly specialized machines.

Just the same, some impulses come from such developments and their pursuit should definitely be continued. For the time being, the application of such techniques and materials may well be limited to the field of pure racing, especially time trialing. No doubt we can expect to see some spin-offs from these innovations used on the normal bicycle some day — be these tires with less rolling resistance, wheels with reduced wind resistance, or hopefully more reliable components.

A development of an entirely different kind, namely the mountain bike, has already had a great impact on both the design of the bicycle and the way it is used. Who would have guessed in the early eighties that this would happen, in a time when mountain biking was purely a leisure activity for the adventurous thrill-seeker. Yet today the mountain bike not only accounts for the majority of adult bicycles sold in many countries, it is also greatly influencing the overall use of the bicycle.

In the second half of the nineteenth century, the bicycle was taken seriously by the engineering and scientific community. It is fascinating to see that this interest is recurring. For scientific pursuits, the bicycle is more interesting than may seem obvious at first. Its apparent simplicity fools many into thinking there can't be much to it. What makes the bicycle so interesting is perhaps the fact that one is always working at the margin: whereas in many other fields it is easy enough to add lots of power or weight, in bicycle matters, very marginal effects have to be considered at all times.

To get just a few watts more power out of the rider is a significant achievement, saving mere grams of weight, decreasing air or rolling resistance by diminishingly small amounts, is often all that can be achieved, but is worthwhile in a sport where the limits are so clearly set by a fine-tuning of the balance between human performance, mechanical perfection and minimal weight.

Today's development again does not only go into more refined mechanical gadgets, although these are the most obvious, featured prominently in the trade press. Much of the information that exercise physiologists have obtained about the human body is derived from the study of the bike as a machine and the role of the cyclist as its propulsive force. The bicycle ergometer and its more recent off-shoots are the devices used to measure human power, endurance, oxygen consumption, heart rate and efficiency, whether related to bicycle use or not.

Similarly, the scientific work done on developing the bicycle pays off in other disciplines as well. But the main benefit of the increased scientific interest in the bicycle is perhaps in the changed social status. Whereas it was considered at best a little odd to ride a bicycle twenty years ago, and that not only in the fully motorized USA, today it is quite accepted, even admired. It seems a bit of the aura of the renewed scientific interest in the bike is rubbing off to make the pursuit more glamorous than it had been for nearly a hundred years.

Despite the renewed technical interest in the bicycle, there is still a lot of junk out there. Yet the vast majority of bikes and their components offered today are qualitatively superior to what has been sold for many years. This is due largely to the commendable shift of the bike buying public from cash-and-carry outlets and department stores to the qualified bicycle trade. In addition, the trade itself has greatly benefited from the rejuvenation that results from the entry of many experienced and knowledgeable cycling enthusiasts.

In the early bike boom of the nineteenth century, American-made bicycles were by and large of excellent quality, but so were English, Dutch, French, Italian and German machines. And all of them cost a lot of money: it was common for a working man to spend a month's wages on a touring bike. Only with the increased interest in motoring, did a period set in when bicycles were not considered worth spending much money on. Thus, by the nineteen-sixties, most bikes sold hardly represented a few days' pay. Lately, however, the trend has been a return towards higher quality — and price.

Today the bicycle is no longer seen as a cheap item for those who can not afford a car. Instead the bicycle has become a status symbol in many circles. That is good for the sport and it is good for the industry — as it is ultimately to the cyclist. Numerous manufacturers have helped upgrade the image of the bicycle, sometimes employing dubious methods including the propagation of ideas that were later dropped again. Even so, the overall effect has been a positive one.

When considering this upgraded image and the high price tag attached to quality components, it should not be simply assumed that expense is always necessarily

Bicycle Quality

1.14. Today's bicycle is the derivative of yesterday's. Essentially, there is not much difference between this turn-of-the century touring bike and most modern high-quality bicycles.

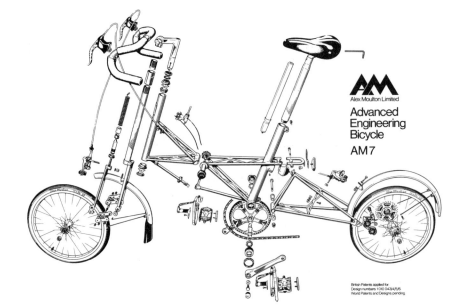

1.15.
One reason for the high price of high-quality bicycles is the amount of work and detail that goes into making such a machine. Although this is not your everyday bicycle, the exploded view of this Moulton shows the intricacy of its construction. Considering most of this is done by hand, the cost can be justified.

synonymous with quality and suitability. Although you usually pay for what you get, you don't always get what you pay for, if only because the high price may be attributable to features that are irrelevant for your particular application. In this book, you will encounter numerous suggestions to help you establish the quality and the suitability of a bicycle and its components for *your* specific circumstances — and detailed instructions on keeping a good bike working properly.

Chapter 2

The Modern Bicycle

In the present chapter, we shall take a closer look at the bicycle in general. You will be shown how a typical bike is put together and what the names and functions of the various components are. In addition, a brief summary of the commonly available bicycle types is included, pointing out their respective characteristics. Even for those who are familiar with the subject matter, this information will be useful, since it will allow the reader to become familiar with the terminology used in this book.

Although clearly not all bicycles are created equal, there are quite a number of common concepts, and all of them are built up quite similarly, based on the same range of relatively standard components. The bicycle manufacturer generally makes only the frame, installing the various other parts that are supplied by manufacturers specializing in those items. Fig. 2.2 depicts a typical bicycle and identifies the various components by their most common designations.

The bicycle can be seen as basic structure (the frame), with groups of components that each fulfill a particular function. The best way to describe and understand the way the bicycle is built up and memorize the names of its many components is on the basis of the functional groups or systems in which the bike and its components can be divided. Thus, the following functional groups can be distinguished:

The Parts of the Bicycle

2.1.
Today's bicycle is mostly made with modern mass production methods. Here the conveyer belt with finished frames before the various components are installed at individual work stations along the way.

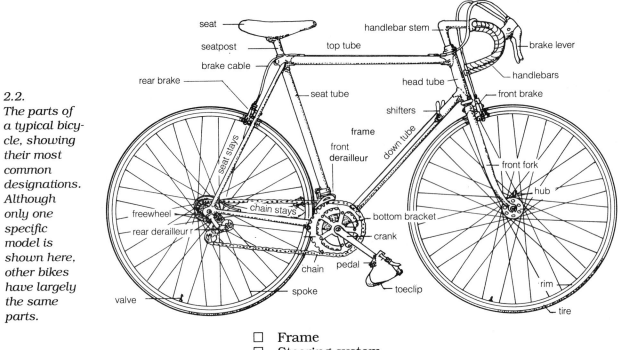

2.2.
*The parts of
a typical bicy-
cle, showing
their most
common
designations.
Although
only one
specific
model is
shown here,
other bikes
have largely
the same
parts.*

☐ Frame
☐ Steering system
☐ Seat and seatpost
☐ Wheels
☐ Drivetrain
☐ Gearing system
☐ Brakes
☐ Accessories.

The same break-down is reflected in the technical chapters of Part II of the book, where the various components and systems will be covered in depth. In the sections that follow here, each of these groups will be summarized only in so far as to aid an understanding of the bicycle as a whole. Although Fig. 2.2 only coincides fully with one particular bicycle type, most of this material is general enough to aid in the understanding of any bicycle.

The frame is the supporting structure of the entire bicycle, to which the various other components are attached. It generally comprises a structure of metal tubes, usually attached to each other either by welding them together at the ends or by means of hollow lugs. In recent years variants that are built up differently have been introduced, and the various methods of construction will be discussed in chapters 4 and 5.

The front portion of the frame is called main frame, the rear portion is referred to as the rear triangle. The main frame consists of the thick tubes called head tube, top tube, seat tube and down tube, respectively. The rear triangle is made up of sets of thinner tubes referred to as seat stays and chain stays, respectively. The lower point, where down tube, seat tube and chain stays come together, is the bottom bracket. Where seat stays and chain stays come together flat plates called drop-outs or (rear) fork-ends are installed.

The steering system, covered in Chapter 6, serves both to steer and to balance the bicycle. It comprises the front fork, the handlebars with the stem that attaches it to the fork, and the headset bearings that allow the system to pivot in the frame.

The seat, or saddle, is held in the frame's seat tube by means of a tubular piece called seatpost, which in turn is clamped in the seat lug. An adjustment mechanism allows for the correct positioning of the seat. These components are covered in Chapter 7.

The wheels are installed in the frame's drop-outs in the rear and the fork-ends in the front. Each wheel itself comprises a central hub with ball bearings that is held to the frame, a rim onto which the tire with its inner tube is installed, and a set of spokes connecting hub and rim. Chapter 8 is devoted to the technical details of the wheel.

The drivetrain, covered in Chapter 9, consists of the components by which the rider's effort is transferred to the rear wheel. These are the crankset, itself comprising cranks, spindle and bearings, as well as the chain-wheels installed on the RH crank, the pedals, the chain and the rear sprockets with their freewheel mechanism on the rear wheel.

The gearing system nowadays almost invariably takes the form of a a set of derailleurs that move the chain sideways into the desired combination of chainwheel and sprocket. In addition, there is a system that relies on a mechanism integrated in the rear wheel hub, still used on many utility and touring bicycles in many parts of the world. The two systems are covered in chapters 10 and 11, respectively.

The brakes also come in two distinct types, namely rim brakes and hub brakes, the latter not only found on cheap utility bikes, but also available in versions that lend themselves to application in tandems and other special bicycles. Chapters 12 covers the rim brake, while hub brakes are described in Chapter 13.

Accessories are anything that can be usefully installed on the bike but are not essential to its operation under

2.3 Campagnolo's C Record, their top racing bike component group.

normal circumstances. These include lighting, fenders and luggage carrying equipment, as well as such things as lock, pump and bicycle computer (electronic speedometer). The most essential of these items will be covered in Chapter 14.

Component Groups

Until recently, it was quite common to find a quality bicycle equipped with components from many different manufacturers. Brakes could be of one make, derailleurs of another, hubs of a third, the crankset might be supplied by yet another.

Not so today, since what I call the 'gruppo-craze' has set in, meaning that most parts are now sold together as a so-called *gruppo*, or component group-set. Due largely to extensive advertising and simultaneous commercial pressure from the two biggest component manufacturers (Shimano and Campagnolo), it has become fashionable to present the unitary look. Manufacturers are virtually forced to choose all their components from one supplier's various component groups, rather than selecting what they consider the most suitable individual makes and models, and the public has unjustly come to expect this.

Nice perhaps for the two big component makers, who indeed make just about everything, but unreasonably tough on those specialist suppliers who have invested all their efforts into particular components. Due to this recent craze, makers of superb brakes, hubs or cranksets have run into serious problems, since the bicycle manufacturers who would like to install these products cannot get the other components individually: they either buy everything from Shimano or nothing. Even when obtaining parts from the same maker, they often have to be selected from one of many different gruppos.

This has sent some of the smaller manufacturers scrambling to also establish gruppos of their own. Thus, hub and derailleur maker SunTour teams up with brake manufacturer Dia-Compe and crankset maker SR to present its own gruppo with the name SunTour engraved on all parts. Similarly, some of the European manufacturers team up with others to present their own Simplex, Ofmega, Huret, Weinmann or Edco sets, each containing selected items from other manufacturers.

The result is that the customer's and the manufacturer's choice is considerably narrowed down. What is even worse, the big manufacturers seem to be steering the bicycle industry away from one of its greatest virtues, namely the interchangeability of parts. Compo-

2.4. An unusual component group from Sachs-Huret, including optional drum brakes.

nents are now no longer designed to be fully interchangeable with other makes and models. Add to this the infuriating tendency not to stock spares of minor bits and pieces, and to change components from one year to the next, and you have arrived at a throw-away bicycle culture.

For the cyclist, this has made it more and more necessary to replace or repair parts by trial and error. No longer is it possible to predict with certainty whether a particular major or minor component will fit for replacement or repair. The moral is to always take the bike — or at least the matching components — to the shop when trying to obtain spares or replacement parts, to make sure things fit together before you buy.

2.5. Conventional American utility bike

In this section, the various different types of bicycles available in the US and elsewhere will be presented. Even though quite a number of different models are described here, there are many more. However, most of these are so uncommon that they can only be briefly mentioned in the chapters of Part III, devoted to special bicycles. Even the regular bicycles covered here often come in many different variants. However, for the vast majority of these bikes, the following definitions apply quite accurately.

Bicycle Types

2.6. German utility bike, inappropriately referred to as Sportrad, (i.e. 'sports bike').

Utility Bicycles

Though somewhat out of fashion amongst serious cyclists since the present trend of fitness and purely recreational cycling has set in, these humblest of all bicycles still have a place. In this context, it is interesting to observe that each country has developed its own kind of utility bicycles, all characterized by a rather upright riding posture.

The American utility bike is the model shown in Fig. 2.5. Weighing about a ton, it rolls on thick low-pressure tires and is stopped by means of a coaster brake.

2.7. The Dutch utility bicycle is the most fully equipped model. It reflects a practical approach combined with a relaxed pace.

The German equivalent is shown in Fig. 2.6. It is invariably equipped with a three-speed hub with integrated coaster brake (in addition to a rim brake in the front), a flimsy luggage rack, chain guard and fenders, as well as dynamo lighting.

In the Netherlands, the Western country with the highest degree of utility cycling, utility bikes take the form depicted in Fig. 2.7. It comes with fenders, a rugged luggage rack, dynamo lighting, as well as fully enclosed chain guards and a rear wheel guard.

The British variant of the utility bike, depicted in Fig.

2.8. *English bikes for recreational or touristic use, equipped with fenders and luggage racks. Unlike their American counterparts, many women in Britain still insist on a frame with a lowered top tube, as in the bike on the left.*

2.9 and 2.10.
Above: Simple racing style bike for fitness cycling (photo: Trek).
Below: Track racing bicycle.

2.8, is called a *roadster*. It is usually equipped with a three-speed hub, rim brakes, fenders (called mud guards locally), battery lights and a saddle bag.

In France and a number of other European countries, the utility function is fulfilled by something akin to the English roadster, though generally with a luggage rack instead of the saddle bag, slightly smaller wheels, and without the hub gearing — these bikes have either no gears at all or a limited-range derailleur just in the rear.

In many other parts of the world, primarily the third world, a type of utility bicycle is in use that derives from the original form of the British heavy-duty utility bike: a stately looking black machine, equipped with stirrup rim brakes (the type operated by means of pull rods instead of cables), a saddle with big coil springs and a heavy-duty luggage rack.

Drop Handlebar Derailleur Bicycles

This term more accurately describes what is usually referred to as *ten-speed* and is shown in Fig. 2.9. It includes models ranging from out-and-out racing machines to models intended for the casual or recreational cyclist — not quite racing bikes, but with their looks — at least from a distance. Since they nowadays usually have at least 12-speed gearing, the term ten-speed is inaccurate and confusing.

Bicycle racers and people who cycle for fitness (as well as many others who have learned to appreciate its virtues of this design) still ride bikes based on this design. The difference between different versions of this basic design are apparent upon closer examination. The real racing bike is much lighter and built more accurately than the run of the mill. Recreational models are often quite a bit heavier and more forgiving. Those intended for touristic use are also a little heavier and sturdier, as well as more extensively equipped.

On racing models, very narrow tires are used, and the gearing tends to be very closely spaced, while the whole bike has a rather short geometry with minimal clearances. Essentially all components are made of strong aluminum alloys, which allows them to be kept very light. The simpler versions may have certain parts made of steel and use weaker types of steel for the frame, making them considerably heavier and giving them a less lively feel.

A rather exclusive and rarely seen type of racing machine is the track bicycle, depicted in Fig. 2.10. This model has the same basic design but lacks brakes and gearing. The frame geometry is usually even tighter than that of other racing bikes, and they are not intended, nor suitable, for use on the road.

Lightweight Touring Bikes

Although this type of bicycle has become almost extinct in the US with the advent of the mountain bike, it is still widely used in other countries. A comeback of this design, be it via the hybrid mentioned below, is anticipated in the US as well.

Shown in Fig. 2.11, it is essentially a high-quality conventional derailleur bicycle with the addition of some utilitarian accessories, such as fenders, luggage rack and lighting. The tires have a greater cross section and more tread than the racing bike, yet less extreme than the mountain bike.

2.11 and 2.12.
Abov: The supreme touring bicycle by Klein.
Below: A high-quality mountain bike by Gary Fisher.

Mountain Bikes and Hybrids

Suddenly, in the eighties, there was a revolution in America that has subsequently swept the rest of the western world as well: The mountain bike has become the most universal adult bicycle, replacing narrow tires with fat ones and dropped handlebars with straight models. This development has had a significant effect on cycling habits as a whole, winning friends for the bicycle amongst those who had never felt at ease on the conventional derailleur bike.

Depicted in Fig. 2.12, the mountain bike is a derailleur bike with very wide-range gearing, a rather upright riding position, due to the use of flat handlebars, and fat high-pressure tires. Although it was originally conceived for off-road use, it was soon adapted for regular cycling as well. The advantages of this design for the average cyclist are obvious enough: easily accessible brakes and gears, a riding posture that allows a clear view of the road ahead, a softer ride due to the thicker tires and a less fragile construction that makes the whole machine more forgiving.

2.13. The ultimate multi-purpose bicycle: This is a Bruce Gordon hybrid bike with interchangeable wheels.

The hybrid is a recent variation on the same theme. It is intended for less rugged terrain but performs better on the road. Different types of this machines may have either flat or drop handlebars, somewhat less widespread gearing range and less bulky tires.

Portable Bicycles

This category is far less common than the models described so far, but it is significant enough not to be

2.14. Simple folding bicycle with relatively small wheels. Quite rare these days, even in Europe, where they were once very popular.

2.15. Moulton's high tech small-wheeled bicycle with built in suspension. It can be separated for ease of transport.

overlooked. These bicycles may eventually increase in popularity again, enabling more extensive use of the bicycle for commuting. As shown in Fig. 2.14, they usually come with smaller than usual wheels (anything from 12 to 20 inch diameter, as opposed to the 26 and 27 inch wheels common on conventional bicycles). Their portability may be achieved by means of a folding or separating mechanism that allows getting the overall package dimensions down to something that can be handled on public transport vehicles.

In the nineteen-sixties, crude versions of this type were all the craze in much of Europe. Today's models are, almost without exception, very much superior in design and execution. The queen of these is probably the Moulton, with built-in suspension but rather limited portability. Other designs generally sacrifice some of the desired riding and handling characteristics to achieve a more compact package. More satisfactory designs are coming on the market, so this concept has a fair chance to ripen to maturity before long.

Special-Size Bikes

Many women and some men have physical proportions that don't allow them to be comfortable on most standard bicycles, because they are too small. Something similar applies to very tall persons of either sex. By and large, the bicycle industry does not adequately cater to these people. Too much attention is paid to the greatest common denominator, and few in the trade seem to be aware how ergonomically disastrous the bicycle can be if it is drastically misproportioned in relation to the rider.

Not only the frame itself, but also many of the components should be adapted correctly. For small riders, that often brings unforeseen problems, since simply downscaling things doesn't work, as will be explained in some detail in Chapter 15. For very tall people, similar problems apply as for those who are short, with the additional drawback of their generally greater weight and the fact that parts become structurally weaker as they are made larger.

Some frame builders have recently shown an interest in the problems of the tall and the small, but much is still left to be desired. The major component manufacturers make their high-quality parts only in a very limited range of sizes, leaving even the best intentioned frame builder little to choose from for his discriminating big and small customers.

Children's Bikes

Although much of what was said with respect to the problems of small adults also applies to children, some additional difficulties should be pointed out. One of the most obvious of these is the fact that children often are not able to define the discomfort of a particular design. If one considers the fact that bringing up children is accepted to be an expensive hobby by most adults in the US, it is astonishing that not more pressure has been brought to bear upon the manufacturers to properly cater to this category of cyclists.

Whereas adult bicycles are available in a wide range of both price and quality, children's bikes are generally available in only one: mediocre. It appears that until a customer fits a bike with 27 inch wheels (or a mountain bike with 26 inch wheels), very little is done to provide quality. The argument that a child's bike is not worth the expense since the child outgrows any bike too fast is a flimsy one indeed, especially coming from an industry that encourages adults to upgrade their bicycle every two to three years. Although a few framebuilders and manufacturers actually make good childrens' bikes, it is very hard to find them.

Amongst the bicycles for children and young teenagers, two designs should be considered separately, since they are available only for this age category: the BMX bike and the more recently introduced Formula-1 bike, depicted in Fig. 2.16 and Fig. 2.17, respectively. The BMX bike may be fun for doing tricks, and has been a great help in raising the standard of the industry, but it is very little use for transportation. Not so the Formula-1 bike, which can be seen as the racing bike for kids. Built for fast acceleration, high speeds and easy maneuvering, this machine is superbly suitable for getting around as well.

Tandems

Since the early eighties, there has been a renewed interest in the bicycle built for two. Whereas formerly tandems often seemed to be modeled on the touring bike, many of the newer tandems may have borrowed the characteristics from either the mountain bike or the pure racing bike.

The design of the tandem is an art by itself, due to the structural problems that occur when making a large, complex structure carry such a heavy load. But there are other problems too, for which experienced tandem riders and tandem frame builders have found adequate solutions over the years.

2.16. *Formula-1 bike, intended for higher speeds than the BMX bike.*

2.17. *BMX bike from Diamond Back*

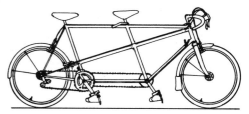

2.18. *Tandem bicycle*

2.18. Recumbent bicycle

Bicycle Sizing

Special Bicycles

In addition to the relatively common bicycles built on conventional lines discussed above, quite different designs are introduced from time to time. These include bikes with built-in suspension systems, recumbents, tricycles and even real or presumed HPV's, in which the rider may be fully enclosed. In addition, bicycles incorporating different solutions for one problem or the other are presented by daring inventors or reckless investors. Chapter 17 will discuss some of these ideas in more depth, while Chapter 18 will take a look at the chances of success for such concepts in the future.

At least as important as the type and quality of a bicycle is its size. Standard bicycles — at least those of any quality — come in quite a range of different frame sizes; yet determining the correct size for any individual is not universally clear. One reasonable way to find the correct frame size is by means of Fig. 2.19. Straddling the top tube with the feet flat on the ground, it should be possible to raise the front wheel off the ground by the distance listed below:

☐ touring bike, hybrid,
  sports bike: 8—12cm (3—5 inches)
☐ racing or fitness bike: 12—15cm (5—6 inches)
☐ mountain bike: 15—18cm (6—7 inches)

Table 8 in the Appendix gives an approximation of the correct basic frame size as a function of the rider's leg size. Use the table to find the nearest size, then experiment with saddle height, handlebar height and stem size to find a position that provides overall comfort.

2.19.
Frame sizing
(also refer to
Table 8 in the Appendix).

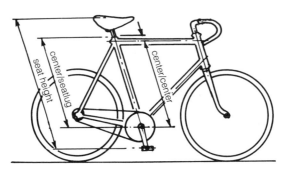

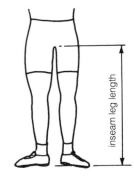

Chapter 3
__ Common Parts and Procedures

In the present chapter, those parts will be described that are commonly used in several different locations on the modern bicycle. Included are descriptions of their operation as well as detailed instructions for their maintenance, which will eliminate the need to repeat these details for each of the individual applications in subsequent chapters. The following details will be covered here:

☐ Screw threaded connections
☐ Ball bearings
☐ Wedge connections
☐ Bowden cables
☐ Quick-releases.

There are a number of other common details that apply not so much to the maintenance as to the manufacture of the bike. Since these are nevertheless of importance when it comes to judging the quality of bike or components, these details will be covered in Chapter 4.

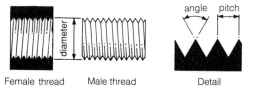

3.1. Screw thread details

Screw Threaded Connections

Most components of the bicycle include some kind of screw threaded connection. This not only applies to conventional nuts and bolts, but also to the attachment of individual parts to the bike and the internals of minor items, ranging from ball bearings to cable adjusters. Consequently, an appreciation of their operation is necessary for all maintenance and repair work on the bicycle and its individual components.

Simple though these things may seem, a more thorough understanding is essential for your own safety. This was recently confirmed by a German survey that showed the likelihood of an accident due to an incorrectly installed or attached accessory is three times as high for items mounted by the cyclist as for those installed by a bicycle mechanic. In the US and Britain, the situation is probably quite similar. Yet it is easy enough to learn to do it right.

Fig. 3.1 shows the parts of a typical screw threaded connection. It comprises a cylindrical (male) part with a thread in the form of a helical ridge wrapped around the circumference and a hollow (female) part with a corresponding groove. The outside diameter of the male part is just a tiny bit smaller than the inside diameter

3.2. Dura-Ace gruppo. These are Shimano's top road racing components.

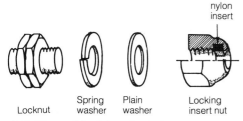

3.3. *Thread locking devices*

of the female part measured at the deepest point in the ridge, so the male part fits inside the female one without undue resistance when it is turned.

Once the male part is screwed fully into the female part until the components that are to be connected (e.g. the head of a bolt and the face of a nut) make contact, the resistance suddenly increases as the surfaces of the threads are pushed hard up against one another over the entire helical contact surfaces of the thread. The resulting friction is adequate to firmly hold the connection.

If there is some obstacle to the mutual turning before this point is reached, e.g. when the threads are damaged or dirty, the resistance becomes so great that it may be impossible to reach the point where contact forces hold the connection properly. For this reason, screw threads must always be cleaned and preferably slightly lubricated before installation, and parts with damaged thread must be replaced — or in some cases a damaged thread can be recut by a bicycle mechanic with the appropriate thread cutting tool.

Locking Threaded Connections

However firmly attached to begin with, many threaded connections come apart after cycling due to vibration. This applies most notably to parts that are attached in only one place, since this causes an imbalance aggravated by vibration. For this reason, care must be taken to attach accessories in two or more locations whenever possible, and to frequently retighten single attachments — or use at least two mounting points.

In order to minimize the effect of vibrations, several locking devices have been developed, some of which are shown in Fig. 3.3: locknut, locking insert nut, spring washer and lock washer. The latter is shaped to match a longitudinal groove cut in the male part to accept the inward pointing key on the washer. Another solution, that cannot be shown in any illustration, is the use of a locking adhesive, such as Locktite. Although all these solutions work to some extent, even these have to be checked and retightened regularly. In the case of the locknut, the inner nut must first be tightened independently, after which the outer nut is tightened against the inner nut.

3.4. *Shimano Dura-Ace track racing gruppo.*

When tightening or loosening screw threaded connections, accurately fitting tools with correct leverage must be used to provide the right torque. Excessive torque can damage parts, while too little torque results in adequately tightened connections (or, when trying to loosen a connection, would not suffice to do so). Some manufacturers specify the torque that should be used, which can be controlled by means of special torque wrenches. For the home mechanic, it will generally be sufficient to make sure tools of the right size are used.

Screwdrivers must match the size of the saw cuts or the size of the cross-shaped recess in so called Phillips-head screws. Allen keys of the exactly matching size must be used on bolts with hexagonal recesses. Use open-ended wrenches or (preferably) box wrenches that exactly fit on hexagonal nuts and bolts. When using two tools that do not have the same leverage (measured as their handle length perpendicular to the axis of the connection) use the tool with the longer lever on the part to be moved, the shorter one on the stationary part.

Wrenches are supplied with increasing handle size as their nominal sizes go up to provide correct leverage. Fastened by hand, with the correct size wrench perpendicular to the axis of the connection, the chance of damaging the connection by overtightening is minimal. When using an adjustable wrench, select a short one for small nuts, a larger one for larger ones to prevent excessive torque. To loosen a particularly stubborn connection, apply penetrating oil, such as WD-40 to the threads before resorting to tricks to increase leverage (e.g. by means of a length of steel tubing stuck around the handle of a wrench).

Bicycles and their individual components, ranging from wheel hubs to cranksets and from pedals to the head-set, largely owe their smooth running properties to the use of ball bearings. These were invented around 1865, initially specifically for bicycle applications. The use of exactly spherical hard steel balls, embedded in lubricant between the fixed and the rotating parts of the bearing assembly reduces the resistance enormously.

The most common type of ball bearing on the bicycle is the adjustable cup-and-cone model, depicted in Fig. 3.5. In this type of bearing, the balls lie between a cup-shaped outer race and a conically shaped inner race, one of which can be adjusted in- or outward by means of screw thread. The cone is the adjustable part on wheel and pedal bearings, whereas on most bottom brackets it is the cup that is adjustable.

Lubrication can be in the form of oil or grease. Although oil has the advantage that it rinses out the wear and dirt particles, it must be replenished frequently and is rather messy. Consequently, bearing

Sizing and Leverage of Tools

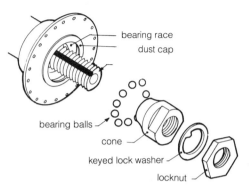

3.5. Adjusting parts of cup-and-cone bearing.

Ball Bearings

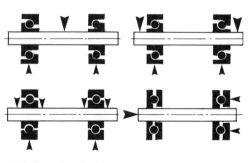

3.6. Bearing loading situations

grease is almost universally used these days. On Wilderness Trail Grease-Guard mountain bike components (also available from SunTour under license), clever V-shaped seals isolating the inside of the bearings makes it possible to grease each bearing through a separate grease nipple, providing the same advantage as oil lubrication, but without the mess.

Bearing Maintenance

3.7 and 3.8.
Wilderness Trail Greaseguard fitting and matching tools for grease injection. A chevron-shaped seal prevents grease from going where it shouldn't.

Ball bearings must be adjusted correctly: they should have minimal lateral play yet rotate freely. To establish whether a bearing is loose, check whether a point with some leverage connected to the rotating part stays in place when applying lateral force relative to a point connected to the fixed part (thus, to check a wheel hub bearing, push and pull the rim relative to the fork blade or the rear stays). Tighten the bearing if free lateral movement is noticed.

To find out whether the bearing is too tight, check whether it can be rotated freely. If it feels rough or if there is noticeable resistance, it is either too tight or, more likely, damaged. Loosen it first and then check again: it should be overhauled if it either does not reduce friction or results in lateral looseness as described above. Although a worn bearing may seem to rotate freely when adjusted just a bit loose, that is not the solution, because the situation will change radically once the bike is loaded, which explains the sometimes mysterious high resistance on bearings that seem to rotate freely when unloaded.

The way bearings are loaded varies quite a bit depending on the location. Relatively simple are those of the wheel hubs being loaded perpendicular to the axis, which is referred to as radial loading. The headset bearings of the steering system are loaded in line with the axis, referred to as axial loading. Pedals and bottom brackets are loaded asymmetrically. Fig. 3.6 schematically shows the various loading cases and the particular bearing designs that are most suitable for each. Unfortunately, this is something too few manufacturers take to heart, with the result that even today few bikes run as smoothly as a 1932 BSA, which used bottom bracket and hub bearings of the type illustrated in Fig. 3.9, now offered only on the exclusive French Maxicar hubs.

Adjustable Bearing Maintenance

To overhaul an adjustable bearing, disassemble it and replace both the ball bearings, which are usually contained in a bearing ring or cage, and any other parts that show signs of wear in the form of irregular grooves, pitting or corrosion. Then fill the bearing with clean grease, reassemble and adjust. The bearing cage must be installed in such a way that only the bearing balls, not the metal of the cage, contacts the surface of cup and cone. The adjusting procedure is given below. Overhauling and other maintenance instructions applicable to the various specific bearings will be provided in the chapters of Part II.

The following description outlines the principle of bearing adjustment in general, assuming the cone is the screwed (i.e. adjustable) part, while the cup is fixed.

Adjust Bearing:
1. Loosen the locknut by one or two turns, while countering at the underlying cone.
2. Lift the locking washer to free the cone.
3. To reduce play in the bearing, screw the cone in slightly — perhaps ⅛ turn at a time, while countering at the opposite locknut.
4. To loosen the bearing (rarely necessary), unscrew the cone slightly, while countering at the cone on the other side.
5. Push the locking washer back onto the cone.
6. Tighten the locknut while countering at the underlying cone, making sure it does not turn.
7. Check and repeat if necessary.

In recent years, more and more manufacturers have replaced conventional cup-and-cone bearings by non-adjustable cartridge bearings, often referred to as sealed bearings. These units, shown in Fig. 3.10, are not adjustable but tend to be more accurate, less prone to wear, and easier to seal against penetrating dirt. Their theoretical disadvantages are their reduced load bearing capacity for the same overall size and the need to replace the entire unit in case of wear. In practice they usually hold up very well.

This method of attachment is used in various locations on the bicycle by means of matching tapered or conically shaped surfaces. Typical applications of this method are found in the attachment of the cranks to the bottom bracket spindle and the handlebar stem to the front fork.

The principle of the wedge connection is that a given axially applied force transfers a much increased lateral or radial force when applied via a slanted surface, proportional to the slope. The maximum connecting force is thus achieved by choosing the angle of the wedge surface relative to the axis as small as practicable.

outer race

inner race

adjusting nut

3.9. Detail of adjustable precision bearing as used on Maxicar hub.

Cartridge Bearings

Wedge Connections

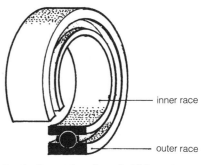

inner race

outer race

3.10. Cartridge ('sealed') bearing

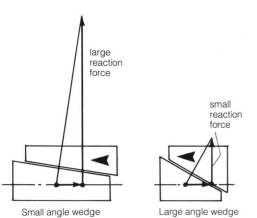

Small angle wedge   Large angle wedge

3.11. Principle of wedge connection

Bowden Cables

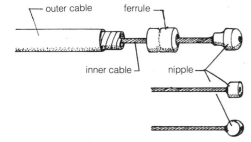

3.12. Bowden cable details

Since, on the other hand, the relative displacement increases inversely proportional to the slope, the parts must be made more accurately matching and of less deforming materials as the angle is made smaller. This applies especially to the connection between cranks and bottom bracket spindle, while the situation is much less critical in the case of the handlebar stem attachment.

When wedge connections come loose, it is mainly because the deformation of one part relative to the other increases the play, thus reducing the contact pressure. This applies mainly to cheaper components, made of relatively soft materials and short contact surfaces.

Any wedge connection, especially when new, must be tightened frequently — once a week or before every long ride during the first month. This prevents damage done by a loosening connection and keeps the connection trouble-free without need for frequent tightening from then on. Another important precaution is to clean and slightly lubricate the contact surfaces, which prevents seizing.

Brakes and gears are usually activated by means of Bowden cables, so named after their inventor Frank Bowden, the founder of the Raleigh bicycle factory. As depicted in Fig. 3.12, a Bowden cable consists of a flexible but unstretchable stranded steel inner cable and a flexible but incompressible outer cable constructed of a helically wound flat steel strip, usually plastic-coated on the outside. The inner cable takes up tension forces, while the outer cable is used to counter these by taking up compressive forces.

A nipple is soldered on at one end of the inner cable — usually the end that is connected with the operating lever. At the other end it is clamped in by means of an eye bolt or a pinch plate. The outer cable is usually finished off at both ends with a metal bushing or ferrule and is restrained at a fixed anchor point.

Generally, cables work more accurately when the inner cable is relatively thick, while the outer cable must be very tightly wound. To check their quality, it will suffice to make sure the former does not stretch under force, while the latter must not compress. Cables used in conjunction with indexed gearing systems usually have a low-friction internal sleeve between inner and outer cable, which makes operation even smoother, while the use of stainless steel inner cables tends to improve things by preventing corrosion and increased friction.

The routing of the cable is critical. Comparative tests

conducted at a German technical university proved that the bending radius is of little effect and can be kept quite tight (a radius of 5cm, or 2 inches, is adequate), while the overall length should be minimized, commensurate with unhindered operation of the cables and associated mechanisms. It will also be advantageous to run as much of the inner cable free between relatively short sections of outer cables, rather than enclosing the full length of it in outer cable, as has become the fashion.

The maintenance-free cables with liner for index gearing systems have double-stranded outer cables that are very hard to cut. Consequently, they are usually sold in fixed lengths exactly corresponding to a particular combination of derailleurs, shifters and anchor points. Other cables are generally sold separately: inner cables to be cut down to the correct length, and outer cable by the yard. All cables must be kept clean. Those without internal low-friction sleeve should be lubricated — use vaseline before installation and enter oil at the points where the inner cable disappears into the outer cable a couple of times yearly afterwards.

The two locations that must be inspected for damage on the inner cable are where the nipple is attached and where the other end is clamped in. Replace any inner cable on which individual strands are broken, since friction is increased and sudden breakage may occur. On the outer cable, the thing to watch out for is that it is never pinched or abruptly twisted, since this restricts the internal diameter locally, leading to so much friction that reliable operation is defeated.

When replacing a cable, cut the outer cable off very carefully to prevent forming an inwardly protruding hook at the end. The outer cable must be cut off about 3cm (1¼") outside the clamping point, using a special sharp tool that does not cause the ends of the cable to

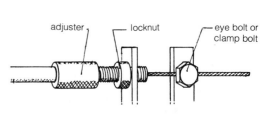

3.13. *Cable adjusting detail*

Cable Care

3.14.
Shimano Deore XT mountain bike component group. Included are a choice of several different brakes and the easy shifting Hyperglide freewheel with matching chain. Although the particular set shown here is a few years old, it is updated regularly and remains Shimano's top-of-the-line mountain bike gruppo.

3.15. Campagnolo Centaur component group for mountain bike use. Beautifully shaped and finished, it is slowly taking its place besides Shimano's and SunTour's top gruppos.

fray. It is recommended to solder the inner cable strands together around the point where it will be cut before doing so, which makes it easier to cut and prevents cable fray for good. To do this, heat up the cable with a soldering iron and then allow some resin core solder to melt at the point where the tip of the soldering iron touches the cable, waiting for the solder to run around and in between the strands before removing the soldering iron.

Adjusting gears and brakes usually amounts to changing the tension of the cable. All systems in which Bowden cables are used include an adjuster, shown in Fig. 3.13, to compensate for wear and real or apparent cable stretch. The (excellent, though in the US rather uncommon) hub gear mechanisms by Fichtel & Sachs use a variation on this theme that uses a grooved pin and a clamp instead of the screw threaded pin and the matching adjusting bushing with locknut.

Cable Adjustment Procedure:
1. Establish whether the inner cable should be tightened (after some wear or use) or loosened (only the case if parts have been replaced).
2. Where possible (on brake cables), untension the cable by loosening the quick-release or by unhooking the transverse cable.
3. Hold the adjuster bushing and loosen the locknut by several turns.
4. Holding the threaded pin, screw the bushing further on or off, as appropriate to increase or decrease cable tension, respectively.
5. Holding pin and bushing, tighten the locknut up against the former.
6. If appropriate, reconnect cable or tension quick release.
7. Check operation and repeat if necessary.

Quick-Releases

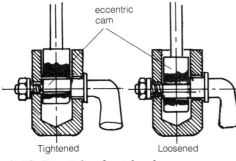

3.16. Principle of quick-release

These handy mechanisms are frequently used to ease installation and removal of such parts as the wheels and the seat, while a similar device is often used to tension or untension the brake cable. Folding bikes may have a similar mechanism to latch the two parts of the frame into place and ease folding them together.

Essentially, any quick-release is based on the eccentric cam principle, which allows applying considerable force over a short range of travel by means of a hand-operated level via a cam that is arranged eccentrically with respect to its pivot point. Figures 3.16 and 3.17 show the principle and the operation of a typical quick-release mechanism, as applied to the hub in this case.

When operating a quick-release system, a few points must be kept in mind, namely:

1. The lever should not be used to screw the system in but only as a lever that is twisted fully to tighten or loosen the assembly.
2. The locknut or thumbnut at the opposite end is not used to tighten it, but only to adjust the system until the length of the assembly is exactly right to allow definite loosening and tightening of the lever by hand.
3. Install the levers in such a direction that they run more or less parallel to a frame member, such as the seat stay, so the latter provides a restraint for the hand when operating the quick- release and so the lever does not protrude excessively.

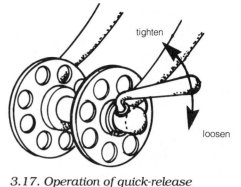

3.17. Operation of quick-release

Working on the Bike

When carrying out repair and maintenance work on the bike, it is recommended that you support the bike in a rack designed for that purpose. Some excellent examples of home-mechanics' work stands are the Blackburn Sportstand and the model offered by Tacx, both of which are small and light enough not to be in the way when not in use and cheap enough to keep the average cyclist's budget intact.

For those who like the home-made touch, I have included a drawing of a handy device that is easily made in Fig. 3.18. This handlebar stand is particularly useful for people who do not really intend to do too much work on the bike themselves or those with very limited space. It is used to support the handlebars of the bike when placed upside-down, thus preventing damage to cables and controls and providing a reasonably stable hold.

Selecting Tools

Although I am not giving a list of tools here, specific tools for each of the operations discussed in the book are listed with the instructions. It will be wise to start off with a very basic kit comprising sets of screwdrivers, allen keys, open-ended wrenches, box wrenches, two adjustable wrenches, a small hammer and the tools needed for fixing a tire. All other tools may be purchased as the need arises.

When buying tools for working on the bike, always select the highest quality available. Generally that does not mean those that shine the brightest, but those that are the most expensive. Don't be fooled by terms such as 'economy tools', because only the best (i.e. expensive) tools provide real economy. Cheap tools are inaccurate and easily deformed, causing damage to the

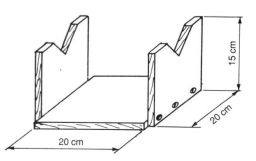

3.18. Simple handlebar support

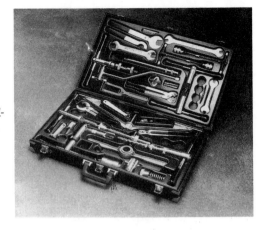

*3.19 and 3.20.
Left: Work stand
from Tacx.
Right: Full set of
special bicycle
workshop tools.
Such sets are avail-
able from VAR and
Campagnolo. The
thread cutting
parts must be
specified for
English, French or
Italian threading.*

bike in addition to their inherently poorer performance. My own experience is that the most expensive tools are invariably worth their money if you get serious about maintaining the bicycle.

Most of the common tools are best bought at special- ized tool or hardware stores, while the specific bicycle tools listed in subsequent chapters should be bought only at a bike shop. Although I don't in general recom- mend patronizing mail order companies except if you don't have access to a bike shop, the limited availability of tools at most bike shops may force you to make an exception when it comes to buying tools. *United Bicycle Tool Supply* and *The Third Hand* are two reputable specialist tool suppliers, and their catalogs are gold mines of useful information on tools and working pro- cedures.

Chapter 4
_____ Materials and Construction

This chapter explains the most significant technical aspects relating the choice of materials and their properties, as well as the construction techniques used. This will apply equally for the bicycle itself as for its individual components. Wherever possible, this will be done in such a way that even the technically uninitiated can understand it. A knowledge of these concepts will enable you to recognize quality when evaluating a bicycle or selecting components. In addition, the purpose of these explanations at this point is to avoid the need for repeated coverage of these technical details for each of the components covered in the chapters of Part II.

A high-quality bicycle is a successful synthesis of materials, dimensions and construction methods that gets the most out of the available potential of each. That means e.g. that when a different material is selected, the relative dimensions and the construction techniques must also be selected specifically to match the potentials and limitations of that particular material. Or conversely, when dimensions are altered to make a very small or big bike, or one for greater tire clearances or specific purposes, the material choice and joining methods may have to be adapted to these dimensions as well.

4.1. An example of the sad result of incorrect material choice and/or manufacturing techniques.

The reason why a modern quality bike may weigh as little as 10kg (22 lbs), without being weaker than a much heavier model, lies in this successful synthesis of materials, dimensions and construction methods. More than for almost any other product today, weight saving is a primary aim of the designers of bikes and components. Everything possible is done to make each component as light as possible within the existing constraints.

Anybody who wonders whether a minor weight reduction is really worth the cost and effort is encouraged to try it out for himself. Just compare the feel of a light bike with that of a heavier model when riding, even if the total difference is only a very small percentage of the total weight of bike and rider. The lighter bike, especially if it also has significantly lighter wheels, is not only easier to get into motion, it also transmits less shocks and occilations. These shocks and occilations

Weight and Materials Selection

4.2. Strain gauge analysis used on a bicycle frame by frame tubing manufacturer Columbus to optimize tubing thickness.

all result in the loss of energy that would otherwise be available for forward motion. Although some shocks can be eliminated by lowering the tire pressure, this increases the rolling resistance, resulting in even more wasted energy. To explain this and other phenomena, the relevant physical and mechanical concepts will be briefly explained below.

Mass and Weight

The most significant effect of the *mass* (often casually referred to as weight) is when increasing or decreasing speed. Mass, measured in kg (kilogram), is the total amount of matter, quite independent of the force by which it is attracted due to the earth's gravitational field, which is represented by the *weight*, measured in N (Newton). At any one location relative to the center of the earth, mass and weight are of course so closely related that there is no harm — except in scientific accuracy of terminology — in using weight as an indicator for mass. At sea level and at most latitudes, an object with a mass of 1kg weighs 9.8N.

Acceleration is the increase in speed, while *deceleration* is speed reduction (negative acceleration), and both are measured in terms of m/sec^2. The *force* required to accelerate a certain mass is a function of the mass and the square of the acceleration. Thus, to accelerate a 14kg bicycle will require considerably more force then a lighter one, while the same force will suffice to accelerate the lighter bike faster. Maintained over a period of distance or time, the force is multiplied by the distance to calculate the *energy*, or *work*, required, expressed in Nm (Newton-meter). The *power*, limited by the rider's output potential, is computed as the quotient of energy and time, and is expressed in Nm/s.

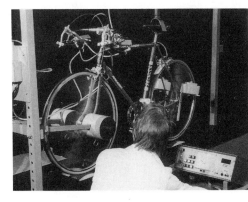

4.3. Fatigue testing of the bicycle under cyclical loading at Raleigh. Done to make sure a bike or a component does not fail after a number of miles of use.

Of course, the rider's weight must be considered too. For a 65kg (145 lbs) rider on a 10kg bike, the difference of one kg amounts to only 1.3%. However, since in bicycling one is always working with marginal values and differences, such a relatively small difference is clearly detected.

The difference becomes even more significant when the effect of rotating mass is considered, such as that of the wheels and, to a lesser extent, that of cranks, chain and pedals. This is due to the fact that such parts are not only accelerated forward, but also around. Simplifying, it can be said that the mass of the rotating parts should be doubled for purposes of acceleration calculations. Thus, if a 10kg bike has 6kg in fixed mass and 4kg rotating mass, the effect will amount to 14kg. Each kg saved on the rotating mass will reduce the mass effect by the equivalent of 2kg — that is 2.5% of the total for a 65kg rider on a 10kg bike.

Weight may be minimized by several different means. As far as the choice of materials is concerned, the most obvious way is by selecting a lighter material of the same strength (if possible). The lighter material has a lower *density* (usually given without indicating the units, but measured in g/cm^3). Given the same dimensions, an aluminum alloy part (density 2.7) will weigh about ⅓ of an identical one made of steel (density 7.8). Of course, it still has to be strong enough, and that may require making it bigger if the lighter material is not equally strong as the heavier one, so the final result is rarely quite as dramatic as the difference in density would suggest.

As suggested above, weight can only be considered in conjunction with other material properties, primarily its strength. The bicycle and its components must be strong enough to withstand the loading without breaking or permanent deformation. The latter is referred to as *plastic deformation*, as opposed to the *elastic deformation* from which the material recovers, or springs back.

The strength of a material is usually determined by its *tensile strength*, which is expressed in N/mm^2 — the force that can be applied when pulling on the end of a rod of the material with a cross section of 1mm^2. Of the various measures used, the *tensile yield strength* is the most useful, being the value at which plastic deformation sets in. Some manufacturers unfortunately still provide this and other technical details in archaic terms such as tons (meaning tons/square inch), lbs (meaning lbs per square inch) or kg/mm^2. Table 10 in the Appendix lists conversion factors for these and other dimensions into their scientific equivalents.

Even the elastic (temporary) deformation should not be so great that stability is affected negatively, even though some shock absorption in the vertical direction may be desirable. *Rigidity* is the quality that determines how well a bike or its components resist this kind of flexing. It is affected by several factors, including a material property referred to as *modulus of elasticity*, expressed in N/mm^3. The greater the modulus of elasticity is, the more rigid a part of given dimensions under a given load.

The bicycle or its individual components should not suddenly break, even after many cyclical changes of loading. This kind of damage, known as *fatigue failure*, is dependent on the mutual coordination of material

Other Material Properties

4.4. Fatigue testing of cranks. Aluminum parts such as these must be tested to the actual maximum number of anticipated load cycles, whereas steel parts only have to meet a certain limit to allow a prediction of their useful life.

strength, loading, cross section and detail design (the latter particularly with respect to sudden changes of shape or thickness). The number of times the load changes may be very high, such as in the case of loads induced by road surface irregularities. The ability of a material to withstand this kind of load is expressed by the number of loading cycles it can withstand. For steel parts, there is a distinct limit above which a part will withstand any number of cycles, so a steel part need only be tested to this value (10 million cycles). Aluminum does not have such a distinct limit, but must be tested at least to the actual number of cycles anticipated.

Hardness is a desirable quality to resist wear. This is particularly important for parts that move relative to each other, such as bearing and drivetrain parts. Unfortunately, harder parts are invariably less ductile, meaning that they may break when subjected to a sudden impacting force. For this reason, many parts are treated to produce a hard, wear-resistant outside, while retaining a ductile, impact-resistant core. Depending on the kind of material, this property is expressed by either *Brinell* or *Rockwell hardness* figures. These figures relate the force applied to the resulting deformation, higher values indicating greater hardness.

The *melting point* of a material is of some relevance in the bicycle trade when the materials are to be joined by means of welding or brazing. Of course, this property is even more significant for the filler materials used in those processes. But the melting point also matters in the selection of such non-metallic materials as those for brake blocks and minor structures — witness the bike stand made of resin-reinforced plastic that collapsed under the effect of the sun behind glass shop windows.

4.5. Testing a drivetrain for shifting ease and wear.

Corrosion resistance, finally, is a property that is less easily measured, yet can be significant for many parts of the bike, especially those that come in contact with each other or cannot be painted for other reasons. In general, the cheapest steels do not corrode as easily as stronger ones, since the latter contain more carbon. Aluminum, titanium and stainless steel all corrode less, although untreated aluminum may suffer badly when subjected to a salty atmosphere.

Not only these material properties, but also the weight and the price of a bike and individual components are determined in a process of weighing up the relative advantages and disadvantages. The designers of the various bits and pieces can predict on the basis of basic engineering knowledge what the properties of certain designs will be. Unfortunately, many forget to take that trouble, so hopelessly improper designs for the selected materials are presented at regular intervals. Just the same, awareness for these finer points has increased significantly in recent years.

The major categories of materials used for bicycle frames and components are steel and aluminum alloys. In addition to these common metallic materials, at least one other metal, titanium, and several other materials may be used for various parts of the bike. The latter include natural and synthetic rubber used for tires, as well as various plastic and resin-embedded fibers (usually referred to as *composites*).

At this point, it should be clarified what the word alloy really means: it is any mixture of two or more materials of which at least one is a metal. Actually, in bicycle engineering circles, the term is usually reserved for materials comprising at least two metals. Steel alloys are mixtures of mainly steel with small percentages of one or more other metals, while aluminum alloys comprise mainly aluminum with minor percentages of one or more other metals. Thus it is patently incorrect to assume that alloy means aluminum alloy only, or that 'chrome-moly' (meaning chrome-molybdenum steel) is not steel, as is often assumed or implied.

Often manufacturers put up a smoke screen of technical sounding terms that mean nothing specific, or at least nothing special. Virtually all frames are made of the same rather limited range of steel and aluminum alloys, while most components are made of one of an equally narrow range of aluminum alloys. The fancy names some manufacturers use to describe their products rarely indicate anything that differs from the standard materials.

Amongst the material properties described in the preceding section, one should distinguish between *physical* and *mechanical* properties. Alloying can be used to improve the mechanical properties — strength, melting point hardness and ductility. The physical properties — density and modulus of elasticity — remain virtually unchanged and can not be affected by alloying. The same applies to the various thermal or mechanical treatments that (either intentionally or incidentally) affect only the physical properties of the material.

Choice of Materials

4.6. Fatigue testing. Here pedals are loaded cyclically in Raleigh's materials and component testing laboratory.

Steel and its Alloys

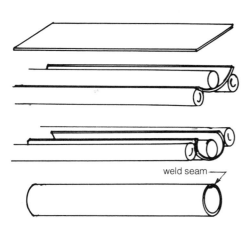

4.7. Welded tubing is rolled into shape and then welded at the seam.

Tubing Types

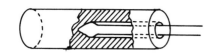

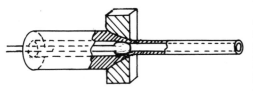

4.8. Seamless tubing is pierced and then pulled over dies until the required diameter and wall thickness are achieved.

Steel is iron to which a small percentage of carbon (usually about 1%) has been added — thus, metallurgically, it is an alloy itself. Steel alloys are mixtures of this material with one or more other metals. Although the tensile strength of various steels and steel alloys can vary widely, the density and the modulus of elasticity remain essentially unaffected. Thus, given a certain dimension, the strongest alloy may resist a much higher force than a weaker one, yet it will bend, twist and torque equally far under this effect, and it will weigh just as much. If made with a smaller wall thickness, the stronger alloy will provide a tube as strong as one made with weaker steel and a bigger wall thickness, but then it will be less rigid, leading to more flex.

Despite its rather high density of 7.8, steel is a very suitable material: strong, rigid, cheap, predictable with respect to fatigue, and easy to work with. Depending on the specific purpose, certain material properties can be enhanced. Thus, the surface hardness can be increased by means of a form of heat treatment to give good wear properties for bearing parts, or the tensile strength may be increased by means of alloying, heat treatment and mechanical work, allowing the use of thin walled tubes to save weight.

There are four different methods of making tubular shapes: welded, drawn, welded and drawn, and extruded. For steel, only the first three are appropriate, while the latter may be suitable for making aluminum and plastic tubes. Figures 4.7 and 4.8 show how the tube is formed by each of these methods.

A *welded* tube is made by bending, or rolling, a flat narrow plate into the appropriate shape, after which the matching ends are butt-welded together. The weld seam remains visible on the inside (unless it is ground off locally, and can generally be felt through the bottom bracket as a distinct ridge. Although this method of construction is not necessarily bad, it is only used for relatively weak, cheap tubes, and the weld seam is generally considered to reduce the overall strength to 80% of that of a seamless tube with the same dimensions.

Drawn tubes are made by pulling a heated steel bar over a form and then repeating this process, also rolling it in from the outside, until the desired dimensions have been achieved. The last stage is done cold — at least that's what it's called in metallurgical circles, meaning at temperatures not exceeding half the melting point temperature (expressed in degrees C). This total operation enhances the strength and hardness of the tube, lending itself to application with strong steels.

Welded and drawn means just that: a welded steel tube is cold-drawn afterwards. This operation removes the weld seam and enhances strength and hardness, although this material is rarely quite as strong as cold drawn tubing. All of these methods can not only be used for the manufacture of frame tubes, but also for other components with tubular cross sections, while the process of cold work for strength enhancement is equally used on non-tubular products.

The tensile strength of ordinary welded carbon steel tubing, as used on simple bikes is about $40N/mm^2$. As a result, frame tubes for normal road bikes constructed of this material, when made with the conventional diameters, must have a wall thickness of about 1.4mm. For mountain bikes, tandems and other heavily loaded machines, they should be at least 0.2mm more. Some cheap bikes have frames of this material that seem quite light; they turn out to have a wall thickness of only 1.0mm, explaining the low weight, but indicating hopelessly inadequate strength, as was demonstrated clearly in a test conducted by the Dutch Consumer Association in which virtually all such bike frames eventually broke after hard use on rough roads.

Increasing Material Strength

The easiest and cheapest way to increase the material strength is by adding more carbon to the steel, resulting in what is referred to as 'High Ten' (for *high tensile strength*) or high carbon steels. This kind of tubing is also welded and has a tensile strength of about 45—$48N/mm^2$. The same strength provided by simple carbon steel tubing with 1.4mm wall thickness can be obtained with a wall thickness of about 1.2mm when this material is used.

To increase the strength further, allowing the use of even thinner wall tubing, other metallic components are added to obtain a steel alloy of greater strength. One percent manganese gives 10—15% more strength, reducing the required wall thickness to something like 1.0mm without loss of overall strength, even for welded tubes.

4.9. 'Honking' test. Done to establish the fatigue limit of aluminum handlebars when used to provide leverage during climbing.

Things start to get quite a bit more expensive when the strength has to be increased even further. This is done by using other materials in the alloy — either more manganese in combination with molybdenum or chromium and molybdenum. These materials, referred to as manganese-molybdenum and chrome-molybdenum steel, respectively (or by their manufacturers' trade names), are usually cold drawn, although some manufacturers offer welded and drawn tubes of the same quality at lower prices.

4.10. Orientation of single and double butted tubing (illustration from Hayduk: Bicycle Metallurgy for Cyclists).

Butted and Reinforced Tubes

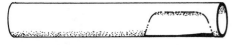

4.11. The three basic tubing types: welded, plain gauge seamless and butted.

Either process results in extremely strong tubes that could theoretically be as thin as 0.6mm, providing the same strength as the 1.4mm simple carbon steel tubes. By means of an additional heat treatment and drawing step, their strength can go up enough to allow even thinner walls, such as those used in Reynolds 753 and Tange Prestige tubing (Vitus 853 and Excel, which also contain vanadium, are at least as strong, but less well known). These very strongest, heat treated and cold drawn tubes are so hard that they can not be bent or shaped afterwards.

It should be noted that all steels used for frame tubing, however exotic, are in a metallurgical sense referred to as *low alloys*, meaning they contain less than 5% total alloying metals besides steel (measured by weight). A few exceptions do exist, such as the stainless steel frames for utility bikes made by the German mass producer Kynast. By and large, stainless steels are not stronger than most of the low alloy steels used for bicycle construction, and their properties cannot be enhanced as readily by means of heat treatment or drawing operations — however attractive it is to have a material that does not corrode and can be left unpainted.

All the thin tubes, starting at about 1.0mm, are usually supplied butted, which means that only the central section is actually that thin, while the ends, or butts, have a greater wall thickness. This increase in wall thickness serves to avoid damage done by the heating and cooling process during welding or brazing of the frame, which will be discussed in a separate section. An additional benefit of differential wall thicknesses over the length of the tubes is that they can be designed to match the local thickness to the relevant loading at any point along the tube, without sacrificing the weight and flexibility advantages of the thinner tubes in those areas where they are adequate to handle the local stresses.

Fig. 4.11 shows, slightly overstated, the way tubes are usually butted. Note that the seat tube and the steerer tube, or fork shaft, are generally single butted, i.e. have a thick-walled section on only one end, to provide a constant wall thickness where seat post and handlebar stem are inserted. Fig. 4.10 shows the locations of the butts in a typical butted frame.

Many frame and tubing manufacturers claim their tubes to be triple or even quadruple butted, a misnomer if there ever was one, since no tube can have more than two butts (ends). What they mean is fair enough though, namely that there are three or four different wall thicknesses along the length of the tube, presumably to best handle the relevant loading locally.

Other methods of reinforcing tubes include helical internal ridges, as used by Columbus, and external butting. The helical ribs have the inherent disadvantage of forming sudden differences in wall thickness at heavily loaded areas (referred to as *stress raisers*), which makes them susceptible to fatigue failure.

Maximizing Rigidity

To increase the rigidity of the tubes, without sacrificing weight or strength, several methods have recently been introduced. Columbus has presented its Max tubes that are flattened somewhat at the ends, with the longer axis coinciding each time with the orientation that calls for the greatest bending force. Another method is to form the tube into a kind of lozenge shape or to put a distinct ridge along the largest part of its length. In the case of the very strongest cold drawn and heat treated materials, this must be done before the final drawing or heat treating operation.

On mountain bikes, tubes have been made to greater outside diameters than has become the standard for road bikes. This provides a greater strength and a significantly increased rigidity, even if the wall thickness is reduced somewhat. This same method, with notably thin walls, was recently also introduced by several manufacturers of road bikes, while many mountain bike manufacturers have been taking this method even further. Tubes made along these lines are referred to as OS, or oversize, tubes.

Aluminum Alloys

Aluminum is frequently used for many bicycle components because its low density of 2.7 promises considerable weight savings over steel components. However, pure aluminum is too weak and soft for this purpose: Its tensile strength is only $120N/mm^2$, which would require three times the steel tube's wall thickness, resulting in the same weight. A number of aluminum alloys have been developed to overcome this problem. However, the modulus of elasticity of aluminum is also about $\frac{1}{3}$ of the value for steel.

Even so, aluminum can be used to advantage — providing it is used with the material's properties in mind. This has long been done by making e.g. aluminum brake arms about 1.7 times as thick as steel versions, resulting in a weight savings without reducing the rigidity. Similar tricks can be played with frame tubes, as aluminum frame pioneers such as Gary Klein and Charles Cunningham initially showed, and has since been confirmed by numerous other frame builders and

4.12. Cannondale bicycle with welded aluminum frame.

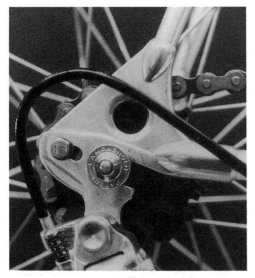

4.13. Detail of bonded ('screwed and glued') aluminum frame.

Titanium and its Alloys

Magnesium

4.14. Bicycle with one-piece cast magnesium alloy frame from Kirk Precision.

major manufacturers.

For many years, alloys designated as *7000 series*, containing about 5—7.5% zinc, have been used, especially for frame tubes. Their disadvantage is that the frames have to undergo heat treatment after welding. Most of these materials owe their high strength to a particular heat treatment procedure during the tube-manufacturing process (i.e. before welding), identified with a suffix such as *-T6* added to the basic material designation number. More recently, several interesting varieties of the 6000 series, which contain magnesium and silicon, and do not require after-weld heat treatment, have been applied successfully.

Aluminum alloys of the 5000 series are not weldable, although they include some of the strongest types. Whenever these are used they are joined either by bonding with an anaerobically setting epoxy resin or by means of some high-tech process based on literally shrinking the tubes around the lugs, fusing them in an electric induction process.

Titanium and its alloys have a density of about 4.6, i.e. 60% of the value for steel, leading to a significant weight reduction. However, it also has a lower modulus of elasticity, which means the way titanium parts are dimensioned is almost as important as it is for aluminum. Other disadvantages of titanium are its high price and the difficulty encountered when it is machined, formed or welded. It is used both for frames and for small components.

This is the lightest of the structurally suitable metals, with a density of 1.7, or 22% of the corresponding value for steel. Its strength is very much lower, as is its modulus of elasticity. Only by means of significant alloying with other metals does the strength come in the useful range for bicycle applications, but even then the modulus of elasticity makes for inadequate rigidity.

At least that's what everybody thought until recently. This view was changed by the British entrepreneur Kirk, who introduced a cast magnesium frame. An interesting construction, it is reasonably cheap (due to mass production techniques and publicity as well as funding from parent company Norsk Hydro, the world's major magnesium supplier), reasonably light, fabulously strong and extremely rigid. Actually, its major attraction is probably its unusual shape. As with most other bicycle frames made with exotic materials, the end result is not really any lighter than comparable steel frames. Just the same, it is a refreshing departure, escaping from the ingrained conventional thinking in the industry that characterizes too many of the other products in the industry.

By and large, you can ignore ordinary plastics for the construction of most useful bicycle components. Of course, ordinary plastic is too imprecise a concept, but the statement applies accurately to all plastics tried so far for load bearing parts on bicycles. An experimental plastic-framed bike, which actually went into production in the early nineteen-eighties, was heavy, noisy and uncomfortable, without solving any of the real problems of the bicycle, such as the fact that the drive-train is exposed to the elements and corrodes easily.

Clearly, too much experimenting with the bike ignores the real problems: there is nothing wrong with a steel frame that a layer of paint can't solve, yet that's all these experimenters seem to think of. After all, innovation in the motor industry has not concentrated on the bodywork, but on what's inside — and during the time when all the manufacturers did was change the body from year to year, there was technical stagnation in that industry.

Just the same, certain plastics have specific applications. One of these is Kevlar, or more correctly *aramid*, the generic name for a substance that has been under dispute between DuPont and the Dutch AKZO company, each claiming to hold the original patent on its manufacture. This artificial fiber is as strong and un-stretchable as steel, yet many times lighter and more flexible, making it suitable for reinforcing structures in tires.

Both aramid and various other (mainly natural) fibers can be used to advantage as harnessing structures in a matrix of epoxy resin to provide light and strong so-called *composite* materials. The other fibers used for this purpose are carbon and boron. As long as the resin selected hardens fully and the fibers are long, very sound structures can be made, suitable for frame tubes and other parts. However, they can also be used to advantage in a mold, in a method similar to what is used 'in fiberglass construction, to form composite frames that differ from the run of the mill, departing from the conventional tubular structure. To date, nobody seems to have been able to make a frame of this material that is as strong as a steel frame without making it equally heavy, which makes you wonder whether there is any justification for such expensive techniques.

Plastics and Composites

4.15. Kestrel frame made of Kevlar fiber-reinforced epoxy resin.

4.16. Yesteryear's composite: Hickory frame with brass lugs wer used on an this early American bicycle (approx. 1900).

Dimensions and Construction

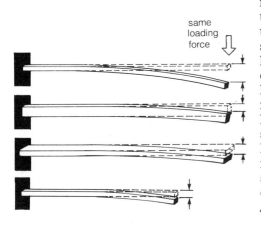

4.17. *Factors that affect rigidity of a simple structural member: The less it bends, the more rigid it is.*

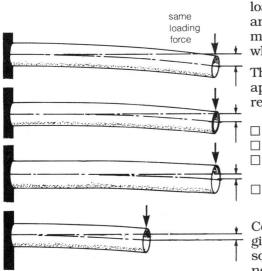

4.18. *Factors that affect rigidity of a tubular member. Again, the more rigid member is the one that bends least.*

These two factors are at least as important as the choice of materials, and must always be considered in conjunction with the latter. Often a part can actually be made lighter with steel than with some of the lighter materials, providing the dimensions and the construction methods are selected to make the most of the material. Thus, recently introduced thin-walled, high-strength steel handlebar stems have proven to be lighter than the aluminum versions that were considered the cat's whiskers up to then. Similarly, it makes little sense to make handlebars and seat posts of aluminum, since given the diameter used, they could be lighter and stronger if made of thin-walled, high-strength tubular steel. Even cranks could be made lighter if hollow steel were used instead of solid aluminum. Lately, there has indeed been a rediscovery of steel, to which the introduction of (small) stainless steel chainrings for mountain bikes testifies.

The answer to many of the bicycle's particular demands seems to lie in the use of tubular members, as was discovered over a century ago when engineers first got seriously involved with bicycles in Victorian England. Under tensile (pulling) loading, it does not matter whether a member is tubular or a simple rod, as long as the same total material cross section is used, expressed in mm^2. Thus, a 6mm (¼") diameter rod would be as strong as a 28mm (1⅛") diameter tube with 1mm wall thickness. However, frame tubes are not loaded only in tension, but alternately in compression and torque as well, and for this kind of loading the dimension perpendicular to the load must be maximized, which is elegantly achieved with round tubing.

The resistance against bending due to perpendicularly applied forces is dependent on a number of factors. The resulting deflection is:

☐ Directly proportional to the force
☐ Directly proportional to the square of the length
☐ Inversely proportional to the width of the member (perpendicular to the force)
☐ Inversely proportional to the square of the height of the member (in the direction of the force).

Consequently, to avoid excessive deformation with a given force and material, components must be designed so that they are as short as possible, and their thickness perpendicular to the direction of the force must be maximized. This explains why brake arms are made as chubby as they are and why the wheel clearances are minimized to make them as short as possible. On the other hand, that does not justify making frames smaller than necessary to fit the rider: it is the finished geometrical structure that counts, and on a frame, the maximum rigidity is achieved if the structure extends to the limits, with the members joined rigidly at the corners of the resulting polygon.

Applied to cylindrical members, be they rods or tubes, these same factors can be expressed slightly differently. In this case, deformation is determined as follows:

☐ Directly proportional to the force
☐ Directly proportional to the square of the length
☐ Inversely proportional to the wall thickness of tubular members
☐ Inversely proportional to the cube of the outside diameter.

Within limits, the biggest diameter is the best, even at the expense of wall thickness, thus retaining the same weight. Fig. 4.18 illustrates this. The limit is a function of the risk of collapse — the aluminum beer can effect. To prevent this in parts that are anchored at both ends, such as frame tubes, the ratio of wall thickness to diameter should not exceed 1:30. However, while cantilevered parts such as the fork must have significantly greater wall thickness, also related to the suspended length and the load, and must be thicker near the fixed point than near the end that is loaded, to avoid collapse.

For aluminum tubing (which has less inherent rigidity than steel ones), the principle of maximized outside diameter, rather than wall thickness is used more and more. After all, the same effect as a 35% increase in wall thickness can be achieved with only a 10% increase in outside diameter — with a correspondingly lower weight penalty. Recently, several manufacturers have applied the same principle to steel tubing as well.

All of the above is not limited to frame tubes. Tubular steel luggage racks and many other components can be designed with these principles in mind, providing increased stability with a minimal weight penalty — even with a weight reduction in certain cases. It is worth noting in this context that the benefit of large diameter tubing only applies to bending and torquing forces. Tension forces are just as well taken up by relatively narrow members of adequate diameter, while the remarks about buckling apply to compression forces. Finally, it should be noted that both tension and compression forces must be taken up in line with the force, since the supporting member would otherwise bend. Thus, e.g. the stays of luggage racks must be straight.

4.19. Detail of a lugless ('fillet brazed') steel frame on an older Gary Fisher mountain bike. Although beautiful, the build-up of brazing metal in the fillet does add to the frame's weight.

Joining Methods

In addition to the replaceable screw-threaded and wedged connections covered in Chapter 3, other techniques are used to permanently connect parts of the frame and other bicycle components. These methods, which will be covered below, include various welding processes, brazing (i.e. hard soldering), and resin bonding. The curiosity of casting a lug around the tubes has been used at times for cheap bikes — technically there is nothing wrong with it, but aesthetically it is an abomination.

Brazing

This is still the most common method of frame construction when steel tubes are used. Brazing is a process by which the tubes are heated to temperatures well below their melting point, after which a filler material with a lower melting point is allowed to melt and run between the joint, forming a permanent bond (the molecules of the filler material intermingle with those of the base metal) when cooled. For steel tubes, it is done at temperatures between 650 and 960°C, depending on the particular brazing material used.

Only relatively thick-walled tubes of the less exotic types of steel should be brazed at the higher temperature, because the sequence of heating could weaken a thin point at a distance of about 10—20mm from the hottest joint, referred to as the *heat affected zone*. Low temperature brazing requires the use of brazing rods with a high percentage of silver. This process is usually referred to as silver brazing, even though the material used is still predominantly copper and zinc.

Welding

In the welding process, the base metal is heated to the melting point and the parts are fused together either with or without the aid of a compatible filler metal, forming one piece after cooling. Because a much smaller area has to be heated for a shorter time, although the temperatures involved are higher, welding is actually more time- and energy-efficient than brazing.

4.20. Unusual industrial joining method: Aluminum lugs cast around the stainless steel tubes on a Bridgestone fame.

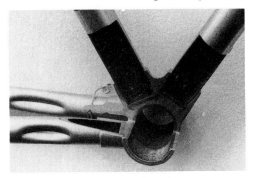

Due to the high temperatures required, the base metal must be relatively thick for successful welding. About 1.2mm is the minimum wall thickness under most circumstances. To prevent corrosion, welding is often done by the TIG (tungsten inert gas) process, by which a tungsten welding element (which itself does not melt, due to its extremely high melting point) is used and the joint is protected against oxidation by means of a blanket of inert gas.

Welding can be used for steel as well as for aluminum and titanium. The TIG process is used when joining the latter two metals, since oxidation would otherwise make a reliable bond impossible. When welding the strong heat treated alloys of the 7000 series, the material properties are affected negatively by the heat that results from welding. This effect must be reversed subsequently by a controlled heating process referred to as *post weld heat treatment*.

Bonding and Other Processes.

If nonmetallic materials have to be joined, it is usually done by other methods, such as bonding, and even aluminum is frequently joined this way. Bonding is usually done by means of an anaerobically hardening epoxy resin, made by mixing two reacting components shortly before applying them. Depending on the substance used, the gaps between the parts may have to be relatively generous or very tight, but the surfaces must always be quite uniform and scrupulously clean. In some cases, the joint is screwed or clamped as well as bonded. Recently, the use of strong non-weldable alloys has led to the development of different joining methods, including a high voltage electro-magnetic shrink-fusion process pioneered in Austria.

Finishing Processes

The different parts of the bicycles are protected against corrosion, or just made to look prettier, by means of several different processes. Steel and aluminum frames are generally painted or lacquered. Sometimes chrome plating is used on steel, while both aluminum and titanium may be anodized. The latter is a galvanic process that transfers the outer layer into a hard, impregnable form of oxide, which in turn protects the rest of the material.

4.21. Another mass-production joint detail: Carbon fiber-reinforced epoxy lug, cast in place around the frame tubes.

Modern paint processes generally use an epoxy resin, which reacts anaerobically into a hard layer. Some frames are still lacquered, using many thin layers of a highly diluted material, usually finished off with a transparent layer. In recent years it has become popular to color even aluminum parts, which may be achieved either by adding a dye to the anodization or by means of resin coating. The latter process is used on cheap parts in order to save the rather expensive polishing that would be necessary to obtain a smooth, clean look on bare metal parts. On components that come into contact with others, a blank finish is preferable, since the coating or anodization soon wears off, making the whole thing look rather shabby.

Increasing Surface Hardness

Finishing processes are also used to increase the surface hardness for increased wear resistance. Thus, rims are often anodized to a greater depth — 0.050mm, rather than the 0.005mm depth used for simple cor-

4.22. An interesting historic bike. This 1890 cross frame may be seen as the prototype for the De la Haye and Breeze frames shown in Chapter 1.

rosion protection. This process may also be used on aluminum chainwheels.

Steel parts are often protected and made wear-resistant by means of hard chrome plating. Even more common is the use of chemical oxidization, which results in a matt black surface (although the use of a dye can produce almost any color effect). Soft metal parts, finally, may be nickel plated, since the harder chrome would easily peal off when the parts are deformed — it is also an excellent finish for frames. This process is used on spoke nipples. Stainless steel parts are usually left completely untreated. Actually, stainless steel does corrode, but this material instantaneously forms its own shiny surface film.

Chapter 5

The Frame

In the chapters of this second part of the book, the various functional groups of components will be presented, including extensive coverage of their maintenance and repair. The first part to consider is the frame, the bicycle's backbone, and the only part generally made by the manufacturer whose name appears on the bike. It forms the basis on which all the other components are mounted.

On most bicycles, the frame represents about 40% of the complete bike's total value. They are sold as complete units comprising the frame and the range of other components selected by the manufacturer for that particular model. However, in the higher price category, it is not uncommon to find what is referred to as custom bikes. In this case, the bare frame is equipped with components selected by the customer in the bike shop. Another step up is the bike based on a real custom frame, which is made to measure for a particular cyclist by a specialist frame builder.

When choosing a custom bike or frame, it is also customary to select frame and components from comparable price categories, so the ratio of 40% frame, 60% other parts usually applies here too. However, if you are on a budget, it may be smart to select the highest quality frame you can afford, and save on components of a lower price category. There are two reasons for this. In the first place, the frame can last a lifetime, while the other parts will probably have to be replaced sooner or later, which will be a good time to upgrade them if desired. In the second place, the difference between components may lie more in their finish than in their inherent quality, and it makes no sense to pay extra for a shiny finish when you are on a tight budget.

Fig. 5.3 shows the different parts that make up the conventional frame. The main frame comprises top tube, seat tube, down tube and head tube. The rear frame, or rear triangle, is built up of seat stays and

5.1 and 5.2. Frame builders at work. Above: Manual brazing as done for small series production. Below: automated brazing in a larger factory.

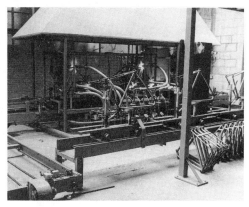

Frame Construction

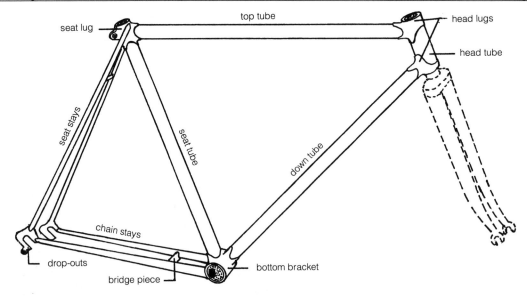

5.3. The frame and its components

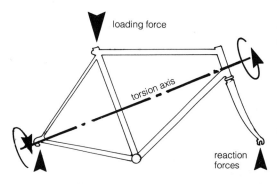

5.4. Dynamic and static loading of frame

Frame Design

chain stays. Main frame and rear triangle are joined at the bottom bracket and at the seat lug. Frequently, the frame is sold together with the fork and is then referred to as frameset. In this book, the fork is covered separately in Chapter 6, which is devoted to the steering system.

The main frame tubes are normally joined by means of lugs into which they are brazed, while the bottom bracket is essentially also a big and complicated lug. The rear stays are connected by means of short connecting bridge pieces. At the ends, where seat and chain stays meet, they are attached to flat parts referred to as drop-outs, in which the rear wheel is installed.

Assuming derailleur gearing is used on the bike, the RH drop-out is usually equipped with an attachment lug for the derailleur. Finally, there are often a number of small parts, referred to as braze-ons, which allow the installation of various components and accessories, and to provide stops or guides for gear and brake cables.

What was said above applies to the conventional diamond shaped frame that is still the most common, if only because it generally offers the best compromise between strength, stability, weight and price. Other frame designs using the same basic construction method have been more or less popular at times, especially for women's bikes or special-purpose machines. In addition, quite different frame designs, often based on specific manufacturing techniques, have been making some inroads in recent years. Fig. 5.6 shows some of the different designs based on conventional manufacturing techniques. Some of the more revolutionary designs based on differing techniques will be covered separately.

To determine which of the shapes shown in Fig. 5.6 is suitable, the purpose must be kept in mind. If the lightest, strongest and most rigid frame possible is desired, then this is the wrong place to look. If, on the other hand, the most important criterion for a particular rider is to obtain a low straddling point, then this may go at the expense of some other factors. To get the same strength or rigidity, the price of increased weight due to the selection of thicker walled tubing must be accepted.

Technically seen, the important thing is to form a strong and direct connection between the tie points. A frame structure should resist both the vertical forces applied by the rider's weight, and the various lateral and torquing forces that are exerted due to asymmetrical loading under movement. Braking, steering and vibrations also cause variable forces that must be absorbed.

All these criteria can be easily considered if weight is not the object. But in bicycle design it is, and to mini-

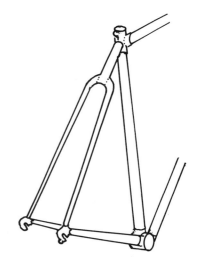

5.5. Wishbone seat stay design

5.6. Some frame design alternatives

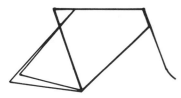

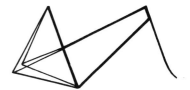

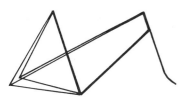

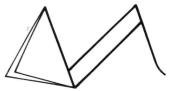

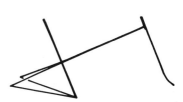

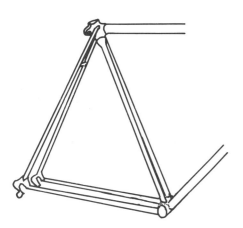

5.7. Split seat stays (short rear triangle)

5.8. Giant's Cadex. It has a composite frame of carbon fiber reinforced tubing and cast aluminum lugs.

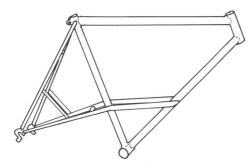

5.9. Raised chain stay design

mize the frame weight, a technically well conceived design must be worked out. It is relatively simple to compare the effect of forces on the various frame designs. To do so, you can make models of thin metal or wood rods, pinned together at the joints, freely pivoted. Only the designs that do not collapse are structurally sound, and you will soon find out that this does not apply to the various women's models shown.

Fig. 5.4 shows the distribution of forces on the conventional bicycle frame resulting from vertical, static loading. As you can see, the various tubes are arranged in such a way that the forces are always applied in line with the tube's linear axis, either in tension or in compression. This design was developed in the late eighteen-eighties and has essentially formed the basis for all bicycle frames since that time. These findings can not only be confirmed in layman's fashion with the modeling technique mentioned above, but also in engineering terms by means of a relatively easily accessible technique known as finite element analysis.

It took a little longer before bicycle designers realized that the asymmetrical and variable forces applied during motion must also be considered. These did not pose such a problem on early bicycle frames, due to the use of very thick-walled tubing or even solid members of significant diameter, which are adequately rigid. In recent times, more attention has been paid to this factor due to the inherent lack of rigidity of very thin-walled tubing. Ideally, the frame should have some vertical flexibility, since this provides shock dampening, while retaining maximum lateral rigidity to prevent instability. Of all the designs used to date, the conventional diamond-shaped frame remains the most satisfactory, especially if large diameter, thin-walled tubing is used.

Some different design details have been introduced at times, especially in conjunction with the use of other materials than steel, not all of which offer real advantages. Take for example the so-called wishbone seat stay design. This brings the stays together just above the rear wheel and carries them as one thicker tube to the seat lug, as shown in Fig. 5.5. The result is a rigid rear triangle — but rigid in the wrong direction: the vertical shock absorption is eliminated without providing additional lateral stiffness. Technically less questionable is the very short frame design that can be achieved by splitting the seat tube into two thinner ones, as shown in Fig. 5.7. The recently popular raised chain stay mountain bike frame design shown in Fig. 5.9 loses its triangulated integrity, just to achieve an amount of chain clearance that is not really needed.

The size of a bicycle is primarily determined by the height of the frame. Fig. 5.10 shows the two methods used to determine this dimension. Although both methods measure along the seat tube, there is some lack of clarity as to the reference points used. French and Italian bicycles, and an increasing number of American mountain bikes, are measured from the center of the bottom bracket to the center of the top tube. The conventional method used in the English speaking world, on the other hand, is to refer to the distance between the center of the bottom bracket and the top of the seat lug. In most cases, the same frame will be quoted approximately 15mm or ½" less when measured center-to-center than when measured from the center of the bracket to the top of the seat lug.

With the introduction of really different frame designs, such as those made of composites, the conventional frame size becomes a questionable reference, as it already is for women's frame designs. Eventually, one should perhaps give a range of sizes: straddle height of top tube, minimum and maximum distance between saddle and bottom bracket, and minimum and maximum handlebar height.

Quite a number of other dimensions and angles, besides the nominal frame size, are important in the design of a bicycle frame, and make one frame more suitable to a particular rider than the other. Fig. 5.10 also shows the most important dimensions that should be considered as they apply to a conventional frame. Just where the rider's hands, feet and seat must be placed on a bicycle for best control over the machine is a matter of basic ergonomics and has been essentially unchanged since the turn of the century (the recent introduction of handlebars allowing a lower and more stretched out posture only works if speed alone, rather than control over the bike, is considered important).

As was explained in Chapter 4, a shorter tube is basically more rigid than a longer one, which in turn is more flexible, providing better shock absorption. Consequently, a small frame, with short tubes due to minimal clearances, would be more rigid than one designed to more generous dimensions. This is the reason clearances are minimized to keep tube lengths to a practical minimum.

On the other hand, it makes no sense to make the frame so small that seat and handlebars have to be raised and extended by means of an overly long seat

Frame Sizing

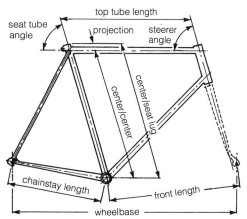

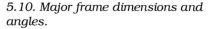

5.10. Major frame dimensions and angles.

Frame Geometry

5.11. Jig to hold frame tubes at predetermined angles during assembly.

63

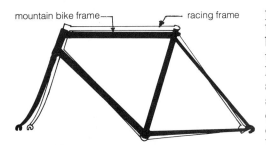

5.12. Comparison of frame geometries

Frame Angles

X (mm)	angle
134	66°
127	67°
121	68°
115	69°
109	70°
103	71°
97	72°
92	73°
86	74°
80	75°

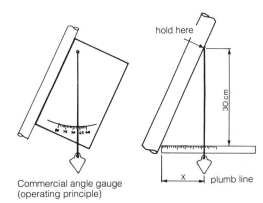

Commercial angle gauge
(operating principle)

5.13. Methods to determine frame angles

post and handlebar stem, since these extensions are themselves less rigid, giving the overall bike not more, but less stability when ridden this way. Another factor that greatly influences overall frame rigidity is the length (and the diameter) of the head tube: frame designs that maximize head tube length, within the given sizing constraints, achieve optimum rigidity. As for the diameter of the head tube, the recent introduction of oversized headsets with matching head tube diameters has greatly contributed to overall frame rigidity and steering predictability.

The relative angles of the frame tubes are as important as the dimensions. The steering angle, i.e. the angle of the steering tube relative to the horizontal plane, greatly affects both the shock absorption and the steering characteristics of the bike. The latter factor will be covered in Chapter 6. With respect to the shock absorption properties, the smaller angle gives a softer ride, assuming equal fork blade thickness.

The seat tube angle, again measured with respect to the horizontal plane, is usually selected so that the seat arrives in the ergonomically best position relative to the bottom bracket. On racing bikes and aggressively ridden mountain bikes, this angle will be 73—74°. The angle is usually somewhat less on touring and recreational bikes, placing the rider closer to the rear wheel. On small frame sizes, a slightly steeper angle may be selected to achieve the relatively short top tube length that is ergonomically required for most women and many short males. To determine the angle of either tube, refer to Fig. 5.13, using the table contained there to convert the dimension measured into degrees.

Although bikes with a small seat tube angle at first seem ergonomically wrong, this only applies when the position is the forward poised one we are familiar with. The same relationship between various fixed points can be achieved with different angles, as it is done most dramatically on the recumbent bicycle design. This can be made to work on relatively normal bikes too: I have ridden bikes with angles down to 60°. In city traffic, this makes it possible for the feet to reach the ground without getting out of the seat, while still maintaining the correct distance between seat an pedals when riding. However, long-term comfort in this position requires a back rest.

The distance between the seat tube and the steerer tube, or rather between the bottom bracket and the front wheel axle, must be such that adequate clearance between the rider's toes and the front wheel remains.

Although this requirement may be waived on racing bikes (since high-speed cycling never requires large steering movements), it is quite critical for mountain bikes, and the use of fenders requires even more clearance. As a guideline, the distance between bottom bracket and front wheel axle is usually about 55cm (22") on a racing bike, about 58cm (23") on a recreational bike and should be at least 60cm (24") if fenders will be installed.

The distance between the bottom bracket and the rear wheel axle is also minimized to achieve a light and rigid bike. Excessive flex, resulting from long chain stays of thin-wall tubing, can cause tire rubbing, chain scraping and unintentional gear shifting when applying maximum pedaling force. There is no truth in speculations about presumed loss of efficiency due to frame flex, either here or anywhere else — after all, any energy that goes into bending the flexible tube quite far would also have gone into bending the less flexible tube less far, and this same energy is released again as the tube springs back. Racing and aggressively ridden mountain bikes may have chain stays that are about 41 and 43cm (16 and 17") long, respectively, while they should be at least 2.5cm (1") longer if fenders are to be installed.

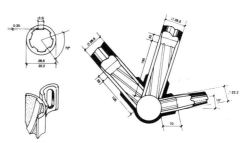

5.14. Helical grooves reinforce this Columbus tubing at the most heavily loaded points.

Frame Materials

Generally, bicycle frames are made of the materials discussed in Chapter 4, i.e. tubular steel or aluminum alloys, while titanium or carbon fiber tubes sometimes find application. Frames constructed of moulded composites or e.g. cast magnesium are still uncommon, although their use may increase in the foreseeable future.

The customary frame tube diameters in mm are listed as follows, depending whether the frame is built to English (international) or French standards:

5.15. Sectioned frame at bottom bracket, showing just how thin the tubes are on a quality frame built with butted tubes.

Road bike	top tube	seat tube	down tube	head tube	chain stays	seat stays
English	25.4	28.6	28.6	31.7	22.0	14.0
French	26.0	28.0	28.0	32.0	22.0	14.0

On mountain bikes, some of these dimensions provide inadequate strength and rigidity for hard use. Consequently, they are generally built with slightly larger, more recently also with oversize tube diameters. Although there are significant variations from one make to the other, the following list shows two typical (though not universal) examples of regular and oversize

5.16. Lugged mountain bike frame made with Columbus OR tubing.

5.17. Carbon fiber reinforced resin bonded around thin aluminum tubes.

mountain bike tubing sizes:

Road bike	top tube	seat tube	down tube	head tube	chain stays	seat stays
Regular	28.6	28.6	31.7	31.7	22.0	16.0
Oversize	28.6	28.6	33.2	35.0	25.0	16.0

Because of the material's much lower modulus of elasticity, aluminum tubes flex too much if built to these standard dimensions. Thus, aluminum frame designers soon found the solution in the use of relatively thin walled oversized tubing. Tube diameters on some aluminum bikes go all the way up to 2" for the down tube — the most heavily torsion-loaded main tube on any bike. Less dramatically oversized tubing dimensions have recently also been introduced on thin-walled steel frames for road bikes, offering increased rigidity without a weight penalty.

Although the difference in weight between a light racing frame and that of a conventional utility bike is quite significant — 1.7kg and 3.9kg, respectively — the difference between frames built of different materials within a certain category is not that dramatic. Thus, the lightest composite frame — that promptly broke when used in the Race Across America — is hardly any lighter than the lightest steel frame, and the same applies to aluminum and titanium. Although lighter frames can be built using these more exotic materials, to make them equally strong, they must also be virtually as heavy.

Frame Joints

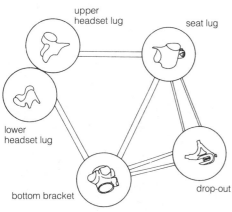

5.18. Lugs and bottom bracket locations

Traditionally, bicycle frame tubes are joined by means of brazing the ends together with the aid of lugs. The American utility bike always was an exception, usually being welded, using thicker wall tube with smaller diameters. This explains their quite sensational weight if adequately rigid, or poor stability if made lighter. The various common frame joining methods are depicted in Fig. 5.19.

On lugged frames, external lugs are generally used, although recently, internal lugs have been applied by several manufacturers. On factory-built frames with external lugs, the brazing material is installed in a notch in the tube before the frame is assembled and then heated, causing the brazing material to run around the joint. On hand-built frames, the bronze is added from the outside, a method also used by some of the factories that build frames in small series. Internally lugged frames are almost always factory-built, and the brazing material is installed in a recess in the lug before assembly and heating.

Lugs are also used on many aluminum and composite frames. However, in that case the tubes are bonded to the lugs, using an anaerobically hardening epoxy resin (meaning that the material hardens in a chemical reaction, rather than by drying with air). Some recently introduced frames have aluminum tubes on internal steel lugs, while others combine thin-wall steel tubes with aluminum lugs. Although these developments are still relatively new and not yet time-proven, they seems to be unquestionable from an engineering standpoint.

Occasionally, especially if odd-size or odd-shaped tubes must be joined, a lugless brazed construction is used. This technique is usually referred to as fillet brazing, since the brazing metal is not only entered in the narrow gap between the tubes, but is built up around the joint to form a reinforcing fillet. It's an expensive way of building, due to its labor- and skill- intensiveness. Optically, the result can be very pleasing. Depending on the type of frame tubes and the maximum temperature specified by the manufacturer, both this and other brazing techniques can be done either with bronze or silver brazing rod. Since the latter material flows very thinly at a relatively low temperature, it is harder to work with, but is specified by most manufacturers of ultra high-strength tubing. Whatever the manufacturers specify, nobody uses silver in locations requiring fillets, since it cannot be built up to a bead.

If thicker-walled (1.2mm or more at the ends) tubes are used, welding becomes a viable option. Thus, this is a common method for the construction of aluminum frames and most mountain bike frames, whether steel or aluminum. Most aluminum alloys must be stress-relieved at an elevated temperature during a prolonged period subsequent to welding to restore the original strength. As pointed out in Chapter 4, some alloys of the 6000 series, though slightly weaker than the strongest tempered types of the 7000 series, make life easier for the manufacturer by eliminating the need for stress-relief by means of post weld heat treatment.

Essentially all welding operations on bicycle frames are carried out in a protective atmosphere. Although some cheaper thick-walled frames are welded under CO_2 gas, inert gas such as argon is used for all quality frame welding operations, commonly referred to as TIG welding (also see Chapter 4 for some comments on this welding process).

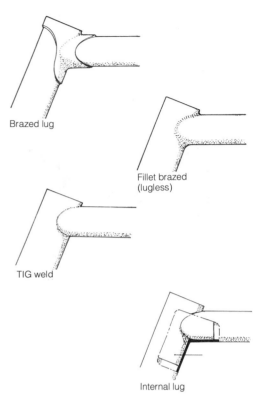

Brazed lug

Fillet brazed (lugless)

TIG weld

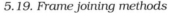

Internal lug

5.19. Frame joining methods

5.20. Seat lug detail on Vitus frame with carbon fiber reinforced resin tubes bonded to internal aluminum lugs. Note the bulging tubes where they are pressed over the lugs.

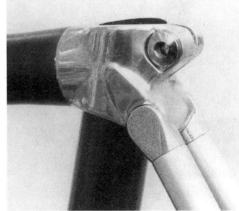

Frame Details

Lugs and Bottom Bracket

5.21. Haden Polaris lug set. Although made of pressed steel, these are accurate enough for high-quality frames. The cut-outs aid brazing metal penetration.

5.22. Investment cast steel bottom bracket by Reynolds.

The details of the bicycle frame include the lugs that hold the frame tubes together, the bottom bracket, the drop-outs, the connecting parts, as well as the minor braze-ons used to mount components and accessories. These are the items that will be discussed in the following sections.

Fig. 5.21 shows a typical set of lugs. For normal brazed steel frames, there are external lugs in several categories, and the same applies to the bottom bracket shell into which the crankset is mounted. The most important factor affecting bonding quality is the consistency of the gap between the tube and the lug, which should ideally be about 0.2mm all around. The highest degree of accuracy is generally achieved when these parts are formed by means of the lost wax casting technique, also known as microfusion. These parts may be recognized by their relatively sharp and somewhat bulky contours. Since a new mold must be made for each item produced, these parts tend to be quite expensive.

Cheaper lugs are made of stamped and welded plate. These range from the cheap and often poorly fitting lugs used on mass production frames to quite nicely shaped and more accurately dimensioned ones used on some quality frames. The best lugs are contoured rather delicately and have cut-outs to aid the penetration and inspection of brazing material, which greatly affects the quality of a brazed connection, even though it is generally accepted that a 70% contact is adequate to achieve sufficient bonding in a brazed joint.

The seat lug and the bottom bracket shell are somewhat special. The former is split in the back to allow clamping the seat post in. The two halves are clamped together by means of a bolt that pushes the eye at the back (or sometimes on the front) together. The gap should end in a round 3—4mm hole to prevent cracking. On mountain bikes, where the saddle is adjusted often, this point is quite critical, as is the attachment of the eye to the lug. Since a cracked lug would essentially ruin a frame, several manufacturers have replaced the eye by a separate external clamp that goes around the top of the lug.

The bottom bracket shell is by far the most complicated lug, connecting down tube, seat tube and chain stays, while providing a mounting for the bottom bracket that must be perfectly aligned perpendicular to the plane formed by the main frame tubes. Usually, the shell is threaded to accept a standard bottom bracket (although some mountain bike manufacturers install their own special bottom brackets by that are held with spring clips). Depending which type will fit, this screw thread may be either of the English, Italian, French or Swiss standard, all of which differ, as is outlined in Table 4 in the Appendix.

On many racing frames, the bottom bracket shell is cut out in the bottom, which is supposed to allow water to drain off and to save weight. The real benefit escapes me, since the weight savings is negligible and the risk of dirt and water entering there is greater than the benefit of it running off. Other details often included are guides for the gear cables, which are more useful. The LH and RH ends should be perfectly faced (squared) to allow accurate installation of the screwed parts of the bottom bracket bearings.

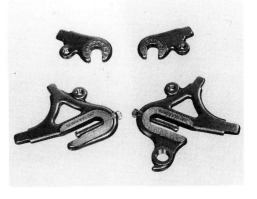

5.23. Shimano front and rear drop-outs

Drop-outs, or rear fork-ends, are depicted in Fig. 5.24. They are also available in several different versions, the most accurate and strongest of which are either forged or cast with the lost wax method described above. These invariably have some adjusting mechanism to position the rear wheel axle and an eye or lug for the installation of the rear derailleur on the RH side. The optimum attachment point of the rear derailleur relative to the rear axle depends on the make and model in question. This is why most derailleur manufacturers also offer their own drop-outs — with the effect that you get locked into their particular brand of derailleur.

Cheaper frames may have relatively thin drop-outs stamped out of flat plate. These usually have neither an adjustment mechanism nor a derailleur eye, requiring a separate adaptor for the installation of the derailleur. Since these drop-outs are so thin, and since the attachment of the tubes is often too far from the wheel axle, these drop-outs bend too easily.

The frames of touring bikes and most mountain bikes have drop-outs with integral eyelets for the installation of stays for fenders and luggage racks. Nowadays, these things are almost always lacking on other bikes, even those meant for recreational riding — purely a fashionable aberration, since they are in nobody's way and add significant practical benefits for anybody not actually racing. In fact, up to the early seventies, even pure racing bikes usually had eyelets, and the toughest bike racers used them without embarrassment.

Vertical drop-outs allow building the rear triangle with smaller wheel clearances, but often lack the adjustment detail, requiring the frame to be built extremely accurately if the wheels are to be aligned properly on

Drop-Outs

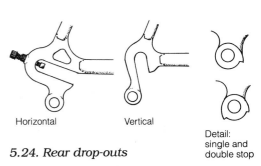

Horizontal   Vertical

Detail: single and double stop

5.24. Rear drop-outs

5.25. This special Mittendorf's off-set LH drop-out allows spoking the wheel symmetrically.

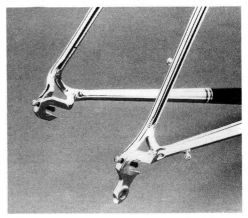

Cable tunnels

Front
derailleur lug

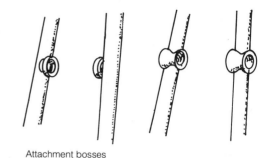

Attachment bosses

5.26. Some typical braze-ons

the finished bike. To produce an extremely short rear triangle, some manufacturers have used what is known as compact drop-outs. These consist of two parts, connected by means of slotted holes and bolts, allowing adjustment and replacement.

The drop-outs on welded aluminum frames had better be extremely thick, to the point of being ugly. Another solution would be a two-part design, with the major part, containing the wheel slot and the threaded holes for derailleur attachment, made of e.g. stainless steel. Bonded frames can be built with steel or aluminum tubes bonded to more or less normal steel drop-outs.

Other Frame Parts

5.27. Racing frame built with Reynolds 531 tubing and investment cast lugs by the same manufacturer.

Most of what was said about the lugs and drop-outs also applies *mutatis mutandis* to the various other frame parts. Thus, the connecting pieces between the rear stays are best when accurately made and shaped to match the respective frame tubes to which they connect. The following is a list of the various braze-ons used on many bikes, briefly summarizing the points that are important in their design or installation:

☐ Bosses for the installation of cantilever or other mountain bike brakes. Attached to the seat stays or under the chain stays, these must be perfectly straight and in the correct position relative to the rim for the particular brake used.

☐ A lug for the installation of the front derailleur on the seat tube. It must be of the type that matches the derailleur selected, keeping in mind that mountain bike and touring front derailleurs are not available for this form of mounting.

☐ Bosses for the installation of shifters. These go on the side or the top of the down tube and must match the particular make of shifters selected, which becomes increasingly important with the advent of indexed shifting, where mis-matching gearing components rarely works reliably.

☐ Cable stops and guides for the brake and derailleur cables. These should allow the shortest possible routing of these cables and eliminate excessive lengths of outer cable. On some bikes it has become fashionable to route the cables through the frame tubes, adding friction and providing another entry point for water, causing internal corrosion.

☐ Bosses for the attachment of one or more water bottles should be located so that the bottle can be reached while riding.

☐ Bosses for the installation of luggage racks. These should be in locations matching the particular make and type of rack selected. Protect the screw thread of these and other bosses when not in use by means of short matching screws or bolts.

☐ On the inside of the RH seat stay, there is often a lug on which the chain can be placed under slight tension when the wheel is removed. This item stops the greasy chain from flopping all over the place, picking up dirt or making other items filthy.

☐ A pump peg is usually installed under the top tube these days. This allows the pump to be clamped between it and the seat lug, leaving the seat tube free for the installation of a water bottle or a lock mounting bracket.

☐ On British touring and mountain bikes, there is often an installation boss for a light or, on some French touring machines, an attachment for a generator, or dynamo. The latter must be in the exact position that allows aligning the generator as described in Chapter 14.

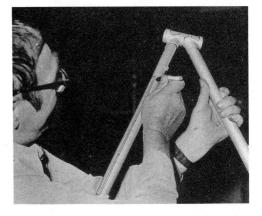

5.28. Some finish detailing is still done by hand, even on relatively simple frames like this.

The subject of finishing processes as covered in Chapter 4 applies largely to the frame. Virtually all steel frames and most welded aluminum frames are painted or lacquered. Chrome plating can be used to advantage on particularly scratch-sensitive locations on steel frames, such as the RH chain stays, the seat lug and the drop-outs. What is not painted or otherwise coated on an aluminum frame should preferably be anodized, although a really good natural polish can look very attractive and remains that way unless the bike gets into a salty atmosphere. Titanium is also anodized or polished, while carbon fiber reinforced epoxy is generally pigmented throughout.

Another excellent frame finish is nickel plating. Popular around the turn of the century, this process was long forgotten, until some mountain bike frame builders reintroduced it recently. It is highly scratch resistant, and although it is less shiny then chrome plating, it is

Frame Finish

5.29. Two-part rear drop-out of cantilever design on Cannondale welded aluminum frame.

more durable than either chrome or paint.

Maintenance and Repairs

Although the frame is the bicycle's major components, it does not rate very high amongst the parts requiring maintenance. If anything does happen, it is often so catastrophic that there is little hope of correcting it: you may have to buy a whole new frame or — more typically — a whole new bike. What little there is to do on the frame will be covered below.

Upon frontal impact, the front end of the bike will be pushed in and this may result in damage to the down tube as shown in Fig. 5.30. This results in a severely weakened frame and usually also affects the steering. Check for this kind of damage after a fall or collision.

On a really good frame, it is often worthwhile to get a damaged tube replaced if you can find a frame builder who will take on this kind of job. After the repair, the frame will have to be wholly or partly repainted, but it may still be cheaper than buying a new frame.

Even if there is no damage of the type described above, you should thoroughly inspect the front fork and the frame for correct alignment after any serious accident, which will be described in the next section.

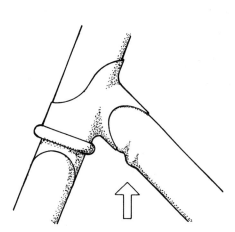

5.30. Typical downtube damage due to frontal collision.

Frame Inspection

Before the actual inspection, the rear wheel and any interfering accessories must be removed. The professional way is by using a special frame alignment gauge, but it can be done quite satisfactorily with 3m (10ft) twine, a ruler with mm marking and a metal straight-edge

5.31 and 5.32.
Left: frame alignment inspection.
Right: drop-out alignment check.

Procedure
1. Place the twine around the head tube and along both sides towards the drop-outs, pulling it taut per Fig. 5.31.

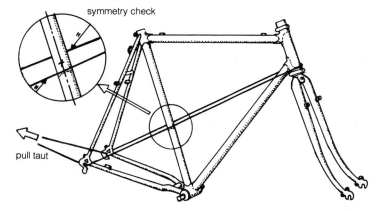

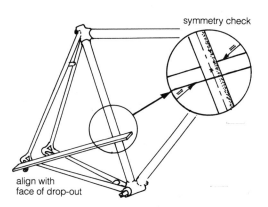

2. Measure the distance between the twine and the seat tube on both sides to one mm accuracy.
3. Compare the two measured values. If they differ by more than 2mm, there is lateral misalignment of the frame.
4. Check whether the drop-outs are still straight. To do this, place the metal straightedge with the thin side against the outside of each drop-out in turn and check whether the distance between the straightedge and the seat tube is the same for both (see Fig. 5.32).
5. If the two values differ by more than 3mm, at least one of the drop-outs is bent.

This is the kind of job best left to a bicycle mechanic. Just the same, it is quite possible to do it yourself if you go about it carefully. It will also give you a much better feel for how bicycle tubes deform and what kind of forces are needed to do so. Generally, it suffices to move the two halves of the rear triangle relative to the center plane of the main frame until a frame check confirms that the deviations are within the tolerances specified above.

Procedure:
1. On the basis of the frame inspection, establish which half must be moved how far in which direction.
2. Place the frame horizontally on a firm flat surface as shown in Fig. 5.33. Let an assistant stand on the main frame, holding the head tube with one leg, the seat tube with the other to assure these points stay flat on the working surface during the bending operation.
3. Using firm but even force, push or pull one side of the rear triangle over its entire length into the desired direction.
4. Check the result by repeating the frame inspection as outlined above, repeating the bending operation until the desired results are achieved.
5. Repeat the drop-out check from point 4 and 5 of the *Frame Inspection* description, and if necessary, perform the following procedure.

First check to make sure the slot for the wheel is still straight and there are no cracks in the drop-outs that will eventually cause them to break. In case of serious damage, a frame builder could replace a drop-out on a high-quality frame at a fraction of the cost you would pay for a new frame.

If the drop-outs are only bent, without serious damage,

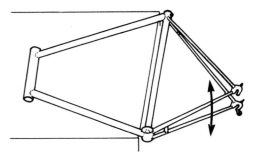

5.33. Crude cold-setting method to straighten rear frame triangle.

Frame Alignment

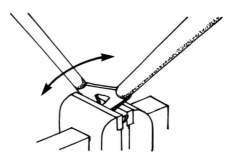

5.34. Crude drop-out straightening method

Drop-Out Alignment

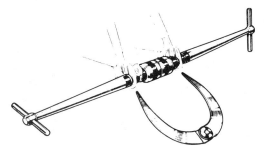

5.35. Professional tools for drop-out inspection and alignment.

you can probably do a repair yourself. This requires a special tool when the RH dropout is bent in such a way that the derailleur eye is affected. In other cases, it can be done with nothing but a heavy metal working vice mounted on a sturdy work bench.

Procedure:

1   Establish which drop-out has to be bent, and determine:
    ☐   how far?
    ☐   in which area?
    ☐   in which direction?

2.   For the LH drop-out, clamp it in the vice as shown in Fig. 5.34, so that the bent location is just above the top of the vice.

3.   Firmly grab both stays on that side just above the drop-out and steadily push the whole rear triangle into the appropriate direction.

4.   Repeat the drop-out alignment check from the *Frame Inspection* checking procedure and repeat until the alignment is within the tolerances given there.

5.   If necessary, use the special tools (borrowed from a bike shop) to straighten the RH drop-out.

Note: If cracks develop, the drop-out must be replaced, which can be done by a frame builder (most bike shops have an appropriate contact).

Chapter 6
The Steering System

The components that make up the bicycle's steering system are illustrated in Fig. 6.1. It comprises the front fork, the head set bearings that hold it in the frame's head tube, the handlebars and the handlebar stem. Before proceeding to the technical details of these components, the steering principle will be described. This greatly aids in an understanding of the way frame geometry and the steering components act together to influence the bicycle's handling characteristics.

The steering system not only serves to control the bicycle in curves, it is equally essential for going straight and for balancing the bicycle under all circumstances. Anybody whose front wheel has ever been caught in a parallel groove, such as a streetcar track, can confirm that even going straight is an impossibility with locked steering. Actually, the bicycle never goes in a completely straight line. Instead, it always follows a more or less curving path, always deviating a little to one side or the other, corresponding to similar deviations in the vertical position of bike and rider.

When the center of gravity is to the right of the point of contact between wheels and road, the bike leaning in that same direction, the rider regains his balance by pointing the steering further to the right. This causes the bottom of the bike to move back under the center of gravity, restoring equilibrium — but only temporarily, because the bike now starts to lean in the opposite direction. In turn, this lean is countered by steering slightly in that same direction, causing it to move back under the center of gravity and beyond, ad infinitum.

Fig. 6.3 illustrates the relationship between speed, lean and deviation. At low speeds, this serpentine-action is quite distinct, with considerable steering deviations. At elevated speeds, the deviations are smaller, although the lean relative to the vertical plane tends to be greater at any steering angle than it is at lower speeds. To get a feel for this movement, low speed riding, consciously trying to follow a straight line, is educational.

To ride a curve, the simplest way is to use the natural lean. To follow a curve to the right, wait until the bike is naturally leaning in that same direction, and then don't do anything for a while. Thus, the bike is not

The Steering Principle

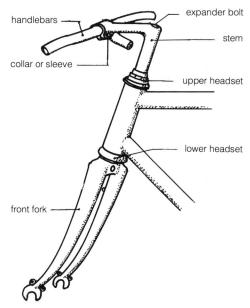

handlebars

expander bolt

stem

collar or sleeve

upper headset

lower headset

front fork

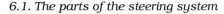
6.1. The parts of the steering system

Natural and Forced Curves

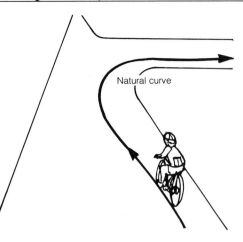

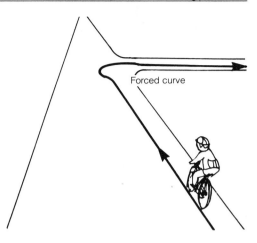

6.2.
Turning techni-
ques compared:
Left: Natural
curve.
Right: Forced
curve.

brought back upright, but continues to lean further and further, until quite a distinct lean angle is reached. Now it is time to steer noticeably in the same direction, avoiding the crash that would have followed the excessive lean, while forcing the bike in the desired direction.

This method of steering is referred to as the *natural* turn and is illustrated in the LH detail of Fig. 6.2. It has one drawback: it requires a lot of time and room to maneuver. If there is not enough of either to follow this method, use the technique referred to as the *forced* turn. This method is illustrated in the RH detail of Fig. 6.2.

To carry out the forced turn, the cyclist first steers in the direction opposite to his intended path. This causes the bike to lean in the opposite direction. Rather than correcting this right away, the bike is first allowed to drift further with increasing lean in the direction of the intended curve. When a significant lean is reached, the rider finally steers in that same direction, resulting in a tight and sudden curve.

Most of this is usually done subconsciously, although this is the very thing that makes learning to ride a bike confidently so difficult at first. It also explains why beginning cyclists, or riders who use a bike with drastically different steering geometry for the first time, feel and act so insecure and often ride so unpredictably.

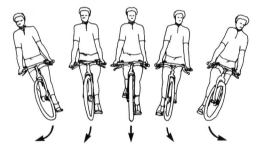

6.3. The cyclist leans into the curve. At higher speeds, more lean is required. At lower speeds, the steering deflection is greater. A sharper curve requires both more steering deflection and more lean.

Steering Geometry

How well a bikes steers and handles, how accurate and predictable, and how comfortable it is to ride, is largely affected by its steering geometry. This is the relationship between angles and dimensions of the parts of the steering system as they relate to the total bike.

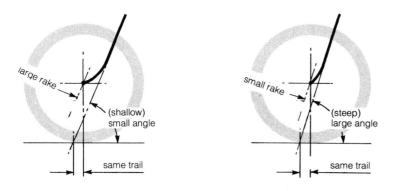

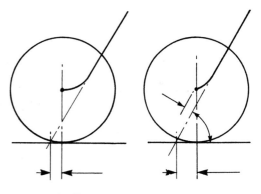

6.4.
The effect of steerer angle and fork rake on trail: The same trail can be achieved with any angle, providing the fork rake is reduced when the angle becomes steeper.

Although the manufacturer of a ready-made bicycle has predetermined the steering geometry, it is quite useful for the technically competent rider to know how a certain characteristic is achieved. This is all the more important if one considers that a remarkable number of manufacturers and bicycle sales people haven't the faintest idea how it is done correctly. The result is that they finish up producing or selling bikes that are less stable than they should be.

Fig. 6.4 illustrates the most important concepts that play a part in determining the bicycle's steering geometry, and indirectly its handling characteristics. How predictably a bike handles and how much stability it has, is largely determined by the dimension called *trail*. This is the distance between the contact point wheel/road (point A) and the point at which the imaginarily extended steering axis crosses the road (point B).

At any head tube, or steerer, angle of less than 90° (and typical values are far below that, namely 66—74°), combined with a straight fork, point A lies well behind point B. Thus the amount of trail, dimension X, would be quite big. This would result in a distinct tendency of the bike to follow a straight course, requiring relatively strong steering forces, or significant external effects, to deviate from this straight path.

As the illustration shows, the fork is usually bent forward — the distance over which this is done is referred to as *rake*. This brings point A forward, closer to point B, decreasing the amount of trail. Thus, the more raked fork on any given head tube angle achieves less trail, decreasing the bike's inherent stability and increasing its agility. Obviously, the same amount of trail, and essentially the same stability, can be achieved with different head tube angles, providing the

6.5. *Trail effect increases with shallower steerer angle.*

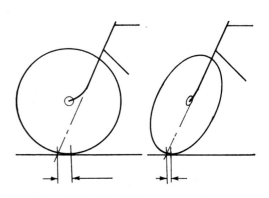

6.6. *The effect of trail decreases when the wheel is turned relative to the direction of travel.*

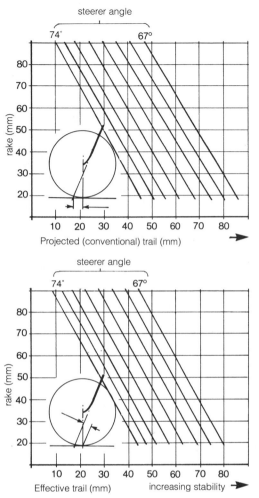

6.7. Graphs to determine conventional, or 'projected,' and effective trail.

6.8. The parts of a typical headset

rake is selected correspondingly to provide the desired trail with each angle.

Even so, there is a difference between the way bikes with the same trail but different head tube angles handle. The bike with a shallow angle is somewhat more sluggish and only responds predictably up to a certain steering deviation, after which a phenomenon called *wheel flop* sets in. This means that the bike oversteers abruptly beyond this point. The advantage of the bike with the smaller head tube angle lies in the increased comfort due to the greater flexibility of the more inclined and more distinctly bent fork, making this solution more desirable for touring on rough surfaces. Trail values typically fall between 50mm for a quick-steering criterium racing bike to 65mm for a stable touring or mountain bike.

Of course, the head tube, or steerer, angle for any given frame is fixed. It can be determined on the built-up bike following the method illustrated in Fig. 5.13 in the preceding chapter. Racing bikes typically have a head angle from 73.5—74°. Touring bikes have an angle of around 72°, while mountain bikes may have one as small as 67—68°, although the trend is towards steeper head angles, 70—71° being more typical these days for most mountain bikes.

Fig. 6.4 shows how the fork rake can be chosen to match any head angle while still arriving at the required trail. Fig. 6.7 simplifies the selection of the appropriate fork rake that gives a certain amount of trail once the head tube angle is known. These graphs is based on the following formulas:

$$X_1 = R \cos \alpha \, Y \times \sin \alpha$$

$$X_2 = \sin \alpha \, (R \times \cos \alpha \, Y \times \sin \alpha)$$

where:
X_1	= projected trail
X_2	= effective trail
R	= wheel radius in mm
Y	= fork rake in mm
α	= head tube, or steerer, angle.

The difference between the two values X_1 and X_2 bears some explanation. The value X_1 is the one commonly used, but does not give as accurate an impression of actual stability as X_2. The latter, which I refer to as *effective trail*, is what some authors call *stability index*, creating the impression that this is a dimensionless value. However, it can easily be determined, as I have done above, and should be used in preference to the conventional value X_1, which I refer to as *projected trail*. The difference between the two values increases as the head tube angle decreases, making it critical to use the right one, especially on mountain bikes and touring or utility machines with a relaxed geometry.

The formula also makes it obvious that the wheel radius enters into the calculation. Small-wheeled bikes should consequently be built with less rake than the values indicated in the table for 650—700mm wheels (nominal sizes 26" and 27"). As the formula and Fig. 6.7 suggest, even a completely straight fork barely provides enough trail for adequate stability on a bike with 20" or smaller wheels — important on folding bikes and children's bikes, as well as on recumbents and some other special designs. Essentially, such bikes with small wheels should have very little or no rake at all if they are to provide adequate directional stability.

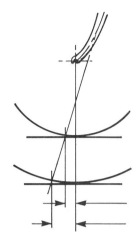

6.9. *The effect of wheel size on trail*

The Headset

The headset bearings form the rotation support for the steering system in the frame. Fig. 6.11 shows how it is typically built up, consisting of a fixed bearing in the bottom and an adjustable one at the top. The lockring may either have the form shown or it may have projecting teeth that match similar teeth in the top of the upper bearing cup. Often on mountain bikes and other machines with high handlebar positions, the locknut is built up with a high collar that stabilizes the handlebar stem. On some mountain bikes, an anchor for the brake cable may be installed between the locknut and the adjustable cup, replacing the lockring.

The ball bearings of the headset are loaded differently than those of most other bicycle applications. Whereas most other bearings rotate constantly and are loaded radially, i.e. perpendicular to the axle, the headset bearings hardly rotate and are loaded axially, i.e. in line with it. This is an unfavorable condition for ball bearings, since impacts from the road are transferred to the balls which remain in the same location, causing pitting of the bearing surfaces in those spots, referred to as *brinelling*. This is the reason mountain bikes are nowadays often equipped with so-called oversize headsets, requiring an oversize head tube and a fork with a matching steerer tube as well. To date, there is no standardization of oversize headsets, so they are not readily interchangeable.

6.10. *EDCO Competition headset with steel races and aluminum fittings.*

Headset Maintenance

Since the headset is so unfavorably loaded, it is quite important to keep it well adjusted and lubricated and to overhaul it occasionally, especially when it is

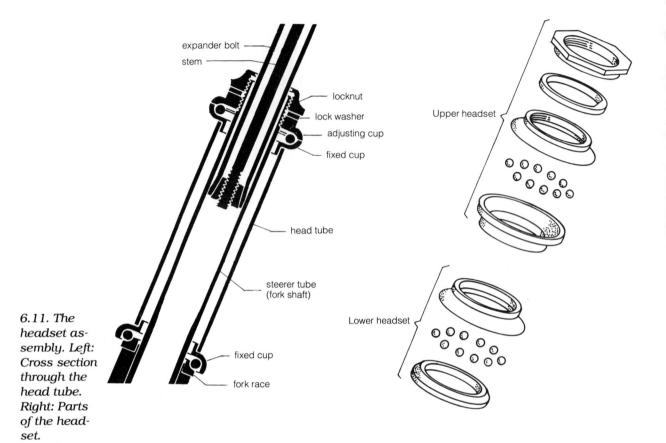

expander bolt

stem

locknut

lock washer

adjusting cup

fixed cup

head tube

steerer tube
(fork shaft)

fixed cup

fork race

Upper headset

Lower headset

6.11. The headset assembly. Left: Cross section through the head tube. Right: Parts of the headset.

noticeably loose or tight. You can check whether it is too loose by lifting the wheel off the ground and checking whether the fork can be moved relative to the frame at the fork crown.

In order to establish whether the headset is too tight, again lift the front wheel off the ground and check whether the steering can be turned from the fork crown (where there is less leverage than at the handlebars) without noticeable or irregular resistance. Unfortunately, the problem of a rough or tight headset can rarely be solved by means of adjustment, although that is the first step. Only too often, it is the result of damage that can only be eliminated by completely overhauling, and perhaps replacing, the headset.

Headset Adjustment

Usually, this can be done without removing anything from the bike. On mountain bikes it may be helpful to remove the straddle cable of the front brake if it is of the cantilever type — just make sure it is replaced again afterwards. It is preferable to use special matching headset wrenches, although it can usually be done with the aid of a large crescent wrench.

Procedure:
1. Unscrew the locknut on top of the upper headset by about two turns (models with toothed lockring: far enough to disengage the teeth).
2. Lift the lockring up enough to free the adjustable cup.
3 Screw the adjustable cup in or out a little, as required to tighten or loosen the bearing, respectively.
4. Push the lockring down on the adjustable cup again.
5. Tighten the locknut, making sure the lockring and the adjustable cup do not turn with it.
6. Check operation of the headset and repeat adjustment if necessary.

This procedure must also be followed to remove or replace the fork. Before starting, the handlebars must be removed, possibly also the front wheel and the front brake, although it usually suffices to undo its cable attachment. You'll need special headset wrenches (or large crescent wrench), a rag, and bearing grease.

If the bearing races must be replaced as well, special removal and installation tools should preferably be used. In a pinch, it can be done with provisional aids, which will be described in the procedure. As with so many parts on the bicycle, care must be taken to replace items with matching ones, since there are several different types of screw thread standards for headsets. The recent introduction of oversize models has added even more confusion. There are other differences as well: for example, the (excellent and reasonably priced) Shimano 600 headset requires that the fork's steerer tube must be cut off shorter than it is for other models.

Overhaul Headset

6.12 and 6.13. Oversize headset (left) and the tools for its installation and maintenance (right). This is the Garry Fisher unit, while many other manufacturers use different sizes, requiring different tools.

Disassembly procedure:
1. Unscrew and remove locknut.
2. Remove lock washer and/or brake cable anchor.
3. Unscrew and remove adjustable cup, while holding frame and fork crown together.
4. Pull the fork out of the head tube, catching the bearing balls from upper and lower headset bearings (usually held in bearing ball retainer).
5. If the inspection that follows indicates the bearing cups and the fork race are damaged, remove these as well. This should preferably be done with special tools, but can also be accomplished by following the illustrations 6.14 and 6.15.

Maintenance and Installation:
1. Clean and inspect all bearing components. Replace any parts that are damaged or corroded. Damage usually takes the form of pits in the bearing surfaces of the bearing races. Ideally, the bearing balls should always be replaced, using either loose balls or a matching retainer. Different manufacturers sometimes use different sizes, although $5/32"$ is the most common.
2. Clean and slightly grease the screw-thread surfaces.
3. If necessary, install the new bearing races, preferably with special tools, although it can be done without, following Fig. 6.16.
4. Fill the scrupulously cleaned bearing cups with bearing grease.
5. Hold the frame upside-down and install the bearing balls in the lower bearing cup, taking care to

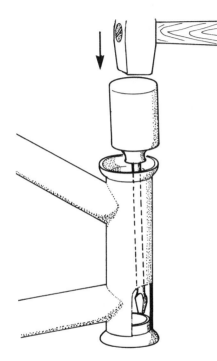

6.14. Fixed race removal without special tools.

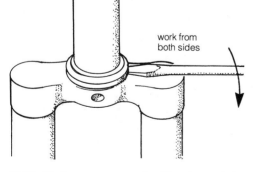

work from both sides

6.15. Fork race removal without special tools.

6.14, 6.15 and 6.16. Headset overhauling work can be done following the provisional methods shown here. However, it is preferable to use special tools.

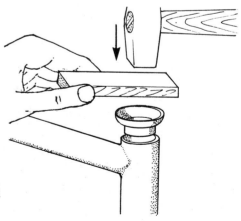

6.16. Fixed cup installation without special tools.

orient it so that only the balls, not the metal of the retainer (if used), contact the bearing cup and the fork race.

6. Install the fork, after checking that the fork race is also perfectly clean and slightly lubricated.

7. Firmly holding the frame and the fork crown together, turn the whole thing upside-down, so the upper headset is on top again, with the fork's steerer tube protruding.

8. Install the bearing balls in the fixed upper cup, again taking care to orient the retainer (if used) so that only the balls, not the metal of the retainer touch the bearing cups.

9. After checking whether the adjustable cup is clean and slightly lubricated, screw it onto the steerer tube until the bearing seems correctly adjusted.

10. Install the lock washer, any brake cable anchor that may be used, and the locknut, tightening the latter relative to the adjustable cup.

11. Check the adjustment of the bearing as outlined above and correct if necessary, following the procedure *Adjust Headset*.

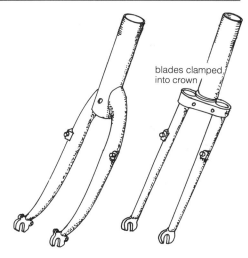

6.17. *Unicrown and switchblades mountain bike forks.*

Fig. 6.18 shows the construction of a typical front fork. It comprises the steerer tube, or fork shaft, two fork blades, a fork crown that connects them together, and fork-ends, also called front drop-outs. Slightly different are two recent variants, called unicrown and switchblade fork, respectively, and illustrated in Fig. 6.17. The two latter versions are popular on mountain bikes, although not better in an engineering sense. The unicrown design is cheaper to make. The (heavy) aluminum switchblade crown design has no virtues at all. It is meant to allow exchanging fork blades, but as we've seen, the steering characteristics are too sacred to fool around with and this fork is quite a bit heavier than other models.

Material selection and construction of the fork are analogous to what was said in Chapters 4 and 5, respectively. Generally, steel and aluminum frames are each equipped with forks of the corresponding material. Composite and magnesium frames usually come with aluminum forks. These tend to be softer than steel forks, providing more shock absorption. The fork-ends should be as thick and accurate as possible, and what was said about the (rear) drop-outs in Chapter 5 applies here too.

The steerer tube of a replacement fork is usually provided long enough to fit even the largest frame, so it may have to be shortened to provide the right length to

The Front Fork

6.18. *The front fork*

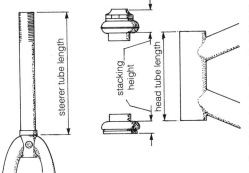

6.19. Steerer tube length depends on headset stacking height and head tube length (adding 2mm spacing).

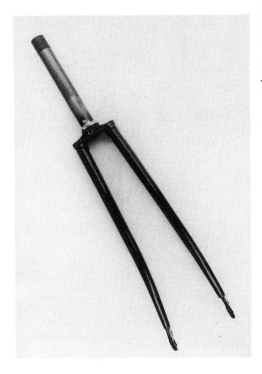

6.20. Typical high-quality fork with investment cast fork crown and drop-outs.

Fork Maintenance

match a smaller frame. The screw thread may then have to be recut, a job for which any bike shop should be equipped. Table 4 in the Appendix summarizes the different common thread types. When cutting a steerer tube down to size, the stacking height of the headset must be considered, measured as shown in Fig. 6.19, add adding 2mm (3/32") clearance. The fork race, which is part of the lower headset, should match the collar, or shoulder, on the fork crown, which may have to be machined for an accurate fit.

The front fork is a particularly heavily loaded part of the bike. Being cantilevered out, it is not loaded only in tension and compression as most other parts are. It is also the first one to be damaged upon collision impact. Even so, it should not be too heavy, to provide adequate shock absorption. Ideally, the fork blades should flex only parallel and remain linearly aligned, while lateral flexing should be minimized, all of which is best achieved with round fork blades. Just the same, most fork blades are made of oval cross section, probably justified only by questionable aesthetic and aerodynamic arguments.

Internal reinforcement of the steerer tube and the fork blades is appropriate. Unfortunately, the shaping process with which the fork blade diameters are made less at the bottom, where the load is minimal, than at the top, where it is greatest, results in increased wall thickness in the area with the smaller outside diameter. To compensate for that, high-quality forks are made of taper gauge tubing, which starts out thicker at the top and finishes up having a nearly constant wall thickness all the way down after forming.

The fork-ends are similar to the drop-outs described in Chapter 5 but do not have an adjusting feature. The slots in the fork-ends point down almost vertically. Recently, mountain bikes have been supplied with Koski forks or imitations made by others than this California mountain bike builder and designer. These forks are characterized by fork-ends with a ridge that traps the axle nuts or the quick-release in place in order to prevent the wheel from coming loose accidentally — and defeat the main purpose of the quick-release.

The front fork tends to get damaged when the bicycle runs into an obstacle. Any of the distortions depicted in Fig. 6.25 may result, depending on the nature and direction of the impact. It should be inspected after any collision, and whenever the steering characteristics seem to have deteriorated. Sometimes it is possible to bend a fork blade back into shape if the damage is not too severe and the material is relatively soft. Otherwise, the fork will have to be replaced, following the procedure outlined under *Overhaul Headset*. For the inspection procedure, a long metal straightedge is required.

Inspection Procedure:
1. With the fork still installed in the frame, sight along the fork blades from the side, to verify whether any damage as shown in Fig. 6.25 is apparent. If so, the fork should usually be replaced, although a straightening suggestion is given below, which sometimes works, depending on the strength of the fork.
2. Leaving the fork in the bike, place the straightedge in line with the center of the head tube and check whether there is a less pronounced bend of the fork blades relative to the steerer tube. If the distortion is slight, you may be able to continue riding the bike only if the steering does not have a rough spot — check carefully as described in the headset maintenance section above.
3. If necessary, remove the fork from the bike, following the procedure *Overhaul Headset*. Place the fork exactly perpendicular to the edge of a perfectly straight, level surface as shown in Fig. 6.23. Verify whether all four points actually make contact simultaneously: the fork-ends and one point each near the top of the fork blades. In case of deviation, measure the difference: if it is more than 2mm, measured at the fork-ends, the fork must either be replaced or straightened.
4. You may try to bend the fork straight by clamping in the steering tube and placing a 60cm (2ft) long metal tube over the fork blade that is bent, trying to force it back into shape. If it does not work, you will need a new fork.

Virtually all modern bicycles use handlebars that are connected with the rest of the steering system by means of an adjustable stem, as shown in Fig. 6.27. The handlebars proper, often referred to as the handlebar *bend* on a racing bike, are clamped in the collar at the end of the stem. The stem is clamped inside the fork's steerer tube by means of a wedge- or cone-shaped clamping device that is tightened with the expander bolt which is usually recessed in the top of the stem (see Fig. 6.30).

Of the two methods shown in Fig. 6.30, the one with the wedge is more popular these days, and is recommended for applications in which the handlebar height is frequently adjusted. The method with the cone,

6.21 and 6.22.
Top: Reinforced mountain bike tandem fork — indestructible but rather heavy. Below: Cinelli investment cast fork crowns.

Handlebars and Stem

6.23. *Simple fork alignment check*

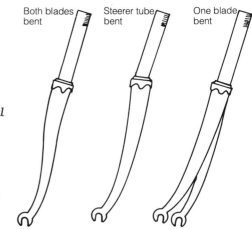

Both blades bent | Steerer tube bent | One blade bent

6.24 and 6.25.
Left: This is what happens in a frontal collision. Although shown on a cheap bike, the same happens to a fancy model.
Right: Three typical kinds of fork misalignment.

though harder to loosen, does not deform the steerer tube as easily, allowing a more accurate angular alignment of the handlebars.

Stems and handlebars are generally made of aluminum, although welded high-strength steel stems and handlebars of the same material are finding their way onto high-quality mountain bikes. This is one application where careful dimensioning of strong steel alloy can provide greater strength and less weight than can be achieved with aluminum. Mountain bike handlebars may also be made of the same material, as well as titanium and carbon fiber reinforced epoxy. On racing bikes, these materials are not practicable, since they can't be easily made in such a complex shape — unless you want to pay as much for the handlebars as for the bike frame.

In order to avoid the possibility of breaking the stem, it should never be clamped in over less than 65mm (2½"). Many manufacturers mark this point of minimum insertion, and if this is not done, you can take care of it yourself with the aid of an indelible marker. Both the height and the reach (or length) may vary, as shown in Fig. 6.29, and should be selected to match the desired posture on the basis of the rider's size. Most bikes are sold with stems that have too much reach to be comfortable for most women, and should be replaced by one that fits at the time of purchase.

6.26. A crude way of making a fork: The ends of the stays are simply flattened.

Handlebar Dimensions and Types

Handlebars are also available in different widths. On a racing bike, the correct dimension is such that the arms are parallel all the way from the shoulders to the wrists when holding the drops (the ends of the racing handlebars). On mountain bikes, the arms spread out slightly, but even here a width of 55cm (22") is as wide as comfort and handling ease allow. Wider handlebars, popular on early mountain bikes, require too much upper body movement when maneuvering at low speeds. If necessary, a hacksaw can be used to cut the bars down to size from both ends, after first having made sure the brake levers and gear shifters can be installed far enough from the ends to allow room for the hands.

Triathletes and time trial cyclists, who typically ride considerable distances without need for difficult maneuvering and braking, like the aerodynamic advantage offered by special handlebars that point far forward and support the arms on pads. These are often referred to as Scott bars. They allow a different, more stretched and forward-leaning body posture, which does reduce wind resistance. A special type of gear shifter is available that is installed at the ends of such bars.

6.27. Handlebars and stem

The diameter of the handlebars is greater in the middle portion than over the remainder of their length, to provide a point where they are clamped, while still allowing insertion in the stem. This thickened section usually contains a reinforcing sleeve or insert. Unfortunately, the ends of the reinforcing sleeve cause a so-called stress raiser, which sometimes leads to fatigue cracking, causing the handlebars to suddenly break apart. This kind of damage is least likely if the reinforcement is put around the outside, even if this is aesthetically less pleasing. Whether inside or out, it should be at least 7.5cm (3") long to distribute the stresses far enough away from the most sensitive location at the ends of the stem clamp.

Drop handlebars, i.e. the kind used on racing bikes, are usually finished off by winding handlebar tape around them. As an alternative, foam plastic sleeves can be used, requiring the brake levers to be removed first. Handlebar tape is available as adhesive cloth, as non-adhesive plastic and in fancy versions made of leather. The ends of the tape are tucked into the handlebar ends, after which the handlebar plugs are installed. Mountain bike bars have plastic handgrips at the ends. Clip-on bars, which have become popular in would-be racing circles should have comfortable grips.

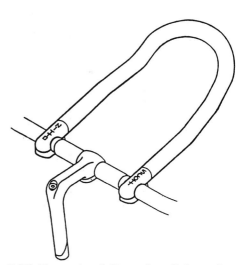

6.28. Example of clip-on handlebars for a lower riding posture and reduced wind resistance. Not suitable for difficult handling situations.

The following descriptions will deal with the height and angle adjustments of the handlebars, and replacement of the individual parts, as well as the installation of tape, sleeves and handgrips.

Handlebar Maintenance

Adjust Handlebar Position

This work usually only requires the use of a wrench that fits on the expander bolt, usually a 6mm allen key. Only simple utility bikes still come with hexagonal, non-recessed bolts, for which an open-ended or box wrench is used, and sometimes you need a hammer or any other blunt, heavy object.

Procedure:
1. Facing the bike from the front, clamp the front wheel between the legs.
2. Loosen the expander bolt by 3—4 turns. If the stem does not immediately come loose, lift the front of the bike off the ground by the handlebars and hit the head of the bolt with a hammer to loosen the wedge or cone inside.
3. Place the stem at the desired height and angle, and tighten the expander bolt partway while holding it in place.
4. Check to make sure the handlebars are perfectly aligned perpendicular to the frame; then tighten the bolt firmly.

Adjust Handlebar Angle

The angle under which the handlebars are oriented relative to the horizontal plane can be adjusted after loosening the binder bolt that clamps the collar of the stem around the handlebar bend. You need a matching wrench.

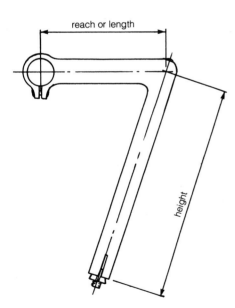

6.29. *Stem dimensions*

Procedure:
1. Facing the bike from the front, clamp the front wheel between the legs.
2. Loosen the binder bolt by 1—2 turns, until the bar is loose enough to be turned
3. Turn the handlebar bend into the desired orientation, and tighten the bolt partway while holding the handlebars in place.
4. Check to make sure the handlebars are perfectly aligned and then tighten the bolt firmly.

Remark:
If it turns out to be impossible to tighten the handlebar bend fully, first try lubricating the binder bolt, which makes it possible to tighten it more easily. If that doesn't work, you may make a shim out of a thin piece of aluminum (e.g. an aluminum beverage can) to fill up the space between the exterior of the handlebars and the interior of the clamping collar — you may have to open up the clamp by wedging a large screwdriver in.

Replace Handlebar Bend

To remove and install the handlebar bend, while retaining the stem, e.g. when the bars are damaged, the brake levers and anything else mounted on the handlebars must first be removed on one side. In addition to a wrench for the binder bolt on the collar around the bars, you may need a large screwdriver.

Removal Procedure:
1. Hold the bike in a work stand or, when not available, clamp the front wheel between the legs, facing the bike from the front.
2. Loosen the binder bolt fully and remove it.
3. If necessary, spread the collar apart as shown in Fig. 6.32, so the handlebar bend is free to move.
4. Twisting to find the most favorable orientation as you work around the bend, pull the handlebar bend out of the stem.

Installation Procedure:
1. Twisting the handlebars in the most favorable orientation as you work, push them through the collar as far as possible.
2. To get the thicker middle section in, spread the collar open with the large screwdriver.
3. Hold the bars in the desired orientation and tighten the bolt partway while holding the handlebars in place.
4. Check to make sure the handlebars are perfectly aligned and then tighten the bolt firmly.

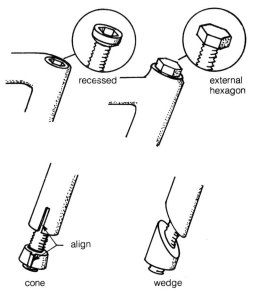

6.30. Expander bolt details

If the handlebar bend should remain attached to the stem, first remove the brake levers or cables and anything else installed on it that is connected to the bike.

Removal Procedure:
1. Hold the bike in a work stand or, when not available, clamp the front wheel between the legs, facing the bike from the front.
2. Loosen the expander bolt by 3—4 turns. If the stem does not immediately come loose, lift the front of the bike off the ground from the handlebars and hit on top of the bolt with a hammer to loosen the wedge or cone inside.
3. Lift the stem out of the front end of the bike.

Installation Procedure:
1. Clean and lightly lubricate the exterior of the stem and the interior of the steerer tube that is accessible through the headset locknut.
2. Place the stem in the desired height, and tighten the expander bolt partway while holding it.
3. If handlebars are installed, check to make sure they are perfectly aligned perpendicular to the frame and then tighten the bolt firmly.

Replace Stem (with or without handlebar bend)

6.31. SunTour mountain bike stem with double clamp (or binder) bolts.

Install Handlebar Tape

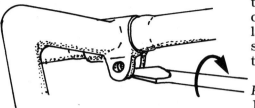

6.32. Opening up stem collar for handle-bar replacement.

Replace Handgrips or Sleeves

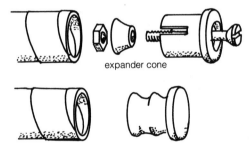

expander cone

6.33. Typical handlebar end plug details

Old handlebar tape is removed after loosening the handlebar end plugs, as shown in Fig. 6.33. Adhesive tape may have to be cut, after which it is advisable to clean the adhesive off with denatured alcohol (methylated spirit). Usually, one roll of tape is needed for each side. First lift the rubber brake hoods off the levers so they clear the handlebars.

Procedure:
1. Adhesive tape is wound starting from a point about 7.5cm (3") from the center, working towards the ends. Overlap each layer generously with the preceding one and wrap in an X-pattern around the brake lever attachments.
2. Non-adhesive tape is wound starting from the ends, after tucking a piece inside. Work towards the center, and overlap as described above for adhesive tape. Fasten the ends by wrapping some adhesive tape around it.
3   Install the end plugs, referring to Fig. 6.33.

To remove old handgrips or foam plastic sleeves, you may either put some dishwashing liquid underneath after lifting the end with a screwdriver, or you may simply cut them lengthwise with a sharp knife, depending whether you want to reuse them or not.

Before installing the new items, remove all traces of detergent (or any traces of adhesive and old tape when replacing tape with sleeves). You may ease the process by softening and expanding the new items in hot water. To make sure the grips stay in place, you may squirt some hair spray inside before pushing them on.

Chapter 7

Seat and Seatpost

Not a technically exciting subject, perhaps, but some sensible and necessary things should be said about the seat, or saddle, and its peripherals. Fig. 7.2 illustrates a typical seat and the seatpost, or seat pin, used to attach it to the frame, as well as the binder bolt used to clamp it in. Several different versions exist of all these parts, and they will be covered systematically in the following sections.

Seats may be made of several different materials. Utility bikes and cruisers have models consisting of a metal frame with springs supporting a plastic cover. Racing, touring and mountain bikes typically have seats made with a stressed, self-supporting cover, usually of leather- or fabric-covered polyamide (nylon), sometimes of firm leather. The ones intended for mountain bikes and touring machines are generally padded and somewhat wider in the rear portion, while those commonly installed on utility bikes tend to have a shape that defies any ergonomic and anatomic principles.

Leather seats easily look the most impressive, and some old-fashioned riders like the author swear by their comfort — which is bought at the expense of many miles of breaking them in and scrupulous care. Most of the nylon-based seats are actually just as comfortable — right from the start — and a lot easier to maintain. If a leather saddle should get wet, you're not supposed to sit on it until it has thoroughly dried. Besides, it should be treated with a special leather treatment (e.g. neat foot's oil or Brooks Proofide) to prevent it from drying out and becoming too absorbent.

The shape of the seat becomes quite critical when cycling over long distances, where the cyclist pedals rather fast and applies noticeable force to the pedals. To allow freedom of movement without chafing, a narrow front end is required, while the rear must conform to the rider's pelvic width. Women generally need a design that is rather wide in the back, as shown in Fig. 7.4: it should be about 6—8cm (2—3") wider than the distance between the two bony protrusions. Due to the typically rather upright position used on mountain and touring bikes, these probably need saddles that are modeled on the woman's seat, but more padded, as

7.1. Lightweight Cinelli seats

The Seat

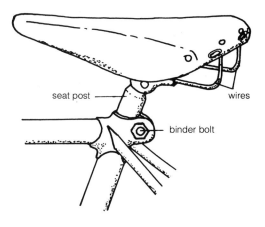

seat post — wires

binder bolt

7.2. Details of seat and seat post

7.3. The ultimate leather saddle: the Brooks Colt.

91

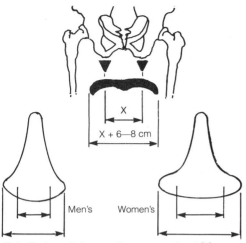

7.4. Determining optimum seat width

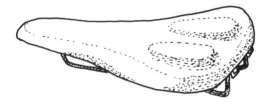

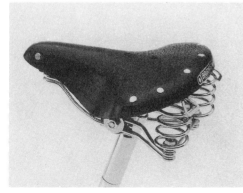

7.5. Padded mountain bike seat

The Seatpost

shown in Fig. 7.5. Excessive springiness, however comfortable it may seem, is not recommended, since it makes for a tiring lateral instability and inefficient pedaling.

Recently, saddle padding made of a gel material that takes on the rider's shape, very much like the filling of modern ski boots, has been introduced. This is still not the ultimate solution to the comfort dilemma, since even this material is eventually penetrated and then feels as hard as a rock. More promising is the special gel material used e.g. as the seating cushion in modern wheel chairs, since this remains flexible even under enduring pressure.

Most seats with a stressed cover are based on a frame with two wires, or rails, usually made of steel. Lightweight solutions with aluminum or titanium wires don't measure up, since the minuscule weight savings is paid for at the price of inadequate strength, often resulting in a broken wire — and a ruined expensive seat. The inadequate strength is easily explained by the fact that it is practically impossible to make the wires any thicker than they are when made of steel, resulting in less strength when these weaker materials are used.

A few expensive leather models for touring, utility and mountain bike use have a double set of wires and incorporate a set of coil springs in the back. Although I am not in favor of excessive springiness in seats, this is probably the most acceptable solution for those who like to ride in a rather upright position, which puts more weight on the seat. These models do require special matching support hardware.

The conventional tubular seatpost shown in Fig. 7.2 is mounted by means of the rather crude clip supplied with most cheap seats. This type does not allow very accurate angular adjustment of the seat relative to the

7.6 and 7.7.
Two attempts to make a more comfortable seat. The two-part design to the right was first introduced in 1898 and offered as a brand new invention during the nineteen-eighties.

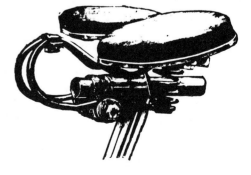

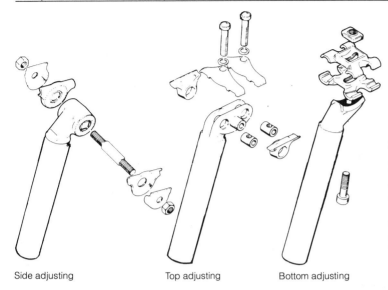

Side adjusting   Top adjusting   Bottom adjusting

7.8 and 7.9.
Left: Seatpost details of various common types.
Below: Saddle testing in Raleigh's product testing laboratory, where wear, shape retention and comfort are evaluated.

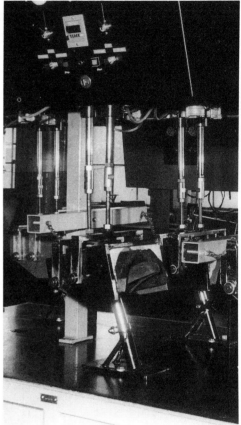

horizontal plane, since the serrated clamp has notches that lie too far apart to find the optimum angle for comfort.

More modern seatposts are illustrated in Fig. 7.8. Usually, these either have an integrated fine-adjusting mechanism of some kind, or they are made up of separate parts: a tubular aluminum post and a separate, precisely adjusting head with clamp to hold the saddle wires. Of all types available, the old Campagnolo model with two hard-to-reach bolts in the front and the rear, as shown in LH detail of Fig. 7.8, is still the most accurate. More recent versions sacrifice some accuracy for ease of access.

As in the case of the handlebar stem, seatposts are not necessarily lighter when made of aluminum than when made of steel. Most of the modern fine-adjusting aluminum models are actually heavier than even a simple steel tubular clamp with matching clip. Due to design and construction constraints, it is often easier to make a really light adjustable seatpost of steel alloy than it is to do so of aluminum. On the other hand, the manufacturing technique for the aluminum version allows mass production and thus a lower price.

The diameter of the seatpost must correspond to the inside diameter of the seat tube. Although many utility bikes and cruisers use 25.4mm (1.00") diameter, the most common sizes for racing and mountain bikes are 27.2mm and 26.8mm, respectively. Even so, there are quite a number of different sizes to fit the various odd-

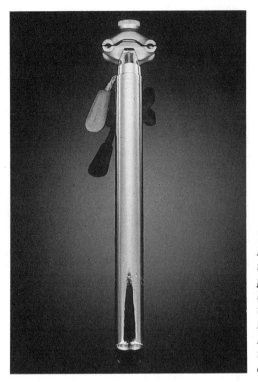

7.10 and 7.11.
Left: Campagnolo mountain bike seat-post, which must be longer than those for regular bikes.
Right: Typical mountain bike seatpost clamping detail.

size inside seat tube diameters, and the variety gets bigger from year to year due to the introduction of non-standardized oversize steel and aluminum tubing.

At least 65mm (2½") of the seatpost must at all times remain clamped in at the top of the seat tube, which requires a long model on mountain bikes. Ideally, the seatpost should be marked to indicate the minimum insertion depth — something you can do yourself using an indelible marking pen, if necessary. The longer seat-posts introduced for mountain bike use, which are 30cm long or more, also seem a nice solution for people with long legs, who previously could never find a frame big enough to achieve the desired seat height. Unfortunately, the likelihood of these long seatposts being available in a size to match the bike in question is rather meager.

Binder Bolt

Nowadays, virtually all racing and high-quality touring bikes are equipped with an allen key operated binder bolt. This has the advantage of allowing adjustment without chance of either chipping the bike's paint or deforming the nut of the binder bolt. On the other hand, some of these require the simultaneous use of two identical size wrenches, which may not always be available. Ideally, one of the two parts of which these bolts consist should have a prong that fits in a matching locating recess to eliminate rotation of that part, thus obviating the need for a second wrench.

Reserved for folding bikes up to the late seventies, quick-release binder bolts, shown in Fig. 7.15, are now readily available and are universal on all mountain bikes. They are quite handy if you want to adjust the seat height frequently, but allow easy saddle theft. Actually, the quick-release is more a fashion item for most people, since many mountain bike riders don't really use the adjusting feature on their bikes very much — or not properly. Instead they randomly set the seat in any one of a wide variety of uncomfortable and inefficient positions. For the mountain bike, you can find appropriate seat height adjustment instructions in my *Mountain Bike Book*, in any of my other books for other bicycle types.

An adjusting aid for mountain bikes is the Hite-Rite. This connects the binder bolt location with the seatpost under spring tension, as shown in Fig. 7.13, preventing theft and vandalism at the same time as easing adjustment while sitting on the bike. The saddle is adjusted by loosening the quick-release binder bolt while applying your body weight in the desired location to bring the seat to that height, and then fastening the binder bolt again.

Mountain bikes that are frequently adjusted sometimes suffer from fatigue-induced cracks. These form either at the end of the split portion at the back of the seat lug or at the eye, or lug, through which the binder bolt fits. The former problem is minimized by drilling a 3—

7.12. Mountain bike seat with coil springs.

7.13 and 7.14. On mountain bikes, it is often helpful to adjust the seat height while riding. The Hite-Rite allows you to do that and return to the original position. Place one side around the seat post, the other around the binder bolt. Tighten when the height is properly adjusted.

4mm (⅛—5⁄32") diameter hole at the base of the slot. The second problem can only be eliminated by correct design. A relatively simple solution used on some bikes is to separate the clamping function in the form of an external clip that is more easily replaced than a cracked frame. If the clamping action does not work properly, the split end can sometimes be filed out just a little, as shown in Fig. 7.17. In that case, also drill a hole at the bottom if the manufacturer has not done so.

Seat Adjustment

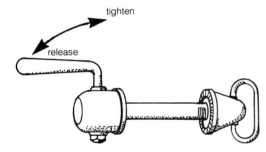

7.15. Quick-release binder bolt as used on most mountain bikes.

Except on bikes with a quick-release binder bolt, this operation requires the use of a matching wrench (two wrenches in some cases). Covered here are the adjustment of the height and the angle of the seat top with respect to the horizontal plane, as well as the forward position relative to the handlebars or the pedals. You will need wrenches to fit the binder bolt and the adjustment bolts on the seatpost or its clip.

Height Adjusting Procedure:
1. Loosen the binder bolt at the seat lug by about one revolution (or undo the quick-release if provided).
2. Move the seat with the seatpost attached up or down — if necessary in a twisting motion per Fig. 7.16.
3. Hold the seat firmly in the desired position, aligned perfectly with the longitudinal axis of the bike, then tighten the binder bolt or the quick-release again.

Angle Adjusting Procedure:
1. Find out which bolt or bolts govern the seat's angular orientation.
2. Loosen the bolt or bolts and place the seat under the desired angle with respect to the horizontal plane.
3. Tighten the bolt or bolts, while holding the seat firmly in place, also keeping it aligned with respect to the longitudinal axis of the bike in case of a seatpost with a separate clip.

Forward Position Adjusting Procedure:
1. Find out which bolt or bolts must be used to loosen the clip from the wires.
2. Loosen the bolt or bolts and move the seat forward or backward to place it in the desired position relative to the handlebars and the pedals.
3. Tighten the bolt or bolts, while holding the seat firmly, it under the correct angle and keeping it aligned with respect to the longitudinal axis of the bike in case of a seatpost with separate clip.

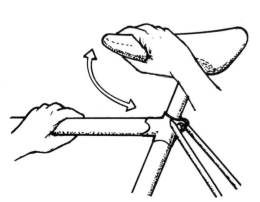

7.16. Twisting motion to adjust or remove seat with tight-fitting seatpost.

Follow this same procedure when only the seat (without the seatpost) must be removed, since it is easier to separate seat and seatpost once they are removed from the frame. Fitting wrenches, a rag and some vaseline are required.

Replace Seatpost and Seat

Removal Procedure:
1. Loosen the binder bolt at the seat lug by about three revolutions. On a bike with a quick-release binder bolt, undo the lever and then unscrew the locknut on the other side by one or two turns.
2. Pull the seat with the seatpost attached out of the frame — if necessary in a twisting motion per Fig. 7.16.

Separating and Installation Procedure:
1. If the seat must be separated from the seatpost, loosen the clip from the seat wires. Usually, only one nut or bolt has to be loosened to achieve this.
2. Remove the seat if desired.
3. If appropriate, attach the replacement seat the same way as the old one was. Don't bother adjusting the seat angle just yet.

Seatpost Installation Procedure:
1. Clean and lightly lubricate the interior of the seat tube and the exterior of the seatpost to prevent corrosion and to facilitate later adjustment.
2. Insert the seatpost in the seat tube to the desired depth.
3. Firmly hold the seat in the desired position, perfectly aligned with the longitudinal axis of the bike, then tighten the binder bolt or the quick-release again.
4. Check and, if necessary, correct the angle and the forward position, following the preceding descriptions.

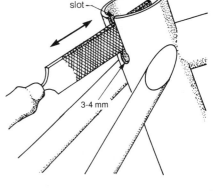

7.17. File out this slot if it is not wide enough to allow proper clamping in of the seat post although it is the right size.

For those incorrigible ones who use a stressed leather seat, here are a few suggestions for its maintenance. First, make sure it never gets wet. To avoid this, it is not enough to keep it out of the rain, you also have to wrap a plastic bag around it when transporting the bike on a car or in a pickup. And if it does get wet, don't sit on it until it is thoroughly dry again, since the application of the rider's weight on the wet seat will deform it hopelessly.

Leather Seat Maintenance

At least twice a year, and anytime it has been wet (but not until it is dry again), apply special leather treatment, preferably from underneath, where the leather is most porous and does not rub off so easily. The leather

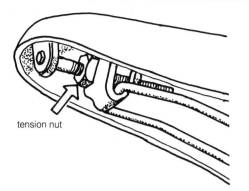

tension nut

7.18. Tension adjuster of leather seat

seat manufacturers Brooks and Ideale each have their own treatment grease or oil for this purpose, although equestrian saddle soap works too.

If the leather seat cover sags, carefully tighten the bolt shown in Fig. 7.18 to tension the cover slightly. This should only be done when absolutely necessary and not too vigorously, since the seat will develop an uncomfortable shape with sharp folds near the sides if it is overstressed.

Chapter 8

The Wheels

The typical bicycle wheel can be considered a minor technical miracle. With a minimal weight of its own, the wheel not only carries a heavy weight by comparison, it also has minimal rolling resistance and even provides some shock absorption. Fig. 8.1 shows such a wheel, built up of hub, spokes, rim, tire and inner tube. These are the parts covered in this chapter.

The hub is the heart of the bicycle wheel, covered here only in its general form, while some special types with integrated gearing and brakes will be described in Chapters 11 and 13, respectively. Since the entire wheel is removed and installed by means of the hub, this section will cover this work as well as the technical details of the hub proper.

Fig. 8.3 shows a cross section through a typical hub. The two main types of attachment are by means of axle nuts and by means of a quick-release. In the latter case the hub axle is hollow, with a quick-release spindle installed through it. Low-end bikes usually have hubs with axle nuts, often with a tab-plate between hub and fork to prevent the wheel from falling out when the nuts are loosened. Another distinguishing factor for different hubs is based on the size of the flanges in which the spokes are attached into high and low, or big and small, flange models, as shown in Fig. 8.4. Although structural virtues are sometimes claimed for the high flange type, low flange hubs are lighter and equally strong (except in a radially spoked wheel, described in the section *The Spokes*).

Another myth surrounds the use of quick-releases, shown in Fig. 8.6: Hubs with them are not inherently better than those without, even though most quality hubs are made with hollow axles and quick-releases for easy installation and removal (and theft). A solid axle of the same material and the same diameter is stronger than the hollow one used with a quick-release, and its overall weight is slightly less. Early mountain bikes and all tandems come with solid axles. The best ones have axle nuts with integrated washers to reduce friction resistance and axle torque when they are tightened.

Fig. 8.5 illustrates the width of the hub. It is measured between the locknuts and must correspond to the in-

The Hub

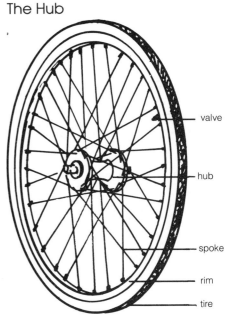

valve

hub

spoke

rim

tire

8.1 and 8.2. Above: Parts of the wheel. Below: High flange and low flange mountain bike hubs from Campagnolo.

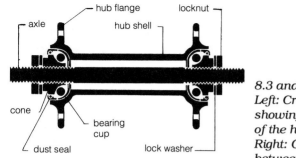

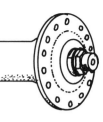

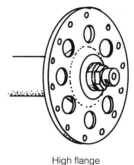

8.3 and 8.4.
Left: Cross section
showing the parts
of the hub.
Right: Comparison
between high
flange and low
flange hubs.

High flange

Low flange

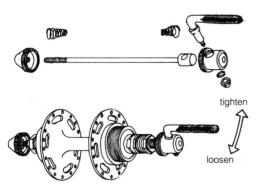

8.5. Hub width dimensions

Wheel Removal and Installation

ternal dimension between the drop-outs or fork-ends of frame or fork. The over-locknut width is typically 100mm for a front wheel, 125mm for a rear wheel with 6- or 7-speed freewheel for regular drop-handlebar derailleur bikes, while hubs intended for mountain bikes and tandems tend to be wider — up to 135mm in the rear for some models. Often the use of solid axles is structurally justified, especially on the rear wheel with its greater width, which more easily leads to a broken axle. The greatest risk of breaking an axle is when the bearings lie rather far inward relative to the drop-outs or fork-ends.

The wheels have to be removed for numerous maintenance operations on the bike. Illustrated in Fig 8.7 and 8.8, this job looks easy enough. Even so, a systematic approach as described here will prevent all sorts of frustration. You may need a wrench to fit the axle nuts and a rag to hold back the chain on the rear wheel.

Removal Procedure:
1. Remove any operating elements that may be attached to the wheel or interfere with its removal.
2. On the rear wheel of a derailleur bike, select a gear that combines the smallest sprocket in the rear with a small chainwheel in the front while turning the cranks with the wheel lifted off the ground.
3. Untension the brake, generally with the aid of the brake quick-release. On mountain bikes or other machines with cantilever brakes, this is typically done by squeezing the brake arms in and then unhooking the transverse cable. In the case of a roller-cam brake, the cam plate must be twisted out from its rollers.
4. On a wheel with a hub brake, loosen the bolt that holds the counter lever to the frame or the fork.

8.6. Assembly of quick-release hub

5. If the hub has no quick-release, unscrew the axle nuts by about three turns each — if there is a wheel locator, far enough to allow opening the fork to free the tab.
6. On a wheel with quick-release hub, twist the lever in the *open* position. If this does not free the hub adequately, loosen the locknut on the other side by 1—2 turns.
7. On a rear wheel, hold back the chain by pulling the derailleur cage away from the sprocket.
8. Pull the wheel out of the bike in the direction of the slot in the drop-outs or fork-ends. If the tire should get stuck between the brake blocks, despite having released the brake, let the air out of the tire. On forks with drop-outs with a ridge that traps the axle nut or quick-release, loosen both nuts (on the former) or the thumbnut (on the latter) until they are clear of the ridge.

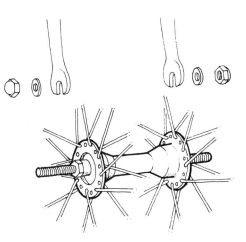

8.7. Installation of hub with axle nuts

Installation Procedure:
1. On the rear wheel of a derailleur bike, first set the shifters in such a position that the gear with the smallest sprocket and the small chainwheel are engaged.
2. If required, release the brake as described in step 3 in the removal procedure.
3. Move any other items that may hinder installation out of the way.
4. Make sure the quick-release is in the *open* position or the axle nuts are undone far enough (and the lock washers are pushed up against them) to pass by the fork-ends or drop-outs.
5. On a rear wheel, hold back the derailleur with the chain so that the wheel can be moved into position.
6. Install the wheel in the fork or the frame, centering it in position by the rim and fully back in the drop-outs (against the adjusters if installed), which may have to be adjusted to center the wheel correctly.
7. Tighten the quick-release or the axle nuts. If the quick-release does not hold the wheel firmly, undo it again, then turn in the locknut on the other side and try again.
8. Retension the brakes, making sure the brake blocks fully contact the sides of the rim when engaged — correct wheel position or brake adjustment correspondingly, if necessary.
9. Reinstall and adjust any other parts that were removed or loosened for removal or installation.

If the hub does not turn freely or is too loose, the problem can generally be solved with bearing adjustment.

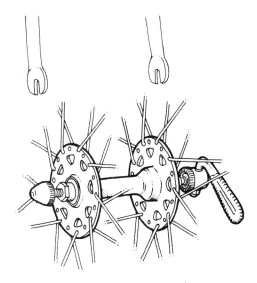

8.8. Installation of hub with quick-release.

Hub Maintenance

8.9. Assembly details of Maxicar sealed, adjustable bearing hub. Although generally used on fine touring bikes, it is equally suitable for tandems and mountain bikes.

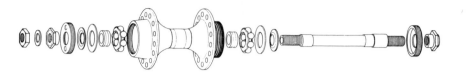

Only if adjustment does not do the trick, will a general overhaul be necessary, although this work is recommended on a yearly or even half-yearly schedule if the bike is used frequently under demanding conditions with dust and moisture.

The hub bearings must be tightened if the wheel can be moved sideways relative to the fork or the frame in the vicinity of the rim. They must be loosened if the wheel does not spin lightly, finally coming to rest after some pendulum movement with the valve at the bottom, when allowed to turn freely. The whole thing must be overhauled if you notice rough spots or crunching noises when the wheel is turned. The same applies if adjusting for too loose a bearing results in notable tightness. Don't think a loosely adjusted hub bearing that allows the wheel to turn freely does not offer excessive rolling resistance: it turns freely only without load, and the rolling resistance may become quite significant when the bike is loaded with the rider's weight.

Hub Bearing Adjustment

Since both the fixed and the rotating parts of the two bearings are connected with each other via the axle and the hub shell, respectively, it will suffice to adjust the bearing on one side (see Fig. 8.10). A hub with axle nuts can be left installed on the bike on one side, so only one axle nut must be loosened. A wheel with a quick-release hub is removed from the bike for this procedure, following the preceding instructions. You will need a cone wrench and a wrench that fits on the locknut.

Procedure:
1. If the wheel remains in the bike (wheel with axle nuts), loosen the axle nut on one side by 2—3 turns. This will then be the side on which to adjust. Retighten after completion of the adjustment procedure.
2. Loosen locknut by one turn, countering from the cone on the same side.
3. Lift the lock washer off the cone.
4. Tighten the cone by ¼ turn to correct a bearing that is too loose, or loosen it by that much to correct one that is too tight.

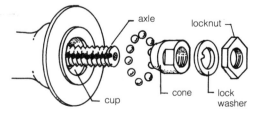

8.10. Hub bearing adjustment detail

5. Install lock washer and tighten the locknut.
6. Check and readjust if necessary.

The wheel must be removed for this work. Once that is done, you will need a cone wrench, a wrench to fit the locknut, rags and bearing grease.

Disassembly Procedure:
1. Loosen and remove the locknut on one side, countering at the cone on the same side. Leave the locknut on the other side installed.
2. Remove the lock washer.
3. Unscrew the cone, countering at the cone on the other side.
4. Remove the axle with the cone and locknut still installed on one side, catching the bearing balls.

Overhauling Procedure:
1. Clean and inspect all bearing parts, including the cups inside the hub. Replace the bearing balls and any parts that are damaged, pitted or corroded.
2. Replace the axle if it is not perfectly straight any more (check by rolling over a flat surface — it is bent if it seems to wobble up and down).
3. Replace the lock washer if the key does not lock in the longitudinal groove in the axle.
4. If replacement parts of a certain make or model are not available, you may sometimes get matching components of another make, providing you try them out to make sure they really fit.
5. To replace the bearing cups, special removal and installation tools are required, so it is advisable to get this done at a bike shop if you don't want to buy such exotic tools
6. If the cone that was left on the axle has to be replaced, first measure exactly how much axle protrudes to its outside, then install the new one in that same location.
7. Fill the cleaned bearing cups with bearing grease and push the new bearing balls in, leaving just a little freedom to move.
8. Insert the axle from the side with the installed cone, making sure the bearing balls are not lost.
9. Install the cone on the free end of the axle, followed by the lock washer and the locknut, and adjust provisionally so the bearing turns freely.
10. Adjust the bearing per the preceding procedure *Hub Bearing Adjustment.*

Overhaul Hub Bearings

8.11. *SunTour low flange hubs*

8.12. *Shimano high flange hubs*

The Tires

The tires not only cause the most misery on the bike, they also directly affect how lightly the bike runs, so it

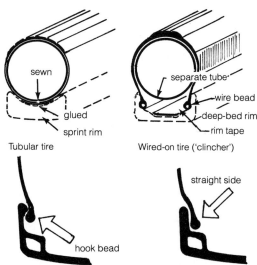

8.13. Tire types with matching rims

Rolling Resistance

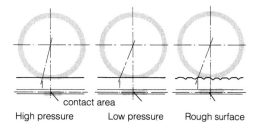

8.14. Rolling resistance is a function of
the pitch-over angle, which depends on
tire pressure and road surface quality.

is well worth selecting and maintaining them properly. In this section we will cover both the mundane maintenance matters and the theory that determines their rolling resistance.

There are two types of bicycle tire: the common wired-on type, also referred to as clincher, and the tubular tire, often called sew-up. Cross sections are illustrated in Fig. 8.13. The wired-on tire is held around a separate inner tube on a deep-bedded rim by means of metal wires (sometimes these are replaced by aramid, such as Kevlar, to save weight and provide flexibility for easy folded storage). The tubular tire is sown around the inner tube and is literally glued onto a much shallower rim.

Certainly at speeds not exceeding 16km/h (10mph), the rolling resistance plays a major part in determining how easily a bicycle runs. Only at higher speeds (or strong head winds) does wind resistance become increasingly important. But even at those elevated speeds, the rolling resistance may make the difference between comfortable cycling and plodding along — if higher speeds are ever reached at all on a bike with poor wheels. Fig. 8.14 gives a graphic representation of the differences between rolling resistance for various tires.

Contrary to common opinion, the rolling resistance is not primarily a function of the tire width. In reality, it depends mainly on the area of deformation. The most important factor that enters into its determination is the tire pressure, and it is easier to make a tire withstand a high pressure by minimizing the cross section width, but it can be achieved with a wide tire too. On the other hand, the condition of the road also enters into the equation. Also important is the load, which is assumed to be 60% of the total weight of bike and rider in the back, 40% in the front for a conventional racing bike; on a mountain bike the figures may be 65% and 35%, respectively.

Fig. 8.16 shows the principle of the pneumatic tire as a suspension element that minimizes energy losses due to road unevennesses. The idea is to provide a very flexible layer that forms around the obstacles, balancing out the forces on either side, so no retarding component results. To approach this ideal, the tire must be both highly compressed (to minimize deformation on level ground) and highly flexible (to minimize the forces required to deform the tire around the obstacles). On an inflexible tire, the higher resistance is mainly due to the energy that goes into lifting the bike up over the obstacle. On a soft tire (or on soft ground), the energy equivalent to raising the bike over the height of the deformation is consumed with each wheel revolution.

To optimize the tires' suspension effect, they should be inflated to the maximum pressure compatible with the road surface (hard on smooth, hard ground, softer on irregular surfaces, very soft on soft ground). Fig. 8.15 shows the effects of different road surfaces relative to the tire pressure. The pressure of front and rear tires should reflect the differences in loading, meaning that the rear tire should have about 20% more pressure than the one in front. The narrower tires do not only allow higher pressures, they usually *require* it, since they don't have as much protective cushioning as the thicker ones. Just the same, in recent years mountain bike tires have been introduced that withstand quite impressive pressures without blowing off the rim.

The following values are based on the use of racing tires with a cross section of up to 25mm. For the rear tire, the optimal value for use on smooth asphalt is about 7—8bar (100—125psig). A rough asphalt or brick road surface would require 5—6bar (70— 85psig), while a cobblestone road can only be mastered at any respectable speed with tires inflated to 3—4bar (45—60psig). When you get off road, soft soil, sand and snow may require pressures as low as 1—2 bar (15—30psig).

Only relatively fat tires, such as mountain bike versions, allow use at very low pressures. Other models do not have enough cushioning to protect the rim or prevent the tire and the tube from getting caught between a rock and a hard spot — the rim and the road, respectively. Special tires with protective layers between the tread and the casing, usually made with aramid (Kevlar), will prevent puncturing upon impacting in the thread area, but will generally not help if the tires are so soft that the tubes get pinched.

Most people who have investigated rolling resistance under the pretense of science have done so in an incredibly incompetent manner. Rather than comparing equal tires under different circumstances or the same tire under different circumstances, they have compared different tires, each inflated to some arbitrary pressure that differed widely, all ridden on a perfectly smooth, hard surface — of course using the fanciest electronic instruments. Not surprisingly, the results simply favored whatever tire was inflated the hardest, since that is all that really counts under such favorable conditions.

Tire Pressure

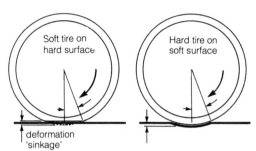

8.15. *Relative deformation of tire and road surface.*

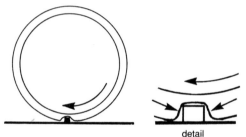

8.16. *Principle of pneumatic tire: Balanced forces instead of reaction force in opposite direction.*

8.17. *Determining tire pressure. The modern designation is in bar, one bar being 14.7 psi.*

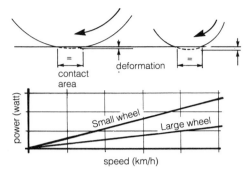

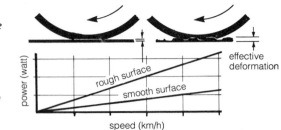

8.18 and 8.19.
Left: Effect of tire
size on rolling
resistance.
Right: Effect of
road surface
quality on rolling
resistance.

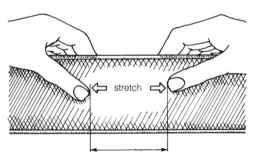

8.20. *Simple check of tire flexibility*

What's needed is less hocus-pocus and more common sense. In a consistent series of simple comparative tests, I have established the criteria that determine the ease of rolling when all are inflated to the same pressure. Even this is of course not the full story. After all, the bicycle wheel is part of the total suspension system of the bike (so the tires on a bike with suspension should only be tested in combination with it), and even the relative flexing of the frame and the steering leads to forces that retard the bike at high speeds. Even so, this simple test has brought a number of significant conclusions about the tires themselves to light:

☐   A cross section that minimizes the volume contained in the rim compared to the volume projecting.
☐   The lightest and most flexible side wall design and construction possible.
☐   A flexible tread surface, which can be tested as shown in Fig. 8.20.
☐   The use of the lightest and most flexible inner tube.

The wheel diameter also has some effect, but this factor is quite insignificant compared to the others: several speed records were established with the Moulton with its 17-inch wheels (compared to the 27-inch diameter customary on racing bikes) and dampened suspension. Fig. 8.18 illustrates the effect of the wheel size on the way the bike travels through unevennesses — unless a separate suspension is used.

Tire Sizing

Although it is still customary in the US to give tires sizes by some archaic method referring to inch sizes that don't even resemble any measurable dimension, there is a more systematic and logical system in use. This is the ETRTO method of tire and rim size designation, developed by the European Tire and Rim Technical Organization, and now integrated in the internationally applicable ISO standards for bicycle components, and referred to as Universal Tire Marking System. This method is illustrated in Fig. 8.21.

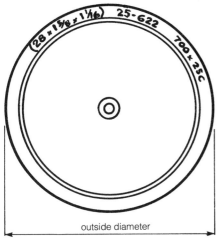

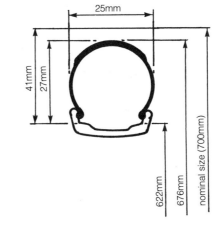

8.21 and 8.22.
Left: Tire size designation in accordance with the ETRTO and ISO standards for Universal Tire Marking. Below: Testing for tire rolling resistance in Raleigh's product testing laboratory in Nottingham, England.

The ETRTO size designation applies to both rims and tires and references the rim bed, or shoulder, diameter. A second dimension quoted is the tire cross section for tires, the inside rim width for rims. Thus, the tires are identified by a code consisting of a 2-digit number followed by a 3-digit number, separated by a dash. The 2-digit number represents the inflated tire cross section, while the 3-digit number is the diameter of the rim bed in mm. Similarly, rim sizes are quoted as the same three-digit code, followed by a two-digit code referring to its inside width in mm, separated by an X. The outside diameter of a wheel is the sum of the rim bed diameter and twice the tire cross section. For mountain bikes, the usual rim size is 559mm, while it is either 622mm or 630mm for conventional derailleur bikes.

The last figures betray the absurdity of the archaic tire size designation method still generally used in the US today, because the 622mm rim used for 700mm (28-inch) tires, is smaller than the 630mm rim used on what is called a 27-inch wheel — given tires of identical cross section, the 27-inch wheel is actually bigger than the 700mm (28-inch) wheel. In the ETRTO system, within reason, any tire with 622 in its code fits any rim of that size, while any tire with 630 matches a corresponding rim size.

The tread of a bicycle tire is generally profiled. Certainly in the case of high-pressure tires, this is of dubious benefit, since the idea of tread profile is strictly unique to the low-pressure condition found on cars. Car tires are inflated much less than bicycle tires for comparable road surfaces. Consequently, the contact pressure (i.e. force per unit area) is much less, which allows water to

Tire Tread

build up between tire and road when it is wet, causing aquaplaning in rainy weather on smooth asphalt.

Bicycle tires do not have this problem since they are inflated to pressures that are up to 3 times as high as car tires (at least for road use). Consequently, there is no need to remove water through channels in the tire tread. Only towards the sides of the tires, where the contact is angular in a curve, is there any justification for a rougher surface to prevent skidding when cornering in wet weather.

Tube and Valve

The inner tube used with the conventional wired-on tire is generally made of butyl, or synthetic rubber. Particularly tough tubes are made of other synthetic compounds that are meant to resist puncturing better. The lightest and most flexible tubes, chosen to minimize rolling resistance, are of latex, i.e. pure unvulcanized rubber. This flexible material is not particularly puncture-prone either, but it allows air to pass through rather easily, and thus daily re-inflation may be required.

8.23. Mountain bike tire profiles. For road use, and for firm ground off-road, smooth tires (slicks) offer less resistance and excellent traction

Butyl tires also lose air, but less so: racing bikes with butyl tires may require inflation twice a week, while mountain bike tires will go at least a week without fresh air. Depending on the material, the size of the tube must match that of the tire within certain limits. Latex tubes must match the tire dimension to within the closest tolerances, while butyl tubes can be stretched e.g. from 47mm to 54mm cross section (typical mountain bike sizes).

Fig. 8.24 shows three valve types, used for letting the air into the tube. In the US, only the Presta and Schrader models are commonly used: the former for racing bikes, the latter for most mountain bikes and utility machines. Each type requires a different valve hole diameter in the rim. Although Schrader valves can be inflated at a gas station, the Presta type is preferable, requiring less pressure to inflate. Tubes with this valve type are available for any tire size, although more readily so for narrow tires than for mountain bikes. Make sure the valve has a section of screw thread on the shaft, since valves without this feature tend to disappear back into the rim when you try to inflate them, making it very hard to do so.

Tire and Tube Maintenance

Of all the problems associated with the bicycle, the flat tire, or puncture, is by far the most common. Although things have greatly improved with the introduction of high-pressure tires in big sizes, such as on the mountain bike, the problem always remains. Just the same, the risk of any damage can be minimized, and it is not insignificant that experienced cyclists have far fewer punctures than inexperienced riders: it's a matter of how you ride and how you maintain your equipment.

The tube must be protected against damage. Only careful path selection will give a safeguard against sharp objects in the road, although tires with aramid (Kevlar) liners are indeed remarkably tough in this respect. Regularly inspect the tires and remove any sharp objects that are embedded. Maintain sufficient tire pressure and watch where you ride, avoiding potholes, rocks and debris in your path, to minimize the risk of pinching the tube and the tire sidewall between the rim and the road. Rim tape, wrapped around the rim bed, should be used to protect the tire from the spoke ends and the sharp outlines of the nipples in the rim bed.

Woods   Schrader   Presta

8.24. The three most common valve types

Although many people seem to think fixing a flat by the roadside is more hassle than it is worth, it is a simple job that almost always can be carried out satisfactorily in reasonable time, even under quite adverse circumstances. If you want to pull out the old tube and install a spare, be my guest, but realize that you can't carry unlimited spares, and sooner or later you will still be confronted with the need to patch a tire anyway. The following description can be followed either in the workshop or by the roadside.

To carry out a puncture repair, you will need a set of (usually three) tire levers, patch kit (containing patches, rubber solution, and sandpaper or a scraper). In addition, you may need whatever tools are used to remove the wheel. If wheel removal is complicated to do (e.g. on a bike with special brakes), you can just leave the wheel in the bike, merely turning the bike upside-down while supporting the handlebars to protect anything mounted on them.

Procedure:
1. Remove the wheel from the bike. Follow the appropriate instructions above for wheel removal.
2. Check whether the cause is visible from the outside. In that case, remove it and mark its location, so you know where to work.
3. Remove the valve cap and the locknut, unscrew the round nut (if you have a Presta valve).
4. Push the valve body in and work one side of the tire into the deeper center of the rim, as shown in Fig. 8.25.
5. Put a tire lever under the bead on the side that has been freed, at some distance from the valve, then

Puncture Repair

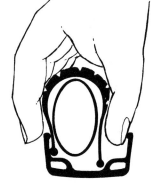

8.25. Pushing the tire bead into the deep center portion of the rim.

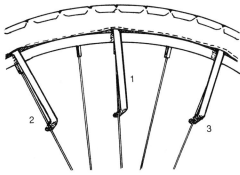

8.26. Use of tire levers

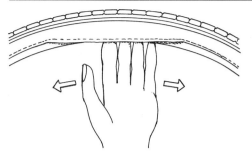

8.27. Removing tire bead from rim

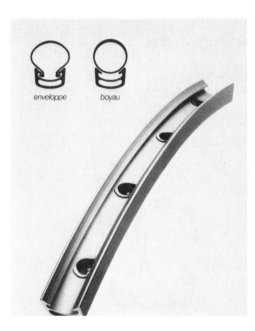

enveloppe   boyau

8.28 Rim suitable for both tubular and wired-on tires — quite superfluous.

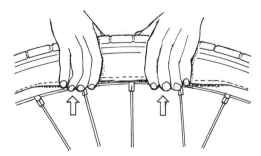

8.29. Pulling tire bead over rim edge

use it to lift the bead over the rim edge and hook it on a spoke, as shown in Fig. 8.26.

6. Do the same with the second tire lever two spokes to the left, and with the third one two spokes over to the right. Now the first tire lever will come loose, so you may use it in a fourth location, if necessary.

7. When enough of the tire sidewall is lifted over the rim, you can remove the rest by hand (Fig. 8.27).

8. Remove the tube, saving the valve until last. Push the valve out through the valve hole in the rim, while holding back the tire.

9. Try inflating the tube, and check where air escapes. If the hole is very small, so it can't be easily detected, pass the tube slowly past your eye, which is quite sensitive. If you still have difficulty finding the hole, and if you have access to water, dip the tube under water, a section at a time: the hole is wherever bubbles escape. There may be more than just one hole.

10. Make sure the area around the hole is dry and clean, then roughen it with the sandpaper or the scraper from the patch kit, and remove the resulting dust. Treat an area slightly larger than the patch you want to use.

11. Quickly and evenly, spread a thin film of rubber solution on the treated area. Let dry about 3 minutes in hot, dry weather, up to twice as long in cold or humid weather.

12. Remove the foil backing from the patch, without touching the adhesive side. Place it with the adhesive side down on the treated area, centered on the hole. Apply pressure over the entire patch to improve adhesion.

13. Sprinkle talcum powder from the patch kit over the treated area, or you can leave the cellophane on the patch so it does not stick to the inside of the tire.

14. Inflate the tube and wait long enough to make sure the repair is carried out properly.

15. Meanwhile, check the inside of the tire casing, and remove any sharp objects that may have caused the puncture.

16. Let enough air out of the tube to make it limp but not completely empty.

17. Push the tire far enough on the rim to allow seating the tube completely in the rim bed under the tire, starting by putting the valve through the hole in the rim.

18. With your bare hands, pull the tire back over the edge of the rim (Fig. 8.29), starting opposite the valve, which is best to do last of all. If it seems too

tight, work the part already installed deeper into the center of the rim bed, working around towards the valve from both sides.

19. Push the valve stem up and make sure the tire is fully seated.

20. Make sure the tube is not pinched between rim and tire bead anywhere, working and kneading the tire until it is free.

21. Install the valve locknut, if appropriate for the type of valve used, and inflate the tube to about a third its final pressure.

22. Center the tire relative to the rim, making sure it lies evenly all around on both sides, checking the distance between the rim and the moulded ridge on the side (Fig. 8.30).

23. Inflate to its final pressure, then install the wheel.

Remarks:

1. If the tire is wider than the rim, you may have to release the brake, and tighten it again afterwards. On the rear wheel, refer to point 1 above for installation.

2. On a particularly narrow rim, points 18—20 are quite important. This same work, as well as the removal of tire and tube, are much easier on wide rims than on narrow ones.

3. Rubber solution and patches have a tendency to dry out if stored at high temperatures. It is a good idea to replace both once a year.

When a tire or tube is hopelessly damaged, it must be replaced. Like the puncture repair, this may have to be done away from home. Although I have rarely found it necessary, most people always carry a spare tube and replace it, rather than repairing the old tube. This must also be done if the valve leaks or if the tube is seriously damaged. To do this, follow only the relevant steps of the instructions for fixing a flat. Replacement of the tire casing is done similarly. Make sure the rim tape that covers the spoke ends is intact (join the ends with a patch if necessary).

Quality bicycle rims are made of extruded aluminum, while cheap bikes may have rims made of bent steel sheet, either chrome-plated or stainless. Steel rims are not usually stronger than aluminum ones, even if the latter are significantly lighter. This is due to the box profile that can be used for extruded sections, while the cross section shape of the steel rim is much less structurally sound. Fig. 8.31 shows the various cross sections used. Steel rims should never be used on bikes

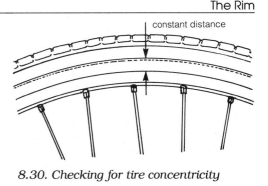

8.30. *Checking for tire concentricity*

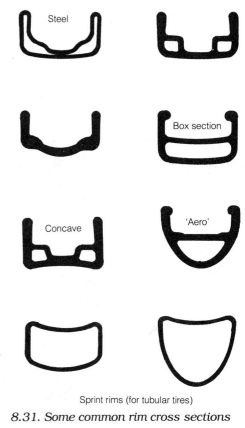

Sprint rims (for tubular tires)

8.31. *Some common rim cross sections*

The Rim

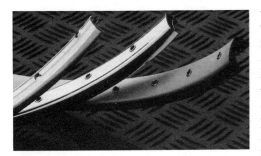

8.32 and 8.33.
Above: Some Weinmann rim types.
Below: Campagnolo racing rims.

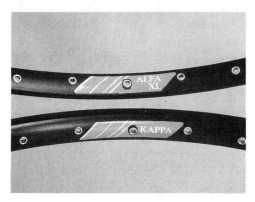

8.34. Hard anodized rim from Sun. Although these are excellent rims, the hard anodization is superfluous and only reduces braking efficiency.

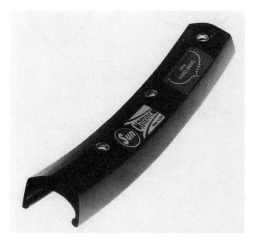

with rim brakes, since the braking deteriorates sharply when steel rims are wet (much more so than for aluminum rims).

Most steel rim manufacturers try to fool the public into thinking that serrating the sides of the rim will improve braking. Actually, there is only one profile that does this trick, though at the price of noisy braking and high brake block wear. This is the patented Van Schothorst design with intermittent diagonal grooves. A new design by the same manufacturer that looks deceptively like an aluminum rim, on the other hand, does not seem to offer improved wet weather braking.

The spoke holes are installed alternatingly off-set to the left and the right of center, corresponding to the direction the spokes run in the assembled wheel. Campagnolo has a series of rims with spoke holes that are accurately aligned, guaranteeing a wheel that maintains its shape and tension. In order to prevent cracking of the rim at the spoke holes, these points should be reinforced by means of bushings, which should connect inner and outer sections on the box-section, or 'double bottom' design. At a minimum, a washer should be installed between nipple head and inside of rim to distribute the spoke forces around the hole.

The size of a rim is determined in accordance with the ETRTO designation and corresponds closely to the size designation for the matching tires. To give an example, a rim with designation 622 X 18 has an inside width of 18mm and a rim bed diameter of 622mm. Most tires with 622 in their designation will fit on this rim.

The strength of the rim is only relevant within the total assembled structure of the wheel. In fact, most kinds of rim deformation are not really the result of a weak rim, but of insufficient spoke tension. Even so, the strength and rigidity of the rim itself do matter, since they help distribute the forces over more spokes. Very, very few rims are made of heat treated aluminum, which is stronger than regular aluminum. Although some of these models are dark gray, it is not generally true that all dark gray rims are heat treated, or particularly strong for that matter. The color is not due to heat treating, but to anodizing with a dye. Anodizing to significant depth increases the surface hardness of the rim, but has no significant effect on its strength. It should also be noted that anodized rims tend to provide poorer wet weather braking than plain aluminum ones.

The easiest way to test the lateral rigidity of a rim, is to place it halfway on a flat table, with the other half

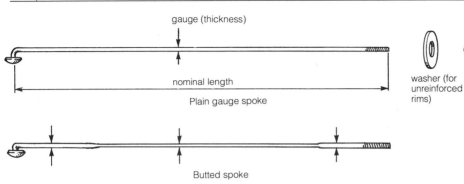

Plain gauge spoke

Butted spoke

8.35.
Details of spoke and nipple. The butted spoke shown below is referred to by the gauge numbers for each of the sections, e,g, 15-16-15 for a 16 gauge inner section and 15 gauge butts.

projecting. Holding it down firmly, while pushing the overhanging part down, will indicate how easily it is deformed (but don't apply so much force that permanent deformation is caused, which may happen on a weak lightweight rim). The radial rigidity is verified by standing the rim on end and pushing it down from the top. By and large, heavier rims, assuming the same material, are stronger; higher profiles lead to more radial rigidity, and wider profiles to more lateral rigidity.

The spoked bicycle wheel is a unique construction, since the spokes are not loaded in compression, as is the case on a wagon wheel (or most other wheels), but in tension. This allows the total forces to be distributed over all but the two bottom spokes, whereas they must always be carried fully by one or two spokes on other wheel types (including in principle the disk wheel, even if that does not have spokes as such — this is one reason for its greater weight). The spokes of the conventional bike wheel can also be kept very thin because the tension loading does not transfer a bending moment on the spokes. Fig. 8.36 compares the loading cases for the wagon wheel and the bicycle wheel.

Despite the obvious technical advantage of the wire-spoked wheel, some manufacturers and would-be innovators never give up on reinventing the wheel. Consequently, we regularly see the introduction of such abominations as cast aluminum or cast plastic wheels built on the basis of the cart wheel. They are heavier all right, and they can't be straightened when bent, but they are by no means technically satisfactory, as was verified by tests conducted at the Aachen Technical University some years ago.

Fig. 8.35 shows two versions of the spoke with the nipple that connects it to the rim and by which it is tightened. In fact, the higher the tension, within reas-

The Spokes

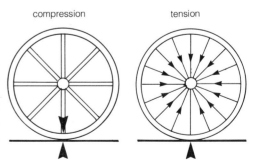

8.36. Comparison of wheels with compression and tension loaded spokes.

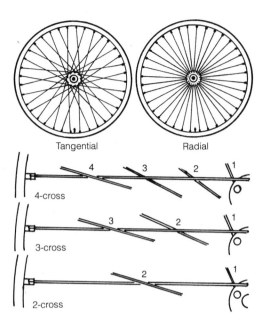

8.37. *Various spoking patterns*

Spoking Patterns

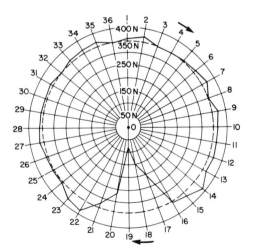

8.38. *The effect of an 800 N rotating force on the tension of individual spokes when these are prestressed at 350N.*

on, the stronger the wheel. When the tension is lower, the sequence of stress variations through which the material goes is more demanding as the spokes are intermittently loaded and released during the rotation of the wheel. This tends to induce metal fatigue, leading to breaking, usually directly at the bend near the head.

The illustration also indicates how the spoke is measured. Its size is quoted as the length from the inside of the bend to the end, while the thickness is usually quoted as a gauge number. Recently, spoke thicknesses are, more logically, referenced in mm — see Table 7 in the Appendix for conversion of the gauge numbers into mm. When two gauge numbers are quoted, the spoke is butted, meaning the ends are thicker than the middle section. This leads to greater flexibility and consequently to greater strength than a spoke that has the same thickness over its entire length — despite the reduced section. Any associated weight savings is insignificant.

Nowadays, stainless steel is commonly used for spokes. Even though this is a fine material, it is not necessarily correct to assume them to be stronger than regular spokes made of galvanized steel. Their advantage is that they don't corrode. Corrosion not only weakens the spokes over time, it also makes it harder to turn the nipple, often causing the spokes to break when an attempt is made to tighten or loosen them.

The spokes are installed according to a certain spoking patterns, some of which are shown in Fig. 8.37. The simplest pattern is that of the radially spoked wheel, where the spokes do not cross each other. Because this pattern does not lend itself very well to the transfer of a torque (the application of a rotating force on the hub, tending to twist it relative to the rim), the various tangential patterns have been introduced. This makes sense on the rear wheel and on any wheel with a hub brake, but there is no reason at all to choose anything but radial spoking for the front wheel of a bike with rim brakes, providing the hub flanges are strong enough to withstand the resulting radially oriented spoke forces.

The various tangential spoking patterns are identified by the number of spokes that each spoke crosses on its way from the hub to the rim: 1-cross, 2-cross, 3-cross and 4-cross. The latter has proven to lead to fewer spoke breakages and is universally used in European professional road racing circles these days. The whole pattern is actually simpler than it appears, since it is repeated every fourth spoke on the rim, every second spoke on either hub flange. The place to start looking is at the valve — it should lie between two nearly parallel spokes, leading to the LH and the RH hub flange, respectively.

Generally, bike wheels have 36 spokes each, although it was customary until the early sixties to use 40 spokes on the heavily loaded rear wheel, and 32 on the less loaded front wheel. Smaller wheels require fewer spokes, down to 20 for na 16-inch wheel. In recent years, the craze for lightness and reduced air resistance has brought back full-size wheels with fewer spokes, requiring matching rims and hubs. For the rear wheel they are only suitable for easy terrain and light riders. Similarly, oval and even more radically sectioned spokes have been introduced to further reduce the air resistance of lightweight racing bikes.

Whatever number of spokes and crosses, the spokes always run alternatingly to the LH and the RH hub flange. Depending whether a particular spokes lies on the inside or the outside of the flange, they are referred to as inside and outside spokes. In the case of the radial spoked wheel, all spokes are outside spokes. On all other wheels inside and outside spokes alternate on each hub flange. Since the outside spokes wrap furthest around the hub flange (and since they stand under a slightly less acute angle), they are generally less prone to breaking. Consequently, the spokes that take the driving forces should preferably be outside spokes — on a rear wheel these are the spokes on the RH side that radiate backward at the top of the hub. On a front wheel with a hub brake, these are the spokes that radiate forward from the top of the hub.

In cross section, the spoked wheel may take any of the shapes depicted in Fig. 8.46. Obviously, the front wheel is generally symmetric (an exception might be a front wheel with hub brake), while the rear wheel is generally off-set to accommodate the freewheel block with its sprockets, pushing the spokes on the RH side into a much steeper angle relative to the axle (or a more acute angle relative to the wheel centerline). This asymmetry is referred to as wheel dishing and leads to proportional differences in spoke tension with attendant breakage probability. Casette hubs, which were previously praised for a favorable bearing configuration leading to fewer broken axles, also excel in this respect, since they require less dish, preventing broken spokes.

The spoked wheel should be seen as an integral structure, so it is hard to distinguish between specific rim and spoke maintenance jobs. When a spoke breaks, the rim deforms. When the wheel wobbles, it is general-

8. 39 and 8.40.
All major manufacturers use automated spoking machines these days. Despite their accuracy, some manual truing and final tensioning is often required.

Spoked Wheel Maintenance

Replace Spoke

8.41 and 8.42.
Very strong hub flanges and straight spokes (in Weco's cheap version above, or Roval's fancy one below) allow radial spoking even on the rear wheel — providing extremely low gears are avoided.

Wheel Truing

check in
3 locations

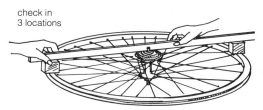

8.43. Simplified symmetry check. There are special gauges to do this more accurately.

ly corrected by means of spoke manipulation. To replace a rim or a hub, you have to replace the spokes. All parts mutually affect each other.

Sometimes it is tricky to replace a broken spoke. The most heavily tensioned and loaded spokes on the RH side of the rear wheel are generally not accessible without first removing the freewheel, or the series of sprockets on a casette hub. This operation is described in Chapter 10. If the nipple also has to be replaced, the tire must be deflated, so tire, tube and rim tape can be pushed over to gain access to the nipple from the top of the rim. You will need a spoke wrench, or nipple spanner, and some vaseline.

Procedure
1. If the hole in the hub that corresponds to the broken spoke lies inaccessibly under the freewheel, remove the freewheel, as described in Chapter 9.
2. Remove the old spoke. If possible, unscrew the remaining section from the nipple, holding the latter with a wrench. If not, deflate the tube and locally lift tire, tube and rim tape off the rim, after which the nipple can be replaced by a new one.
3. Locate a spoke that runs the same way as the broken one: every fourth spoke along the circumference of the rim runs similarly. Check how it crosses the various other spokes that run the other way, using it as an example.
4. Thread the nipple on the spoke until the latter has the same tension as the other spokes.
5. If the spokes do not seem to be under tension, tighten all of them half a turn at a time, until they all seem equally taut and the wheel is reasonably true. If necessary, follow the instructions for *Wheel Truing* below to correct the situation.

If the problem is a serious one, the wheel being bent quite far over a large area, first straighten it roughly. Do this with the wheel removed from the bike. Support it in its two 'low' points, e.g. against the pavement and the curb, while pushing against it in the 'high' points. Push and check and push again, until it begins to look like it is level, and none of the spokes are excessively loose. Then proceed to the truing operation outlined below. For tools, you'll need a spoke wrench and preferably a truing stand — a tool into which the wheel is held, with gauges indicating how far it has to be corrected. In a pinch you can install the wheel in the bike and use fixed reference points, such as the brake blocks).

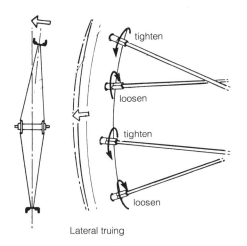

Lateral truing

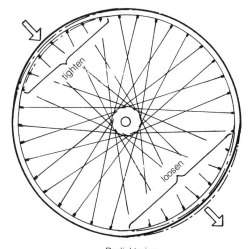

Radial truing

8.45.
Wheel truing is done by tensioning and loosening spokes selectively, as shown here for lateral and radial deflections, respectively.

Procedure:
1. Check where it is offset to the left, where to the right, by turning it slowly while watching at a fixed reference point. Mark the relevant sections.
2. Loosen the RH spokes in the area where the rim is off-set to the RH side, while tightening the ones on the LH side — and vice versa, as shown in Fig. 8.45.
3. Repeat steps 1 and 2 several times, until the wheel is true enough not to rub on the brakes.

In the assembled bike, the two wheels must be perfectly aligned one behind the other with the centerline through the bike, so it stays on track without undue steering and balancing corrections. One factor that comes into play here is the wheel dish on the rear wheel: it must be just enough to place the rim on the centerline through the front wheel and the rest of the bike. If necessary, the wheels are centered correctly to achieve this.

If the wheels are not in line, you may notice balancing problems, especially when riding a straight line with the hands off the handlebars. The person riding behind you can usually confirm the problem when he tries to visually align the two wheels. To establish how much correction is required, it is best to use a wheel alignment gauge, which may be bought ready made. On the other hand, you may also use the technique illustrated in Fig. 8.43. The idea is to correct spoke tension so that the rim is centered between the lock-nuts over the entire circumference (check in at least three locations equi-spaced around the circumference). When you have finished, you may have to follow the *Wheel Truing* procedure above. A bike mechanic can carry out this

Wheel Symmetry

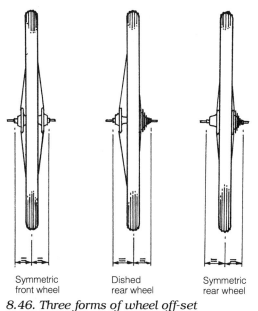

Symmetric front wheel

Dished rear wheel

Symmetric rear wheel

8.46. Three forms of wheel off-set

Wheel Spoking

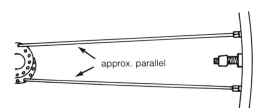

8.47. Orientation of spokes either side of the valve.

whole operation in little time, in case you despair.

This must be done to replace hub, rim or spokes. It is rather a time consuming and fidgety operation, only worth doing yourself if you value its therapeutic value, since any bike mechanic can do it incomparably faster and usually more accurately. Even so, the operation is not half as difficult as might at first appear, once one brings to mind how the wheel is built up. In my *Bicycle Repair Book*, you will find a step-by-step account of this work. However, it is also possible to figure it out yourself on the basis of the following description.

First check on a completed wheel, always looking at it from a certain side (e.g. from the RH side). First check the configuration at the valve, noticing how one spoke runs from the first hole to the right to the RH side of one hub flange, while the spoke from the first hole to the left runs virtually parallel to the LH side of the other hub flange. Then notice how the pattern repeats itself every fourth spoke. Make a sketch of the configuration at the valve and of one set of four spokes. This will be your pattern for the entire wheel.

The correct spoke length may either be selected on the basis of the old wheel, or by asking at the bike shop, consulting a spoke sizing table such as those from *Sutherland's Handbook for Bicycle Mechanics*. To establish the correct size with the aid of such a table, you have to know detailed dimensions of the hub and the rim as well as the desired spoking pattern. Also note that on the rear wheel, the spokes on the LH side may have to be about 3mm (1/8") longer than on the RH side to accommodate the different angles relative to the

8.48 and 8.49. Left: Simple wheel truing stand from the Dutch manufacturer Tacx. Right: professional model from the US manufacturer Park Tools, to do the same job faster and more accurately.

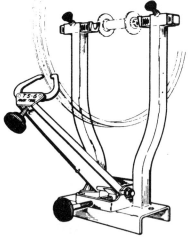

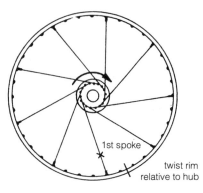

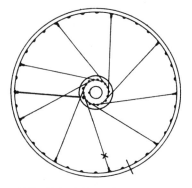

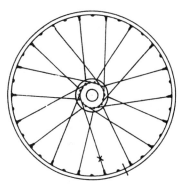

1. The first 9 outside spokes

2. The first outside spoke

3. All spokes on one side

wheel centerline. You will need a spoke wrench, some vaseline, a rag, a screwdriver, and preferably a wheel truing stand.

Apply some vaseline to the threaded nipple ends, so the nipples will be easy to install and subsequent adjustment remains assured. Work in groups of 9 spokes (assuming a total of 36 spokes): first all inside spokes on one hub flange, followed by all spokes on the inside of the other flange, then all outside spokes on that same flange, and finally all outside spokes on the remaining flange. Refer to Fig. 8.50 for a sequence in detailed steps, referring also to your own sketch representing the required configuration. Finally, squeeze all spokes together in groups of four to release tension, and then follow the procedures entitled *Wheel Truing* and *Wheel Symmetry* to bring the wheel into the desired shape.

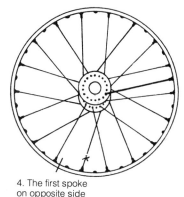

4. The first spoke on opposite side

8.50. *Four stages of the wheel spoking process.*

Disk Wheels

Since the mid eighties, disk wheels have been all the craze in time trial events. They offer markedly reduced air resistance compared to the conventional tension spoked wheel, especially at higher speeds. Since the upper portion of the wheel actually moves against the air at twice the bicycle's speed, it can be seen that this factor is more significant than may appear at first.

Interestingly, disk wheels had been on the market as early as 1893, and their benefit was established even at that time, although few people realized their potential. Only after Shimano introduced all sorts of other supposedly aerodynamic components in 1980, and it was soon established that none of them did anything significant, did one begin to realize how much more could be gained with more aerodynamic wheels.

The international sanctioning organization for bicycle racing, the UCI, did not allow the use of aerodynamic fairings on the bike or its components, but did not ob-

119

8.51. *Full disk in the rear; tension wire construction, using aramid fibers, in the front.*

8.52. *Aerospoke wheel for roughly the same wind resistance and less side wind sensitivity compared to a full disk. And the weight is remarkably low too, thanks to aramid fiber reinforced epoxy resin.*

ject to wheels constructed as one piece — as the disk wheel is. Thus, the disk wheel was given an artificial boost, even though, from a technical standpoint, these wheels were inferior to spoked wheels with added lightweight covers (which remained illegal in sanctioned races). At ridiculously high prices and at first excessively heavy, disk wheels soon appeared on any bike used for time trials. Ironically enough, this also became customary in triathlon, where the UCI regulations did not apply and where wheel covers would have been more appropriate.

The technical disadvantage of the disk wheel is obvious: it's essentially the same heavy construction as the wagon wheel, which was so elegantly overcome by the tension-wire spoked bicycle wheel. The result was both a very difficult construction if the wheel is to be perfectly trued, and a high weight. Oddly enough, this high weight has been used as an argument in their favor, since the increased momentum is supposed to even out the movement. Actually this is correct, but it is no advantage, because these heavier wheels first have to be accelerated to the desired speed, which requires more energy than is needed to bring a lighter wheel to the same speed. For time trials, where the bike is only accelerated up to speed once or twice, while subsequent acceleration and deceleration is insignificant, the disadvantage is minimized, but it would make no sense to use disks for other events, where weight is a more important factor.

The other disadvantage of the disk is its sensitivity to cross winds, or any kind of wind on a curved course. One way around this is the three-, four- or five-bladed wheel. This too is a design that was available as early as 1893, and at the time advertised with the same arguments as today. It is almost as heavy as a full disk of the same materials — and even more expensive.

Recently, more sophisticated materials and construction methods have produced disk wheels of remarkably light weight that begin to compete with tension-spoked wheels, although they are incredibly expensive — and less flexible and less durable. Finally, the interesting Tioga *Tension-Disk* wheel, which is marketed by several Japanese manufacturers, should be mentioned. In this design, the conventional spokes are replaced by a kind of spider's web of tensioned aramid (Kevlar) fiber, embedded in a lightweight plastic membrane. It is still sensitive to cross winds, but it is technically as sound as the conventional spoked wheel and even lighter.

Chapter 9

The Drivetrain

The present chapter deals with the system of components that transmits the rider's effort to the rear wheel. It comprises the pedals, the crankset, which is made up of cranks, bottom bracket spindle and chainrings, as well as the chain and the rear freewheel block with cogs, or sprockets. Not included in this chapter is the selection of the sizes of chainrings and sprockets, since this subject will be covered fully in Chapter 10 for derailleur gearing, in Chapter 11 for hub gearing.

The Crankset

Known as chainset in Britain, this unit forms the heart of the drivetrain. It is made up of the bottom bracket (comprising the bearings with an axle, or spindle), the cranks and the chainrings that are mounted on an attachment device incorporated in the RH crank. Although it is generally sold as a unit of components made by the same manufacturer, a certain degree of interchangeability remains. On bicycles without derailleur gearing, a single chainring is used, permanently attached to the RH crank.

Bottom Bracket Bearings and Spindle

9.1. The bottom bracket is the heart of the drivetrain. This is Fisher's special bearing unit with Shimano cranks.

These parts are installed in the frame's bottom bracket housing. The four different models available are depicted on the following pages. Generally, derailleur bikes and other high-quality machines are equipped with either a BSA bracket or a cartridge type unit, the latter with non-adjustable bearings. The Fauber system, better known as one-piece or Ashtabula crankset in the US, is still found on some utility and BMX bikes. The Thompson bracket is mainly used on some low-end European utility machines.

On the BSA bottom bracket, the bearing cups are open towards the center and are screwed into the bracket housing from both sides. The axle is forged out of one piece with integral cones facing out, the bearing balls (usually in retainer rings) lying between cup and cone. The RH cup is screwed in all the way, whereas the LH one is adjustable and locked in position by means of a lockring. The space between the two bearing cups is usually bridged by means of a plastic sleeve to keep dirt and water out. The BSA bottom bracket is the most universally available type, and consequently recommended for anyone who plans to cycle far from home: In case of damage, it can be repaired or replaced almost anywhere with minimal tools and parts.

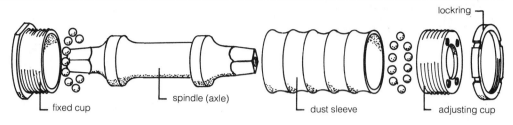

9.2 and 9.3.
Right: Assembly
sequence of BSA
bottom bracket.
Below: Cross sec-
tion through a
BSA bearing.

lockring

fixed cup — spindle (axle) — dust sleeve — adjusting cup

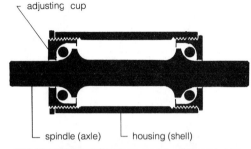

adjusting cup

spindle (axle) — housing (shell)

9.4 and 9.5. Above: Cotterless
'Glockenlager'. Below: Pressed-in
cartridge bearing unit.

The cartridge bearing, often referred to as sealed bearing unit, is not adjustable, being based on conventional machine bearings, or Conrad bearings (some manufacturers display their ignorance by referring to these things as ball bearings, apparently oblivious of the fact that adjustable bearings also qualify for that name). On most models, it is installed in the bottom bracket as an integral unit and held in position either by means of lockrings (Fig. 9.16) or with circular spring clips (Fig. 9.1). Their design is quite critical, since the fixed bearings used are essentially only suitable to support radial loads, and significant wear and resistance could result if the design does not prevent the application of an axial load when tightening the unit in the bracket.

The Thompson bottom bracket has cups that are press-fit into the ends of the bracket shell with the open end facing out, while the cones installed on the spindle face in. Theoretically, this is the right way of doing it, because the off-set pedaling forces are supported most effectively this way. Unfortunately, the construction of this item is generally so hopelessly primitive that any theoretical advantage is more than lost by the practical drawback caused by inadequate precision and the lack of a seal against the penetration of dirt and water. The predecessor of this bearing type, the German *Glockenlager* ('bell bearing') combines the theoretical superiority with a labyrinth seal for protection — and a cotterless crank attachment. Unfortunately, it is now virtually extinct.

The Fauber one-piece design is perhaps the most interesting, not on account of its bearings, but because here both cranks and the spindle form one unit (the crank-to-spindle attachment causes headaches on all other versions). As is the case on the Thompson bracket, the bearings face the right way here. Similarly, the general quality and sealing is far below par, making this an item that rarely works satisfactorily for very long.

All bottom bracket types exist in several different versions. In the first place, the axle length has to correspond to the bracket shell width and the number of chainrings installed. Besides, the way the crank is attached to the spindle comes into play. Cotterless and cottered attachments are each available in different dimensional variants.

In addition, the screw thread diameter and other details of the installation in the bottom bracket shell may vary. For BSA and threaded cartridge bearings, there are at least four different standards: English, Italian, French and Swiss. Apart from differences in dimensions, the English and Swiss versions have LH thread on the RH (or fixed cup) side; Italian and French versions have RH threading on both sides, the former otherwise closely corresponding in size and thread details to the English standard, while the French system has dimensions that are similar to those used on the Swiss version. The only foolproof way to avoid mismatching parts is to take the entire old unit to a bike shop when buying replacement parts, although Table 4 in the Appendix gives some guidance.

9.6. Bottom bracket tools

Bottom Bracket Maintenance

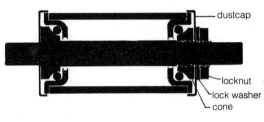

9.7. Thompson bottom bracket

This work is required when the cranks seem to turn poorly — either too tight, too loose or too irregular. The adjustments are made on the LH side. To establish whether the bracket bearings are too loose, try to move the end of a crank in and out relative to the frame. It is too tight, on the other hand, if there is a noticeable resistance when you try to turn the spindle by hand after the cranks have been removed. Unfortunately, if the latter is the case, it usually is necessary to do more than adjust the bearing: you may have to overhaul the whole unit, but adjustment should remain your first step.

Adjust BSA Bottom Bracket

Bottom bracket maintenance goes best with special bottom bracket tools (a set of special wrenches to match the lockring and the adjustable cup). In a pinch, you can get by using provisional methods such as a hammer, a punch and a screwdriver, but fitting tools are preferable since they prevent damage and are easier to operate. Refer to Fig. 9.9 for this work.

Procedure:
1. Loosen the lockring on the LH side by one turn.
2. Tighten or loosen the adjustable cup by one quarter turn at a time.
3. While holding the adjustable cup in place, tighten the lockring again.
4. Check and repeat, if necessary. If perfect adjustment cannot be achieved, overhaul the bottom bracket bearing, following the next procedure.

9.8. EDCO sealed bearing unit. This model allows lateral adjustment.

Overhaul BSA Bottom Bracket

Do this if adjusting does not lead to a satisfactory result. To carry out this work, the cranks must first be

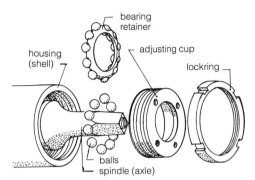

9.9. Adjusting detail of BSA bearing

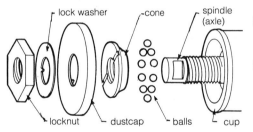

9.10. Adjusting side of Thompson bottom bracket bearing.

Adjust Thompson Bottom Bracket

removed, following the relevant description below. Use bottom bracket tools (including a fixed cup wrench, if necessary), a rag and bearing grease.

Procedure:
1. Loosen the lockring on the LH side by one turn.
2. Loosen and remove the adjustable cup on the LH side, catching the bearing balls and the spindle as it comes out.
3. Remove bearing balls (usually in retainer) on the LH side, the spindle and the RH side bearing balls. Also prize out the dust sleeve if installed.
4. Clean and inspect all parts. Replace the bearing balls (complete with retainer or loose, whatever your preference) and any parts that are damaged, worn or corroded. Damage is usually evidenced by pitting or grooves in the contact area.
5. If the fixed RH cup also shows signs of wear, re-place it too, unscrewing it to the right if the bike is built to English or Swiss standards, to the left if it conforms to French or Italian standards. When re-placing parts, make sure to get matching versions.
6. After thorough cleaning, install the fixed cup, if necessary, tightening it firmly.
7. Fill the bearing cups on both sides with bearing grease and push the bearing balls in. If you use bearing retainers, make sure only the balls, not the metal of the retainers, touch the cones and cups. If loose balls are used, don't try to put too many in: leave just a little play between the individual balls.
8. Install the dust sleeve, followed by the spindle, the longer end in first (towards the RH side), since that's where the crank with the chainring will fit.
9. Install the adjustable cup, making sure you don't lose any bearing balls.
10. Install the lockring
11. Adjust the adjustable cup and tighten with the lockring as described above: loosen lockring, adjus-table cup looser or tighter, tighten lockring again while holding the adjustable cup.

The cranks can remain on the bike. The only tool usually needed is a large wrench that fits on the lock-nut underneath the LH crank. Refer to Fig. 9.10.

Procedure:
1. Loosen the locknut under the LH crank one turn to the right (LH thread).
2. Turn the dust cap underneath the locknut, while pushing it in: to the left to tighten the bearing, to the right to loosen it. This dust cap has a prong

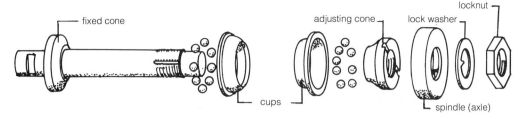

9.11. Assembly drawing of the Thompson bottom bracket bearing.

that penetrates a groove in the bearing cone underneath — if it does not work, remove the nut and the dust cap and then turn the cone directly, e.g. with the aid of a screwdriver.
3. Tighten the locknut holding the dustcap in place.
4. Check and repeat if necessary. If adjustment does not do the trick, proceed to overhauling the unit, following the next procedure.

Remove the LH crank before starting this work. Tools needed for this work include a large wrench, a rag and bearing grease.

Overhaul Thompson Bottom Bracket

Procedure:
1. Loosen and remove the locknut under the LH crank by turning it to the right (LH thread).
2. Turn the dustcap underneath the locknut to the right, while pushing it in, to loosen it.
3. Remove the dust cap, then remove the cone by turning it to the right.
4. Remove the bearing balls in their retainer.
5. Pull out the spindle with the RH crank attached towards the right, catching the bearing balls with their retainer on the RH side.
6. Clean and inspect all parts and replace any parts with damage (rust, pitting or grooves).
7. If necessary, remove the bearing cups by hammering them out from the opposite side, and hammering the new ones into place while protecting them with a block of wood.
8. Fill the clean bearing cups with bearing grease and place the bearing ball retainers inside, orienting them so that only the balls, not the retainer, contact the cups and the cones.
9. Install the spindle with the RH crank attached from the RH side.
10. On the LH side, make sure the bearing ball retainer is in place, then install the cone, followed by the dust cap and the locknut.
11. Adjust the bearing as described above: loosen locknut, turn dustcap to the left to tighten or to the right to loosen the bearing; then tighten the lock-

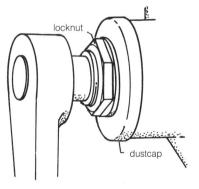

9.12. Thompson adjusting detail

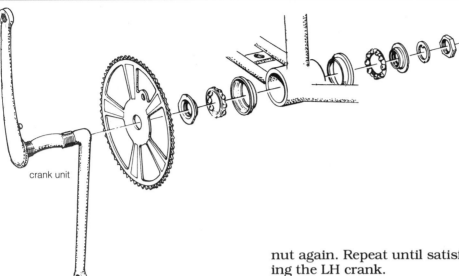

crank unit

9.13.
The one-piece bottom bracket, also known as Ashtabula in the US, Fauber in the rest of the world, comes with a continuous crank assembly, so the crank-to-spindle connection problem is eliminated.

nut again. Repeat until satisfactory before installing the LH crank.

Adjust One-Piece Bottom Bracket

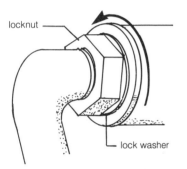

locknut

lock washer

9.14. Adjusting detail of one-piece crank-set bearing.

Being one piece with the spindle, the cranks obviously don't have to be removed. All you need is a large adjustable wrench. Refer to Fig. 9.14 for this work.

Procedure:
1. Loosen the locknut under the LH crank one turn to the right (LH thread).
2. Lift the lock washer under the locknut to free the cone that lies below it.
3. Turn the cone to the left to tighten the bearing, to the right to loosen it.
4. Put the lock washer back on the cone and then tighten the locknut.
5. Check and repeat, if necessary. If adjustment does not do the trick, proceed to overhauling the unit, following the next procedure.

Overhaul One-Piece Bottom Bracket

Before commencing, remove at least the LH pedal. Once more, you will need a large wrench, a rag and bearing grease.

Procedure:
1. Loosen and remove the locknut under the LH crank by turning it to the right (LH thread); twist it around the crank and remove it.
2. Remove the lock washer, then unscrew and remove the LH cone by turning it to the right.
3. Remove the LH bearing balls in their retainer.
4. Pull out the Z-shaped crank and spindle unit to the RH side, twisting it free.
5. Catch the bearing balls with their retainer.
6. Clean and inspect all parts and replace any parts

with damage (rust, pitting or grooves).

7. If necessary, remove the bearing cups by hammering them out from the opposite side, using a big screwdriver, and hammering the new ones into place, protecting them with a block of wood. If the RH cone has to be replaced, unscrew it off the spindle and screw the new one into place, clamping the chainring(s) underneath.

8. Fill the clean bearing cups with bearing grease and place the bearing ball retainers inside, orienting it so that only the balls, not the retainer, contact the cups and the cones.

9. Install the Z-shaped crank and spindle unit from the RH side.

10. On the LH side, make sure the bearing ball retainer is in place, then install the cone, followed by the lock washer and the locknut.

11. Adjust the bearing as described above: loosen LH locknut, turn cone in or out a little, tighten locknut again. Repeat until satisfactory before installing LH pedal.

9.15. Interesting crank unit. This design is from Prof. von Osten-Sacken of Aachen Technical University's Vehicle Engineering Department.

Although the bearings of these units usually cannot be adjusted to compensate for play or wear, at least the screw threaded versions allow something that cannot easily be done with other bottom brackets: their lateral position relative to the centerline of the bike can be adjusted. This makes it relatively easy to correct the chain line (the alignment of chainring and sprocket, which will be covered below). You will need the special lockring wrenches for the unit in question. Just loosen the one lockring and tighten the other one until the bearing unit is moved over sideways into the desired position.

Lateral Adjustment of Cartridge Bottom Bracket

Except on one-piece Fauber units, the cranks are separate parts that are attached to the ends of the bottom bracket spindle. On older simple bikes, they are held by means of a cotter pin, illustrated in Fig. 9.17. The moment transmitted by the cranks on the connection, calculated as the pedal force multiplied by the crank's leverage, is quite considerable at this point. Consequently, the force on the connection can be 20 times the cyclist's pedaling force, and cotter pins, with their small contact area, often come loose.

The Cranks

For that reason, a solution is used on high-quality bicycles that increases the contact area between connecting parts. Whereas the contact area of a cotter pin is only about 1cm^2, it is typically 8 times larger on a cotterless crank, illustrated in Fig. 9.18. The spindle here has square tapered ends, matching square tapered

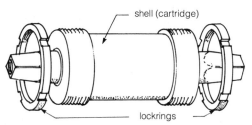

9.16. Cartridge bottom bracket unit

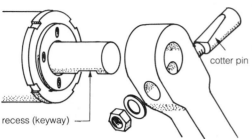

9.17. Cottered crank attachment

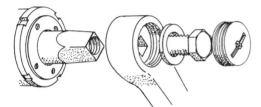

9.18. Cotterless crank attachment

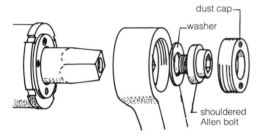

9.19. One-key cotterless attachment

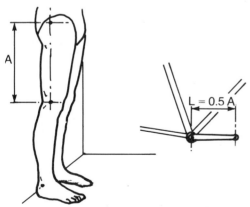

9.20. Optimum crank length as a function of upper leg length.

holes in the cranks. A bolt, or on cheaper versions sometimes a nut, pushes the crank sideways onto the end of the spindle.

When replacing any parts of either the cottered or the cotterless crank assembly, keep in mind that there are several different versions. Cotter pins come in different dimensions, matching different cranks and spindles. Cotterless connections may have slightly different angles for the tapered ends. It would be preferable to match make and model, or at least to refer to *Sutherland's Handbook for Bicycle Mechanics* (most bike shops have a copy of this expensive reference work) to make sure parts will match perfectly.

An interesting variant of the cotterless connection is the one-key attachment depicted in Fig. 9.19, which does not require a special crank extractor tool but can be operated by means of a simple Allen key (older versions of Shimano and some more recent Campagnolo cranks use this technique, which has unfortunately not become common).

Although most cranks have a length of 170mm, measured per Fig. 9.20 from the center of the spindle hole to the center of the pedal hole, long-legged riders may wish to use slightly longer models, short-legged riders will be better off with shorter cranks. Some makes come in quite an array of different sizes between 160 and 185mm, while the cheaper models do not offer much choice.

Cottered cranks should always be made of steel, since aluminum is so soft that the hole (which is much smaller than it is on the cotterless crank) would deform and the connection would never hold up. The largest European crank manufacturer paid a high price to learn this after it introduced aluminum cottered cranks in the early eighties. (Recently the same manufacturer proudly showed me an aluminum one-piece crank that holds more promise). Even cotterless cranks could be made of steel and then have the advantage that their connection is very reliable, while aluminum cotterless connections have to be retightened several times on a newly installed one.

Apart from the kind of deformation of the hole due to insufficient tightening, the most common problem is a crack extending from one of the corners of the square hole. This is typically a fatigue failure, usually leading to sudden fracture across the crank. Another problem is that the crank can get bent in a fall. Don't try to straighten the crank yourself, since it only works without damage if you use the right bending tool, which most bike shops have. If the thread with which the pedal is screwed onto the crank gets seriously damaged, the hole can be drilled out and a Helicoil insert can be installed, essentially providing a new screw thread (Fig. 9.22).

The RH crank has an attachment flange for the chainring or chainrings. On cheap, simple cranksets, a single chainwheel may just be swaged (pressed) on, while they are simply inserted between RH crank and bearing on one-piece cranks. On quality bikes with cotterless cranks, the RH crank is a forged unit with a star-shaped attachment onto which the chainrings are held with special bolts, typically following the kind of detail depicted in Fig. 9.21. The bolt circle diameter for superficially similar versions can be quite different. It will be easiest to verify the dimension by measuring the distance between the centers of two neighboring holes, then using the appropriate formula below to establish the bolt circle diameter this dimension corresponds to:

3-hole attachment:
BCD = 0.58 X

5-hole attachment:
BCD = 0.85 X

where:
BCD = bolt circle diameter
X = center-to-center distance between neighboring holes.

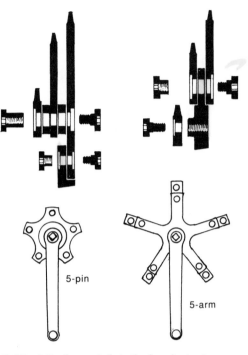

9.21. Attachment details for chainrings to cranks.

The connection between spindle and cranks may come loose, especially on a new bike or one on which the cranks were recently replaced. Left unchecked, this leads to deformation, eventually making it impossible to tighten the cranks properly. Consequently, they should be fastened on a regular basis (every 25 miles during the first 100) at first, and checked once a month afterwards. To carry out this simple maintenance job, there is a crank extractor tool that corresponds to the make and model of cotterless crank in question (the US manufacturer Park Tools offers one that universally fits all).

You will only need the wrench part of the crank extractor, in addition to something to fit the dust cap (usually a coin does the trick). On one-key models, use a fitting allen key, and then you just tighten the Allen bolt — the following description applies to all other types.

Crank Maintenance

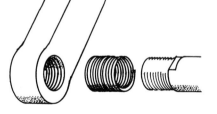

9.22. Helicoil adaptor for pedal thread

Tighten Cotterless Crank

Procedure:
1. Remove the dustcap.
2. Tighten the bolt or the nut that becomes visible in the recess in the crank, countering firmly from the crank.
3. Reinstall the dustcap to protect the screw thread.

Exchange Cotterless Crank

For this work you need the entire crank extractor including its wrench (or a separate wrench) as well as a rag and some vaseline.

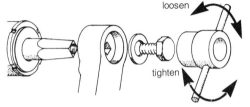

9.23. *Tightening or loosening cotterless crank.*

Removal procedure:
1. Remove the dustcap.
2. Remove the bolt or the nut, countering firmly from the crank (if necessary placing a firm rod between the frame and the crank).
3. Remove the underlying washer (this is an essential step, since the crank extractor will not work unless the washer is removed).
4. Retract the internal part fully into the crank extractor and then screw the tool into the threaded recess in the crank as far as it will go, but at least 4 full revolutions.
5. Holding the crank firmly, screw the internal part of the crank extractor in until the crank is being pushed off the spindle (if it does not work, you have probably forgotten to remove the washer).
6. Remove the tool from the crank.

Installation procedure:
1. Clean and slightly lubricate the square ends of the spindle and the square hole in the crank, as well as the bolt or threaded stud.
2. Place the crank onto the spindle in the correct orientation (the crank with chainring attachment on the right, both cranks 180° offset).
3. Place the washer in the recess and then install the bolt or the nut.
4. Tighten the nut fully, using the wrench part of the crank extractor and countering firmly at the crank.
5. Check and retighten at least every 40km (25 miles) during the next 160km (100 miles) of cycling.
6. Reinstall the dust cap.

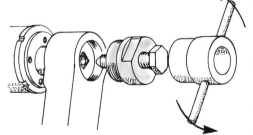

9.24. *Use of crank extractor to remove cotterless crank.*

Tighten Cottered Crank

Although this type is slowly disappearing on newer bikes, it is still used and has the same advantage as the simple BSA bracket: parts are available everywhere in the world. By way of tools you will need a wrench (preferably a box wrench, which is more likely to grip the nut without damaging it) to fit the nut on the cotter pin, while a hammer or any other blunt object comes in handy too. Refer to Fig. 9.25.

Procedure:
1. If possible, support the crank near the spindle and hammer the cotter pin in further.
2. Tighten the nut fully.

In addition to a matching wrench you will need a hammer and something to support the crank, a rag and some vaseline.

Removal procedure:
1. Loosen the nut just so far that the screw thread of the cotter pin lies just below the surface of the nut.
2. Supporting the crank close to the spindle, but keeping the cotter pin free, hammer the pin loose from the side of the nut, preferably protecting it with a block of wood.
3. Unscrew the nut and remove the washer, then push the cotter pin out all the way.

Installation procedure:
1. Clean the spindle, the cotter pin and the holes for spindle and cotter pin in the crank, then lightly grease these parts. Replace a damaged cotter pin or nut.
2. Install the crank — the one with the chainring attachment on the right and both cranks 180° offset.
3. Install the cotter pin from the side of the larger hole in the crank.
4. Install the washer and the nut, then tighten fully.
5. To allow further tightening, support the crank near the spindle and hammer the cotter pin in further, then tighten the nut again.
6. Check and retighten at least every 40km (25 miles) during the next 160km (100 miles) of cycling.

Depending on the kind of gearing used on the bike, the RH crank will be equipped with either one, two or three chainrings. The choice of the number of teeth will be treated in the chapters devoted to gearing, but their installation and maintenance will be covered here. Replaceability criteria include both the construction and the attachment details: bolt circle diameter (covered above) and the number of bolts.

As concerns the quality of chainrings, the best ones are not simply stamped but are machined (sharp contours and a regular, fine groove pattern are telltale signals). Machining allows the use of stronger (i.e. more wear resistant and less easily deformed) aluminum alloys. This is the reason Campagnolo chainrings are usually

Replace Cottered Crank

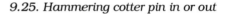

cotter pin — support

9.25. Hammering cotter pin in or out

The Chainrings

9.26. EDCO Competition crank unit

so much better than superficially similar looking items that cost a little less. Wherever the bolt circle diameter of your cranks corresponds to one of the Campagnolo standards, it may be smart to select these when the old ones are worn.

Chainring and sprocket teeth wear according to Fig. 9.27, and the smaller ones wear fastest, as do models with special shaped teeth to ease shifting (actually, the very simple solution of cutting back a few teeth as done on Shimano's Superglide chainrings does not by itself increase wear, it is merely the use of thinner teeth that does). Wear of chainrings, chain and sprockets is minimized by selecting the former and the latter with such numbers of teeth that prime numbers (numbers that are not multiples of some other whole number except one) result. This minimizes the repeated correspondence of particular teeth, which is one of the major reasons for wear. Special shaped teeth that are designed to ease shifting work very well, especially for the less experienced cyclist when new. However, they also wear faster, due to the fact that they are thinner in certain points of contact with the chain. The recent introduction of stainless steel chainrings (used as the smallest chainring on some mountain bike cranksets) is a big step forward, since they are much more wear-resistant and not significantly heavier than aluminum chainrings.

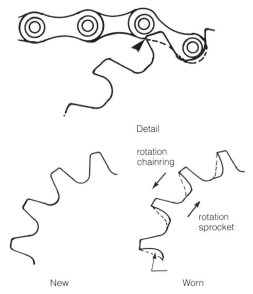

Detail

9.27. Typical wear of chainwheel or sprocket teeth.

In the late eighties, there was a craze of non-round chainrings, with Shimano leading everybody into believing they will cycle more efficiently with chainrings that are oddly shaped (and every other manufacturer followed). Today, it is generally agreed that the most efficient shape (if there is any difference at all) is round. This also eliminates the question in just what orientation the off-round chainrings ought to be installed for greatest efficiency (the results of efficiency tests have been different for different riders). If you still have non-round chainrings, don't worry: the difference is minimal, once you get used to the slightly unnatural pedaling movement, and you can always change to round chainrings when they are worn.

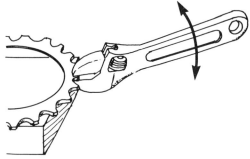

9.28. Straightening individual teeth of chainring.

Chainring Maintenance

Check, and if necessary tighten, the chainring attachment bolts once a month. Prevent chainring wear by keeping chainrings, sprockets and chain clean and lubricated on a regular schedule — once a month plus whenever you have used the bike in inclement weather or muddy or dusty terrain. See the section *The Chain* for comments on establishing when to replace the chain. To clean the chainrings in the area of the teeth, wrap a rag around a small screwdriver and work around each of the teeth.

If individual teeth of the chainring are bent, it is often possible to straighten them with the aid of a small adjustable wrench. Follow the general procedure illustrated in Fig. 9.28, but you may generally leave the chainring on the bike. You will have to replace the entire chainring if a tooth should break when trying to straighten it.

If the entire chainring is warped, this will usually be evidenced by intermittent scraping sounds between chain and front derailleur cage. First establish which section is bent which way by slowly turning the cranks backward, while watching the distance between the outside of the chainring and a fixed reference point on the bike. Mark the location of the bend e.g. with a felt pen or chalk.

In case of a short sudden bend, it is usually the chainring itself that is warped, while a longer, more gradual bend indicates that the attachment spider on the RH crank is deformed, meaning that one of the legs is bent in or out.

To correct a bend in the chainring itself, straighten it by forcing a wooden wedge between the chainring and a frame tube (usually the RH chainstay), or between two chainrings. To straighten the attachment spider, give a sharp blow with a hammer against the bent leg in the appropriate direction, and repeat until the chainring runs level.

The bicycle chain is a remarkably efficient transmission device. This explains why other, technically more complicated drive systems have never made it to success on the bicycle, however often they have been tried. However, the superior efficiency only applies to a well maintained, cleaned and lubricated chain. Whereas such a chain delivers 95% of its input as output, this figure can drop to 80% for a rusty, dirty, unlubricated chain.

All bicycle chains have a link length of ½" (measured between two consecutive link pins). The width is measured between the inside of two inner link plates and measures a nominal 3/32" for derailleur chains, 1/8" for non-derailleur chains. Even so, there are some differences in construction resulting in slightly narrower chains, measured on the outside, and sometimes with slightly narrower inside dimensions. These are preferable for use on gearing systems with 7 or 8 sprockets.

Straighten Chainring

9.29. Shimano Biopace crankset with off-round chainrings. Nowadays, only the smaller chainrings are given this curious shape, while the larger one is usually round — at least on high-end bikes.

The Chain

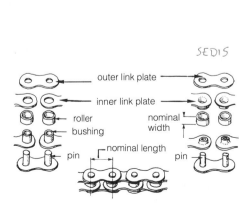

9.30. The two types of chain construction

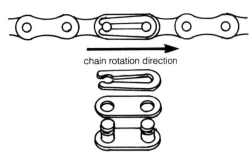

chain rotation direction

9.31. Master link for chain on utility bicycle without derailleur.

The wider ½" x ⅛" chain for the utility bike without derailleur is usually equipped with a master link, or connecting link, to join the two ends. As shown in Fig. 9.31, this device must be installed so that the closed end of the spring link faces in the direction of rotation. Since the master link projects further than the other links, it cannot be used on derailleur bikes, where it would hit the derailleur cages. For this reason, an endless chain is used there, which is formed by attaching the outer link plates of the one end with the inner link plates of the other by means of a regular pin. A chain extractor tool is required to remove, install or shorten such a chain.

Fig. 9.30 shows the two basic chain designs. On the Sedis design, which is copied by some other manufacturers these days, the inner link plates are shaped to carry out the same function provided by the inner bushings on the conventional chain construction. The Sedis design leads to less wear and flexing but is not as suitable for most index gearing systems except those of the same manufacturer (e.g. Sedis chains works poorly with SunTour index derailleurs, whereas the similar Shimano chain works very well with the same company's index derailleurs). The special chains for index shifting usually have bulging link plates. Although they indeed aid shifting, they tend to stretch under load and often have to be replaced.

Chain Line

To assure optimum efficiency of the drivetrain, the chain should preferably be straight, with chainring and sprocket perfectly aligned as shown in Fig 9.33. Obviously this is illusory in the case of derailleur gearing, since the various chainrings and sprockets lie side-by-side. The best that can be done is to align the central point between the extreme chainrings with the central point on the freewheel block. Thus, the middle chainring should be lined up with the fourth sprocket on a system with three chainrings and seven sprockets.

Check this alignment perhaps once a year and whenever new drivetrain components are installed on the bike. Adjustments can sometimes be made by installing a spacer on the rear wheel or by means of lateral adjustment of a cartridge type bottom bracket unit. In extreme cases, the frame's rear triangle may turn out to be misaligned and can be bent back as described in Chapter 5. When spacers are used on the rear wheel, note that this affects the alignment of the wheels and it may become necessary to retension the spokes of the rear wheel in order to line up both wheels.

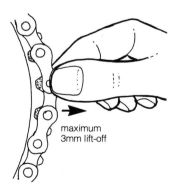

maximum 3mm lift-off

9.32. Simple check for chain wear

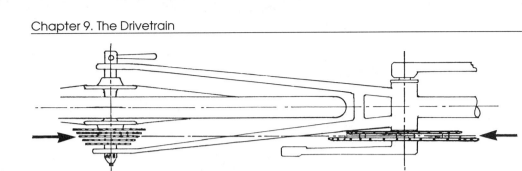

9.33
Chain line: The highest efficiency and least wear is achieved with minimal lateral deflection of the chain.

Chain Maintenance

Cleaning, lubrication and replacement are the jobs occasionally required on the chain. Replace the chain if it is (seemingly) stretched so far that it can be lifted off the chainring as shown in Fig. 9.32. Alternatively, you can remove it and measure a 100-link section hanging down: it is worn too far if it measures more than 51", representing a 2% increase in length. Actually, what seems to be stretch is nothing but the wear of the pins and bushings, which can be minimized with regular cleaning and lubrication. A well maintained chain can last 5000km (3000 miles) in road cycling, or about half as long in off-road use, and even less if used off-road under unfavorable weather and terrain conditions.

Chain Lubrication

There are handy aids available to clean the chain without taking it off the bike. Here the chain is run through a bath of solvent between rotating brushes. Alternatively, remove the chain from the bike and rinse it in a bath of solvent containing about 10% mineral oil to prevent rust, then let it drip out briefly and wipe dry, followed by lubrication.

There are effective chain lubricants on the market that do not attract as much dirt as the old-fashioned types. The ultimate in lubrication, hardly known in the US, used to be Castrol chain grease. This is a waxy grease containing graphite particles, which is melted in a pan of hot water, after which the chain is dipped in. The chain is left to soak in the hot lubricant and then removed to drip and wiped clean on the outside.

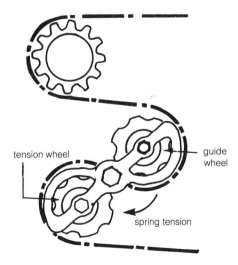

Modern chain lubes are also typically wax-based lubricants, sometimes containing molybdenum disulphide (like graphite, this material works well on the kind of bearings represented by the chain's pins and bushings). They come in spray-cans, and therefore tempt the user to forget cleaning the chain first. Don't make that mistake: only use lubrication on a chain that has previously been cleaned thoroughly.

9.34. *Chain routing at rear derailleur*

Replace Chain

If it should be a chain for a utility bike with a master link, simply remove it by prizing open the spring link

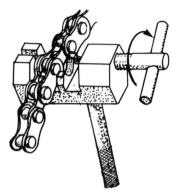

9.35. Use of chain tool to withdraw or install link pin.

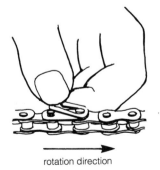

rotation direction

9.36. Installation of connecting link on bike without derailleur.

with a screwdriver — later reinstall it per Fig. 9.36. Many non-US utility bikes on which this kind of chain is used have an enclosed chainguard, which will have to be opened or removed first to allow this work (which will rarely be necessary, since this guard protects the chain against dirt and rust).

The narrow derailleur chain is separated with the aid of a chain extractor tool. When reinstalling, keep in mind that chains wear asymmetrically, so when the old chain is installed, make sure it is the opposite way round to stretch its life considerably — the instructions are set up to achieve this.

Removal procedure:
1. Place the chain on the smallest chainring and a small sprocket by means of the derailleurs.
2. Install the chain extractor tool on the chain as illustrated in Fig. 9.35 from the outside (RH side of the bike when it is standing upright) on one of the pins between two links, turning it in just far enough to be clamped in place firmly.
3. Screw the punch of the tool in by 6 turns (or 7.5 turns on a ⅛" wide chain). This will push the pin out of the chain, but not so far that it will drop out the other end.
4. Retract the punch by screwing it back. Twist the chain links on either side apart — if it does not come apart, reinstall the tool and push the pin a little further if necessary, then try again.

Installation procedure:
1. Set the derailleurs in such a way that the chain runs over the smallest chainring and the smallest sprocket.
2. Place the chain over chainring and rear sprocket and through front and rear derailleur cage, referring to Fig. 9.34.
3. The chain has the right length if it just does not hang through in this position. If this is a new chain, also check whether it fits over the combination large chainring and large sprocket. Then return to the original combination with smallest chainring and sprocket.
4. Bring the two chain ends together with the projecting pin on the RH side of the bike. Hold the chain ends in position with the free link at one end hooked on the slight protrusion of the pin on the other.
5. Place the chain extractor tool on the pin and push the pin in by turning the lever while holding the chain together to assure proper alignment. Tighten

until the pin projects just as much as the other pins.

6. Flex the chain sideways at the connected point to free the connection enough to assure smooth running of the chain. If it does not work, place the chain link joint on the chain tool in the position marked 'spreader position' in the illustration and screw in the handle just enough to free the links, referring to Fig. 9.38.

This sometimes happens on a derailleur bike and can have one of several different causes. Certainly if the chain was recently replaced, chances are it is merely due to a stiff link. To check whether this is the cause, set the derailleur to engage the smallest sprocket in the rear, then turn the cranks back slowly, while watching what happens as the chain runs over the rear sprocket. In one position, the chain will lift off the sprocket — check this link for stiffness, loosening it per point 6 of the preceding description.

If the problem cannot be eliminated this way, it is usually due to the use of a new chain on an old sprocket, and virtually always happens only on the smallest sprocket, which tends to wear down faster than the others. Since the chain pitch (distance between link pins) does not correspond to the worn and therefore changed pitch of the sprocket, it will ride up and give a jerking action. The only solution is to replace the sprocket, following the description in Chapter 10.

The pedals, which are shown in cross section in Fig. 9.37, are installed at the ends of the cranks. Fig. 9.40 shows several standard versions. In recent years the so-called clipless pedals have become quite popular. Actually, these are far from clipless: they integrate their own patent clipping device instead of the conventional separate toeclip hitherto used on racing bikes. Whereas the latter can still be ridden with any kind of shoes, the clipless pedals cannot, confining you to the particular type of matching shoes.

Conventional toeclips are either regular types with straps or open strapless types, which lend themselves well to city riding. The ones with straps are available in several sizes: small, for shoe sizes up to 7 (European size 40), medium up to shoe size 8½ (European size 43), and large for anything bigger than that.When installing the strap through the pedal housing, twist it one full turn between the pedal's side plates so it does not slip. Supposedly adjustable toeclips with matching pedals are not better than old fashioned clips of the

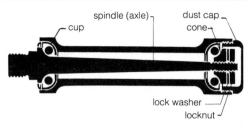

9.37. Pedal cross section

Chain 'Jumps'

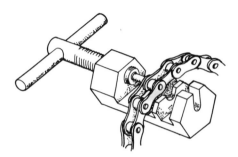

9.38. Using the chain tool to spread, or free, a tight link.

The Pedals

9.39. Lightweight platform pedals from the Italian manufacturer Gipiemme.

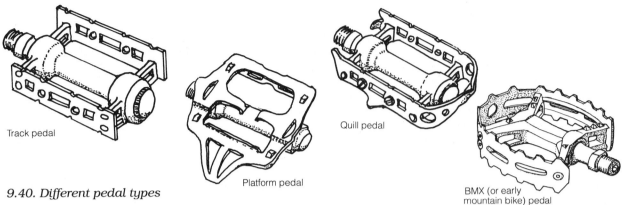

9.40. *Different pedal types*

Track pedal

Platform pedal

Quill pedal

BMX (or early
mountain bike) pedal

9.41. *MKS Samson clipless pedal. This
is probably the lightest full clipless
pedal on the market.*

Pedal Maintenance

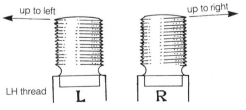

up to left

up to right

LH thread

L   R

9.42. *Threading for LH and RH pedals*

Replace Pedal

right size, since the former do not place the toe strap in the right position for smaller feet.

There are different thread standards for the pedal-to-crank connection, summarized in Table 4 in the Appendix. Whether English or French, the LH pedal always has LH thread and the RH pedal normal RH thread, whereas non-conforming thread sizes, introduced by Shimano during its brief flirtation with aerodynamic pretense in the early eighties, have disappeared as fast as they were introduced (meaning both pedals and cranks may have to be replaced if you still run into one of these on an older bike).

An important dimension for pedals, certainly if intended for fast riding, is the one that determines under what angle the bike can lean when cornering without scraping the pedal on the ground. Since this also depends on the bottom bracket height and the spindle length, comparative values are not very reliable except when comparing models by the same manufacturer. By and large, low and narrow pedals clear the road in a sharper corner better than high and wide models, which is important at high speeds.

Here we shall cover pedal replacement as well as adjustment and overhauling of the bearings. Maintenance is often hampered by the fact that spare parts are not available. While a fall can lead to a bent axle — which is basically a cheap and simple repair, only Campagnolo makes it possible with their admirable policy of spare part availability. The pedals may have to be removed when the bike is transported, and the thread may get damaged if it is not done carefully. Here's how to do it right.

By way of tools, you will either need a special pedal wrench, any thin, fitting open-ended wrench (usually

15mm), or — if the pedal stub visible from the back of the crank has a hexagonal recess — a matching allen key. In addition, use a rag and some vaseline.

Procedure:
1. To remove the pedal, hold the crank firmly and unscrew the RH pedal by turning the tool to the left (as seen from the pedal), the LH one to the right.
2. To install, first thoroughly clean the screw thread stubs and holes, then lubricate lightly with vaseline to prevent seizing and ease subsequent removal.
3. If you often remove the pedals, install a flat steel washer between the crank and the pedal to protect the soft aluminum of the crank and ease subsequent removal.
4. Install the RH pedal by turning to the right (seen from the pedal end), the LH one by turning to the left.

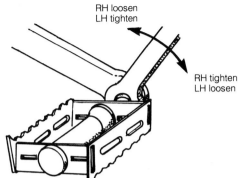

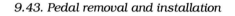

9.43. Pedal removal and installation

The pedal bearings must be adjusted if there is play or they turn poorly. If adjusting does not solve the problem, proceed to the overhauling procedure that follows. This description applies to regular pedals on which the outer bearing is accessible from the end of the pedal, shown in Fig. 9.45. Many newer platform and clipless pedals are not accessible from that end — instead, unscrew the bearing from the body at the stub end. For regular pedals, you will need a pair of pliers or special wrench to remove the dustcap, a wrench to fit the outer bearing locknut, and something to adjust the cone (usually a small screwdriver does the trick).

Adjust Pedal Bearings

Procedure:
1. Remove the dustcap.
2. Loosen the locknut on the outer bearing by unscrewing it by one or two turns.
3. Lift the lock washer clear from the cone.
4. Adjust the cone — turn to the left to loosen the bearing, to the right to tighten it.
5. Put the lock washer back down on the cone and tighten the locknut, making sure the cone and the lock washer do not turn with it (if they do, the lock washer's key is worn and it must probably be replaced).
6. Check and repeat if necessary (or overhaul if correct adjustment can not be achieved).
7. Install the dustcap.

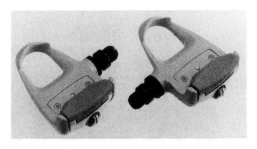

9.44. Shimano's elegant clipless pedals are based on the Look patent.

Again, this procedure applies to regular pedals — see the note in the introduction to the section *Adjust Pedal*

Overhaul Pedal

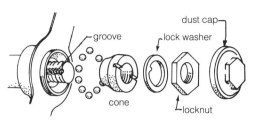

9.45. Pedal bearing detail

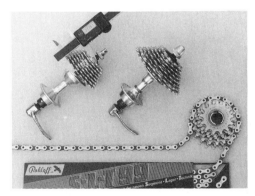

9.46. Highly compact Hügi casette hub with 8 sprockets and matching narrow Rohloff chain.

Freewheel with Sprockets

Bearings for pedals without externally accessible outer bearings. You will need a dustcap wrench, a wrench for the locknut, something to turn the cone, bearing grease and a rag.

Disassembly procedure:
1. Remove the dustcap.
2. Loosen and remove the locknut on the outer bearing by unscrewing it.
3. Lift the lock washer clear from the cone and remove it.
4. Unscrew and remove the cone, catching the bearing balls.
5. Pull the pedal housing off the axle and catch the bearing balls on the other side.

Overhauling procedure:
1. Clean and inspect all bearing parts and make sure the axle is not bent.
2. Replace any damaged or bent parts where available — if not, replace the entire pedal.
3. Fill the bearing cups with bearing grease, then place the bearing balls inside, leaving just a little space between them.
4. Place the housing back over the axle with the end without thread for the dust cap first, taking care not to push the bearing balls out.
5. After assuring the outer bearing balls are in place, install the cone on the spindle.
6. Adjust the cone: turn to the left to loosen the bearing, to the right to tighten it.
7. Put the lock washer on the cone and tighten the locknut, making sure the cone and the lock washer do not turn with it (replace the lock washer if they do).
8. Check and repeat, if necessary (or replace the pedal if correct adjustment cannot be achieved).
9. Install the dustcap.

Except on track racing bikes, all regular bicycles have a freewheel mechanism on the rear wheel hub to allow the wheel to turn forward while holding the cranks still. On utility bikes, the freewheel is often an integral part of the hub (together with brake and gear mechanisms). On derailleur bikes, it is either a standard assembly that is screwed on to the RH side of the hub, or it is a unit that, though strictly separate, remains part of the hub, as is the case on so-called casette hubs. To ease shifting, specially designed teeth sequences are incorporated in some designs, such as Shimano's Hyperglide, providing two locations around the circumference where the teeth are so small that the chain is eased over sideways very easily.

Fig. 9.49 shows a typical assembly of a screwed-on freewheel block with its range of sprockets. Although rarely seen in the US, there are also similar freewheels with only a single sprockets for one-speed bikes, such as those often used in countries like France, Belgium and Italy. Whatever number of sprockets, and whether built-in or screwed on, the principle of these freewheel mechanisms is always as depicted in Fig. 9.51. Turning the internal body relative to the fixed outer part in one direction engages the pawls, causing the two to turn together. Turning it in the opposite direction, the pawls ride over the teeth against their spring tension, resulting in the familiar freewheeling sound. Only on some bikes with a coaster brake, is a different type of freewheel used, which will be described in Chapter 13.

When selecting the freewheel block with its sprockets, the major criterion is the number of teeth of the latter. Not all combinations are available for all freewheels, and not every combination makes equal sense for all purposes. This subject will be extensively covered in Chapter 10, which is devoted to derailleur gearing.

The other considerations mainly concern the kind of screw thread: here too, there are different standards, even for normal screwed-on freewheel blocks. Most bikes sold in the US and Britain have rear hubs with Italian standard thread, while others have French standard threading, which do not fit one another without doing serious damage. See Table 4 in the Appendix.

Whether to use a 5-, 6-, 7- or even 8-speed freewheel block, largely depends on the hub dimensions. If the over-locknut size of the rear hub is 120mm, only 5-speed versions fit. On 124 to 126mm hubs, all 6-speed and narrow 7-speed blocks fit. Standard width 7-speeds and all 8-speeds require widths of 128mm or more. Of course, the frame's rear triangle width (measured between the drop-outs) also has to match these dimensions. Most casette hubs are designed for matching 7-speed units, the freewheel mechanism itself being a (removable) part of the hub, while the sprockets and the spacers are installed on splines with the last one or two screwed on. The two parts of a casette hub can be separated with a special tool (although it is rarely done), while the conventional freewheel block is unscrewed with a crank extractor, as will be described below.

9.47. Calorie counter pedal: This gadget has strain gauges and an indicator that registers how much energy is given off over time.

9.48. Look clipless pedal (photo: Trek)

Maintenance of Freewheel with Sprockets

The maintenance operations described here are limited to replacement and lubrication. Usually, what is needed is the replacement of either the entire freewheel block or of an individual sprocket. If there is too much play in the freewheel, evidenced by wobble, it is possible to adjust the bearing play. Finally, we shall cover the replacement of the sprocket on a bike without derailleur.

Replace Freewheel Block

This work is often necessary merely to replace a broken spoke on the RH side of the rear wheel, which is generally inaccessible without removing the freewheel block. The other reasons for replacement are when the mechanism or the individual sprockets are worn, or the sprockets are of the wrong size for the required gearing. If this is a screwed-on freewheel, the freewheel extractor for the make and model in question will be needed, in addition to a large wrench or a metal-working vice mounted on a workbench. In addition, use a rag and some vaseline. Refer to Fig. 9.52 once the wheel has been taken off the bike.

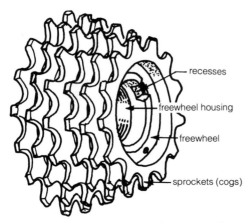

9.49. Freewheel block with six sprockets

Removal procedure:
1. Remove the hub quick-release or the axle nut on the RH side.
2. Place the freewheel tool as far as possible on the splines or recesses of the freewheel body.
3. Install the quick-release or the axle nut over the freewheel tool, leaving about 2mm clearance.
4. Either hold the freewheel tool face down in the vice, or hold it face up with the large wrench.
5. Turn the tool to the left relative to the wheel or, in case it is held in the vice, turn the wheel relative to the tool. You may have to give a firm jolting twist to loosen the freewheel body from the hub's screw thread.
6. After one revolution, loosen the axle nut or the quick-release one turn and continue until the freewheel can be removed by hand.

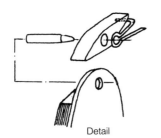

Detail

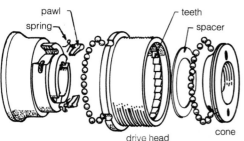

9.50. Construction of typical freewheel

Installation procedure:
1. Clean and lightly lubricate the thread on the hub and in the freewheel.
2. Very carefully align the screw thread on the freewheel with that on the hub and screw it on by hand — don't force it, but remove and start again if any resistance is noted.
3. Once it is screwed on as far as it will go by hand, install the wheel in the bike, allowing the normal pedaling force to tighten it further once you start riding.

4. On index gear bicycles, the gearing may not match at first. Just ride the bike about a mile to make sure the freewheel is on as far as it will go before attempting to readjust the gears.

In addition to a rag, you'll need a sprocket remover, or cog wrench. Quite a few different versions are available, but all achieve the same: they allow you to turn one sprocket relative to the one underneath. The wheel must first have been removed from the bike. Refer to Fig. 9.53.

Removal procedure:
1. While holding the sprocket underneath steady with one part of the tool, turn the one above it to the left relative to it to unscrew it. On some models, there is a screw-threaded ring on top holding the whole assembly together — it too can be unscrewed relative to the underlying sprocket.
2. Depending on whether the other sprockets are screwed on or held in splines, remove them as appropriate until you have reached the one to replace, keeping track of the sequence of spacers.

Installation procedure:
1. Clean and lightly lubricate the various parts and then start assembling them in the appropriate sequence, not forgetting the spacers. Specially shaped sprockets, such as those on the Shimano Hyperglide freewheel, must be installed in the same orientation as the originals.
2. Screw the screwed-on sprockets on with the help of the tool, making sure you tighten them firmly.

This operation is not usually necessary, but it may be a solution if the freewheel does not turn properly. Some models have a special lubrication hole through which thick oil or light grease can be squeezed. On other models, first remove the wheel from the bike. Place the wheel with the freewheel facing up on a receptacle and start pouring in thick mineral oil while turning the freewheel as shown in Fig. 9.54. Continue until it comes out clean on the other side and the freewheel turns freely. Let drip and wipe with a rag.

A wobbly freewheel can usually be adjusted by removing a shim under the bearing cone on the outside. To do this, remove the wheel from the bike and place it flat down, freewheel side up. Although some freewheels are constructed differently, you will generally find a pair of recesses in one end of the freewheel, with which you

Replace Individual Sprockets

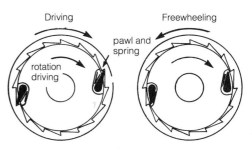

9.51. *Operating principle of typical freewheel mechanism.*

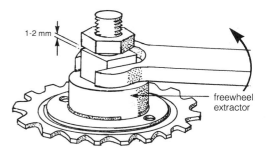

9.52. *Freewheel removal*

Lubricate Freewheel Mechanism

Adjust Freewheel Bearing

143

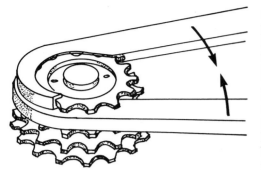

9.53. Sprocket removal

Replace Single Freewheel Sprocket

Replace Fixed Sprocket

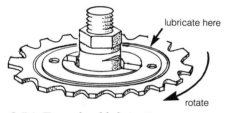

lubricate here

rotate

9.54. Freewheel lubrication

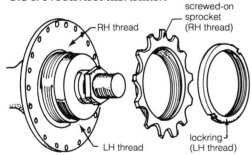

RH thread

screwed-on sprocket (RH thread)

LH thread

lockring (LH thread)

9.55. Fixed sprocket installation

can screw the cone out of the body. This is done with a pin wrench or e.g. with a pointed object and a hammer. If the cone is accessible from the outside, it has to be turned off to the right, installed by turning to the left (LH thread).

Be very careful not to lose the bearing balls under the cone when disassembling. Remove the cone and take one of the shims underneath it out, again without losing the bearing balls. Reassemble the cone on the body, and check whether the freewheel runs better. If this did not do the trick, you may have to replace the whole freewheel block.

To do this, the wheel has to be removed from the bike first. If it is a separate screwed-on freewheel (similar to that used on a derailleur bike), follow the same procedure as described above. On hubs with an integral freewheel mechanism, remove the spring clip that holds the sprocket on the hub. Remove the sprocket, clean all parts and reassemble, clamping the spring clip back into place.

This operation applies to a wheel without a freewheel, such as used on a track bike (also used to advantage on a road bike for training purposes). Fig. 9.55 shows the way this kind of sprocket is installed on the special hub. The hub has two different types of screw thread: a LH threaded section for the lockring and a RH threaded one for the sprocket. You will need a cog wrench, a rag and vaseline.

Removal procedure:
1. Hold the sprocket with the cog wrench and turn the lock ring off to the right (LH thread).
2. Unscrew the sprocket to the left, while countering at the wheel.

Installation procedure:
1. Clean and lightly lubricate all parts.
2. Thread the sprocket on firmly to the right.
3. Countering at the wheel (rather than at the sprocket), screw the lock ring into place, turning it firmly to the left.

Chapter 10
Derailleur Gearing

Fig. 10.2 shows the components that make up a typical derailleur system. The rear wheel hub is equipped with a freewheel block with a whole range of different sized sprockets, while two or three different sized chainrings are used in the front. The front derailleur, or changer, shifts the chain sideways between the chainrings, while the rear derailleur selects the appropriate sprockets in the rear. These derailleurs are operated by means of shift levers on the down tube or the handlebars, to which they are connected by means of flexible cables.

Since the various sprockets and chainrings each have a different number of teeth, the ratio between the rate at which the cranks are turned and that at which the rear wheel turns can be varied accordingly. Given a certain pedaling rate, the speed with which the rear wheel turns is proportional to the quotient of the number of teeth in the front and the number of teeth in the back.

The number of different gearing options is expressed by the product of the numbers of sprockets and chainrings: 2 chainrings and 5 sprockets gives ten speeds, 3 chainrings and 7 sprockets 21. Actually, there is a certain overlap, so the actual number of significantly different gears may be less than that. Racing bikes generally have 12 or 14 speeds (2 chainrings up front), while mountain bikes and touring machines generally come with 18 or 21 speeds (3 chainrings). On cruisers and similar simple bicycles, 5- and 6-speed systems are often used, using a single front chainring and thus eliminating the front derailleur as well — a sensible approach for inexperienced cyclists.

The principle of the gearing system is the idea of adapting the transmission ratio between cranks and rear wheel to the difficulty of the terrain. Under favorable conditions — when the resistances are low — the driven rear wheel can rotate quite a bit faster than the cranks, propelling the bike at a high speed without pedaling excessively fast. This is referred to as a high gear and is achieved when a large chainring is combined with a small sprocket. Under unfavorable conditions, when resistances are high, a low gear is selected, achieved with a small chainring and a large sprocket, so the rear wheel does not turn much faster than the cranks.

10.1. This is what happens when you change gear: The derailleur shoves the chain over onto the next smaller or bigger chainwheel.

Gearing Theory

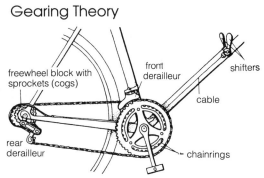

10.2. Parts of the derailleur system

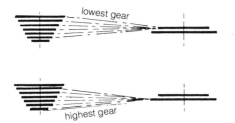

10.3. Gear combinations

10.4. Nothing new: This precursor of today's derailleur was introduced around 1910.

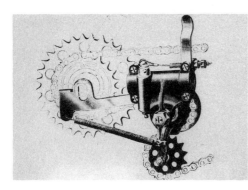

It will be instructive to compare the situation on a level road with that on an incline. The example will be based on a cyclist who can maintain an output of 100W (i.e. about 0.13 hp). On a level road without head wind, this will suffice to progress at 30km/h (about 20mph). If the road goes up by 8%, the same output only allows a speed of 10km/h (about 6.5mph).

If the gearing ratio were fixed, the pedaling rate would have to be three times as high in the first case as it is in the second. Conversely, the forces applied to the pedals would be three times as high when pedaling slowly uphill as they would be pedaling fast on the level road. However, the muscles and joints work better if the pedal force is limited, even if this requires a higher pedaling speed. Thus, the uphill ride is particularly tiring, even though the same total output is delivered — not because of the output, but because of the high forces at low muscle speeds.

This predicament is solved with the use of gearing: it allows selecting the ratio between pedaling and riding speed in such a way that the pedaling force remains within the limits of comfort by allowing an adequately high pedaling speed, regardless of the riding speed. Conversely, it is possible to keep the pedaling rate within the comfortable range when conditions are so easy that one would otherwise have to pedal extremely fast to deliver the available output.

To achieve this, the relatively untrained fitness cyclist might select a gear in which he maintains a pedaling rate of 70rpm while each crank revolution brings him forward by about 7.15m. This results in a speed of 70 x 7.15 x 60 = 30,030m/h, or 30km/h. On an incline, he may maintain the same pedaling rate and output level, but might select a gear that brings him forward only 2.30m per crank revolution, which results in a speed of 70 x 2.40 x 60 =10,080 m/h, or 10km/h. Either way, pedaling speed and muscle force remain unchanged.

Actually, it is unrealistic to assume that the same output level and pedaling speeds are always maintained. All riders put in more effort when climbing than when riding on the level. The example shows what is possible, even though the actually selected gears and speeds may vary a little one way or the other. To adhere to the example would require a very wide range of gears, even for rather moderate terrain differences.

A typical configuration for a racing bike might include a range of 13 to 21 teeth in the rear and 52 and 42 teeth in the front, resulting in a top gear that is (52/13) / (42/21) = 2 times as high as the lowest gear. For a

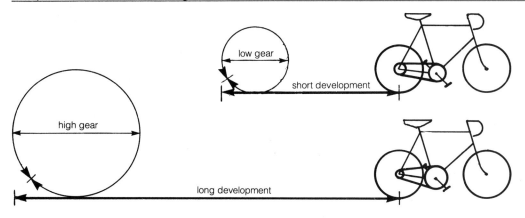

10.5. Development and gear number as designations for gearing ratios.

mountain bike, the range might be determined by front chainrings of 46, 36 and 26 teeth, rear sprockets ranging from 13 to 26 teeth, resulting in a top gear that is (46/13) / (26/26) = 3.54 times as high as the lowest gear.

Virtually all bicycles except the mountain bike are equipped with gears that are insufficiently spread for most applications. Even if you ride a racing bike, the range between favorable and unfavorable conditions is much greater than can be comfortably mastered with the narrow range of gears usually installed by the manufacturer. It is simple enough to adapt the system to more sensible gearing by installing a freewheel block with more widely spread sprockets.

Although one could refer to the particular gear ratio by simply stating the size of chainring and sprocket, this is not a satisfactory method. It would not easily reveal that e.g. 52/26 gives the same gear ratio as 42/21 (curiously enough referred to as 52 X 26 and 42 X 21 respectively, whenever this method is used). Obviously, it becomes completely impossible to compare bikes with different wheel sizes. To overcome these problems, two methods have been developed, referred to as *gear number* and *development*, respectively. The two methods are illustrated in Fig. 10.5.

Gear number is a rather archaic method that is inexplicably used to this day in the English speaking world. It references the equivalent wheel size of a directly driven wheel that would correspond to the same gear. To calculate the gear number, use the following formula:

$$N = D_{wheel} \times T_{front} / T_{rear}$$

where:

Gear Designation

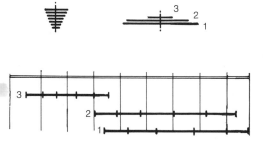

10.6. Graphic representation of the gearing steps using the combinations 'half step plus granny.'

147

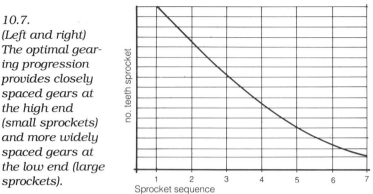

10.7.
(Left and right)
The optimal gear-
ing progression
provides closely
spaced gears at
the high end
(small sprockets)
and more widely
spaced gears at
the low end (large
sprockets).

N	= gear number in inches
D_{wheel}	= actual outside wheel diameter in inches
T_{front}	= number of teeth, chainring
T_{rear}	= number of teeth, sprocket.

Typical high gears are in the vicinity of 100 inches, while very low gears may be nearer 30 inches.

The internationally used development designation is easier to visualize: it represents the distance traveled per crank revolution, measured in meters. To calculate it, use the following formula:

$$D = \pi \times D_{wheel} \times T_{front} / T_{rear}$$

where:

D	= development in meters
π	= 3.14
D_{wheel}	= actual outside wheel diameter in m
T_{front}	= number of teeth, chainring
T_{rear}	= number of teeth, sprocket.

A typical high gear may be around 8—9m, while a typical low gear may be 2.5—3m.

Neither of these gear designations needs to be calculated once you know how they are determined. Tables 1 and 2 in the Appendix provide quick a reference for their determination on the basis of 27-inch and 700mm wheels, while they can be determined for other wheel sizes by multiplying with the following ratio:

$$X_{wheel} = X / 0.675 \times D_{wheel}$$

where:

| X_{wheel} | = the required value for the wheel size in question |
| X | = the value for development or gear number for 27-inch or 700mm wheels |

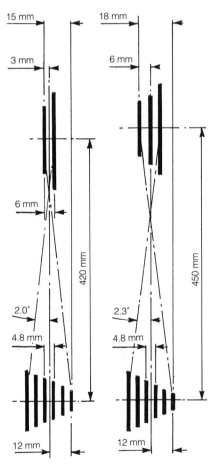

10.8. Chain deflection as a determining factor for the suitability of gearing combinations.

0.675 = the wheel size in meters on which the tables are based

D_{wheel} = the actual outside diameter in meters of the wheel in question.

Ergonomically, it is best to select the gears in such a way that the difference between them is larger in the range of low gears than it is in high gears. This is achieved by selecting the sprocket sizes so that the smaller sprockets differ less from each other than the biggest sprockets. The best ratio is obtained when the percentage steps of the sprocket sizes remains approximately the same. Thus, the high gears are closer together than the low ones.

Take, as an example, a series of 7 sprockets from 13 to 25. At first, it may seem logical to assign them as follows: 13, 15, 17, 19, 21, 23 and 25. The difference is always 2 teeth. However, between 15 and 13 that amounts to $2/15 = 0.15$, or 15%, while between 23 and 25 it is only $2/25 = 0.08$, or 8%. This incongruity becomes even more dramatic as wider range gearing is used.

It will be more accurate to adhere to a progression that keeps the percentage steps similar throughout the range, using smaller steps between small sprockets than between big ones. An example for the range between 13 and 25 would be 13, 14, 15, 17, 19, 22, 25. In this case, the steps can be calculated to be 8%, 7%, 7%, 12%, 11% and 12%.

This too can easily be selected with the use of a graph, referring to Fig. 10.9. Place a copy of the strip over the graph in such a way that the first and last arrows (depending whether it is a freewheel block with 5, 6 or 7 sprockets) coincide with the values for the smallest and biggest sprockets. At the intermediate points, read off the closest intermediate sprocket sizes, deviating slightly to the left or the right only if done consistently to the same side.

There are several different theories for the selection of the chainring sizes. My preference goes towards something referred to as *half step* for systems with two chainrings, to something called *half step plus granny* for systems with three chainrings (see Fig. 10.6). In both cases, the term *half step* refers to the principle of selecting the smaller chainring of such a size that intermediate gears between steps with different sprockets are achieved (this is done by choosing the second chainring only a few teeth smaller than the biggest). The term *granny* refers to a very small third chainring,

The Gear Progression

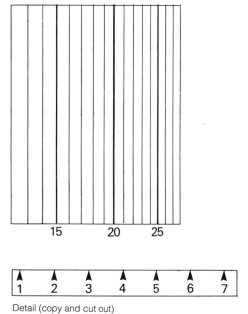

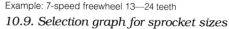

Detail (copy and cut out)

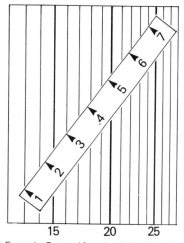

Example: 7-speed freewheel 13—24 teeth

10.9. Selection graph for sprocket sizes

149

10.10. Shimano SIS started the trend towards indexed shifting in the mid eighties. Today, hardly a bicycle is sold without index gearing, whether mountain bike or road machine.

The Rear Derailleur

10.11. Shimano Dura-Ace derailleur

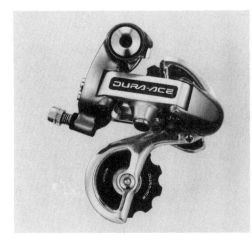

that makes an entirely different low range available when it is combined with any of the sprockets.

The more common selection of chainrings results in achieving a different range of gears with the smaller chainring than with the larger. On mountain bikes, often ridden under conditions where shifting with the front chainring must be minimized, this makes perfect sense, but I find it a crying shame to equip touring bikes and fitness machines with the kind of gearing that provides such overlaps that fully 40% of them are wasted.

When selecting chainrings and sprockets, remember the comments about their wear: they wear less if they are selected with a number of teeth that represents a prime number. This is the reason why 41, 43, 47 or 53 tooth chainrings and 13, 17, 19 or 23 tooth sprockets should be selected in preference to slightly different sizes. They not only wear better, they also run more smoothly.

Finally, it should be pointed out that, especially when systems with seven sprockets are used, the extreme gears that cross over the chain from the smallest sprocket to the smallest chainring, or from the largest sprocket to the largest chainrings, should be avoided (see Fig. 10.8). The resulting lateral chain deflection causes both high wear and reduced efficiency of the drive train. It will be virtually impossible to adjust the derailleurs in such a way that the chain does not rub against the derailleur cage in the extreme gears.

Essentially every rear derailleur consists of a hinged, spring-tensioned parallelogram mechanism with which a spring-tensioned cage with its two chain guide wheels can be moved sideways, shifting the chain from one sprocket to another. The most significant difference in design is that between models with a hanging parallelogram and a more horizontal one, between models with long cages and short ones, between the location at which the cage is pivoted, and between straight and slanted parallelogram mountings (referred to as slant pantograph design).

Figures 10.12 and 10.13 show the two major types. In general, the models with nearly horizontal cages, referred to as pantograph types, lend themselves better to indexing (although the indexing is contained in the lever, rather than the derailleur). The slant design minimizes the distance between the chain and the sprocket teeth, making for more positive shifting. The models with a long cage, preferably pivoted at a point between

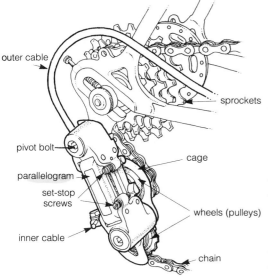

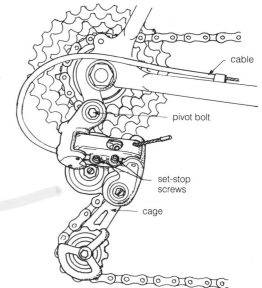

10.12 and 10.13. The two basic rear derailleur types. *Left: Conventional straight parallelogram derailleur as was long the standard for all European makers. Right: Pantograph model as used by all Japanese manufacturers and increasingly also by European companies.*

the two chain guide wheels, are more easily adapted to large differences between sprocket sizes (i.e. wide-range gearing).

Most models are marked to show the range of sprocket sizes and the amount of chain wrap for which they are suitable. In some cases, the cage can be attached to the body in several different locations, each representing a certain range of sprocket sizes. The amount of chain wrap for which a derailleur is suitable indicates how big the difference between the combinations *largest chainring, largest sprocket* on the one hand, and *smallest chainring, smallest sprocket* on the other may be.

The most important adjusting device for the modern derailleur (certainly if it is suitable for index gearing) is the cable tension adjuster. In addition, the extreme limits of travel are adjusted with the set-stop, or limit, screws. In the case of the slant pantograph model there is an additional adjusting screw with which the angle between the parallelogram and the horizontal plane can be adjusted, as described in the manufacturer's instruction leaflet, to achieve the greatest degree of chain-wrap around the sprocket consistent with smooth shifting.

Although most derailleurs nowadays are installed directly to a threaded lug on the RH rear drop-out, simple bikes may lack this feature. In that case, the derailleur is mounted on an adaptor plate that is held between the drop-out and the wheel axle nut or quick-release. Both adaptor plates and drop-outs are general-

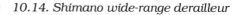

10.14. *Shimano wide-range derailleur*

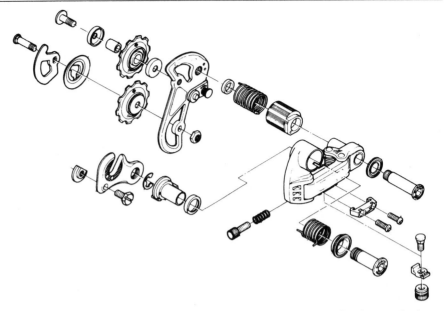

10.15.
Assembly of typical modern rear derailleur. The mounting plate (lower left) is only used on frames without derailleur mounting lug (Shimano il-lustration).

ly designed for specific derailleurs, which work best when certain distances are adhered to. This locks you into equipment from a specific manufacturer, so it is preferable not to experiment with a different make or model of derailleur than those for which the drop-out on the frame was designed.

The Front Derailleur

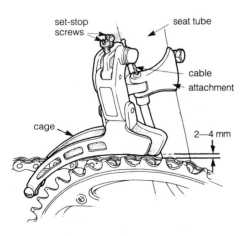

10.16. Front derailleur, showing installation position.

Fig. 10.16 shows a typical front derailleur. It simply consists of a hinge mechanism that moves an otherwise fixed cage sideways to guide the chain over one chainring or another. The differences between the various models are primarily associated with the size of the cage and the lateral travel: there are distinct differences between models suitable for triple chainrings and those suitable only for double chainrings. A long, low dropped cage indicates that it will shift down to a really small chainring, as is necessary for touring and mountain bikes. The adjustment mechanism is usually limited to a set of set-stop screws to adjust the range of lateral travel.

Most modern versions have a hinge mechanism that does more than just move the cage sideways. Instead, they tend to lift the chain towards the larger one as they move to the right, drop down as they move to the left. Especially for triple chainring use, the (long and thus sensitive) cage should be ruggedly constructed. Most racing models (for twin chainrings) are nowadays designed to be installed on a lug attached to the seat tube, while mountain bike models always have a clamp with which they are attached to the seat tube, a solution that allows more flexibility, since the lugs brazed on to the frame tend to be suitable only for one particular make and model of the front derailleur.

Instead of a regular front derailleur, there is one system on the market that does the same job in a more sophisticated manner. This is the Browning system, available from SunTour under the name BEAST. It is an electrically controlled system in which sections of the chainrings are hinged and move sideways to deliver the chain to the next chainring. Although one may object to battery-powered technology on the otherwise perfectly manually operated bike, there is no doubt something to be said for the ease with which this system shifts the chain even under the most difficult conditions (all other front derailleurs shift only very reluctantly as long as the chain is under tension, as when cycling uphill).

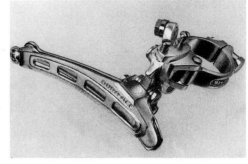

10.17. Shimano road bike front derailleur

Both front and rear derailleurs are operated by means of shift levers via bowden cables. The shift levers may be installed on the down tube, on the handlebars, on the stem or at the handlebar ends. The stem mounted location is inherently unsuitable and is only found on drop-handlebar bikes intended for people who don't know how to handle them. Fig. 10.20 shows several versions.

In addition to these regular models, there is the so-called Grip-Shift for installation at the ends of forward reaching triathlon handlebars, such as used in time trial racing. Campagnolo and Sachs-Huret both have something similar for installation on the ends of regular mountain bike handlebars. Whatever design is used, the shifter for the rear derailleur is mounted on

Derailleur Controls

10.18. SunTour mountain bike front derailleur.

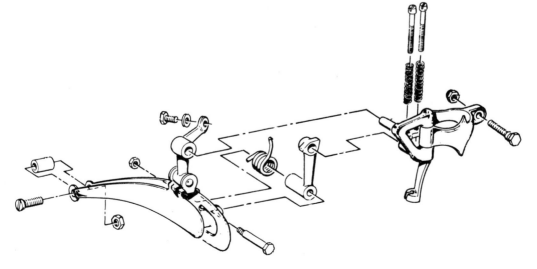

10.19. Assembly of conventional front derailleur. Nowadays, many road frames are equipped with a lug for front derailleur installation, so the mounting bracket is eliminated.

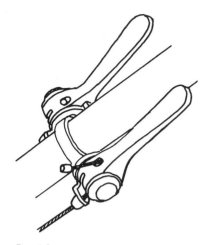

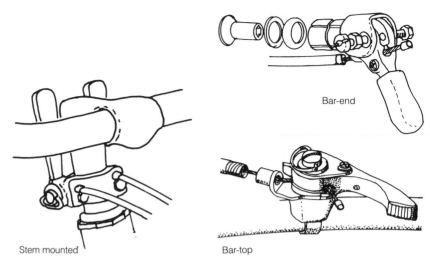

Downtube

Stem mounted

Bar-end

Bar-top

10.20. Conventional (non indexed) shifters.

Index Derailleurs

10.21. Early indexing: It had a ratchet mechanism in the derailleur.

the right, the one for the front derailleur on the left. The Browning system (which only works in the front) is operated by means of a double push button switch.

The difference between the modern index derailleurs and old-fashioned friction models lies mainly in the shifters and the cables. These index shifters have a stepped ratchet mechanism inside, which stops the cable in predetermined positions, coinciding with derailleur positions for particular sprockets. Most of the older versions have a supplementary lever that allows shifting between the index mode and a mode in which intermediate positions can be reached (to allow full use of the gears even when the index system is out of adjustment).

The cables used for index gearing are thicker and stiffer than conventional cables to eliminate real or apparent stretch, which would throw the system out of adjustment. Their length is usually preset for a certain configuration, since they are very hard to cut. These cables also have a nylon low-friction liner and do not require lubrication.

Since 1990, most mountain bikes come with double-button levers mounted under the handlebars. These allow operation without moving the hands: push the top button to shift up, the bottom button to shift down. There are some differences between the available models, but most are so complicated that the manufacturers rightfully warn against taking them apart when they don't work properly: you'll have to replace the whole unit.

Shimano's version no longer has a friction mode to allow for maladjustment, while it also is available only as a combined unit integrating brake lever and gear shifter. This is a particularly consumer hostile approach. SunTour's version is mounted separately and also includes a small-step ratchet to allow non-index shifting, if necessary. Recently introduced Shimano shifters combined with racing brake levers work very well. Unfortunately they also force you into a certain system with specific brakes, and they are very heavy.

Once a month, it will be smart to clean and, if necessary, lubricate front and rear derailleur and other associated parts, especially the chain, the cables and the sprockets. Shifting depends on all of these components working properly. The other operation regularly necessary is adjustment if there is any deterioration of shifting. Non-index versions in particular may require re-adjustment of the set-stop screws if the chain is shifted too far or not far enough.

Sometimes the chain is shifted beyond the last chain-ring or sprocket or, conversely, not far enough. In the first case it will drop by the side and may get caught; in the second case certain gear combinations just cannot be reached as a result. These things can generally be corrected by adjusting the set-stop screws, shown in Fig. 10.27.

Before you resort to adjusting these little screws with the spiral springs under their heads on the rear derailleur, though, check to make sure the problem is not caused by a bent drop-out or adaptor plate. This may be the result of a fall, and will result in a non-perpendicular alignment of the derailleur cage, and no amount of set-stop screw adjustment will solve the problem: get the drop-out aligned instead. Similarly, the front derailleur may have shifted on the seat tube: the cage should be perfectly parallel to the chainrings.

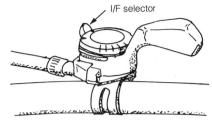

10.22. Above-the-bar index shifter

Derailleur Maintenance

Adjust Derailleur Travel

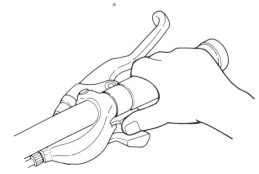

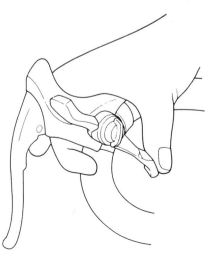

*10.23 and 10.24. Left: Under-the-bar shifter for mountain bikes.
Right: Brake lever mounted shifter for road bikes. (SunTour illustrations).*

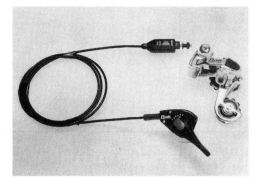

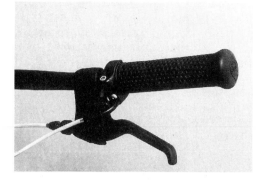

10.25 and 10.26.
Left: Sachs-Huret
Elisee index derail-
leur with a clip-on
cable attachment
and adjusting me-
chanism.
Right: Campagnolo
Bullet twist grip
for mountain bike
use.

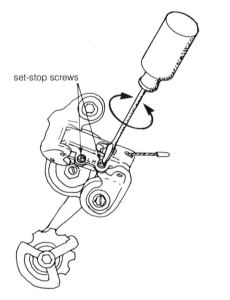

set-stop screws

10.27. Adjusting set-stop screws to limit
derailleur range

Adjust Index Derailleur

When you have established that the problem is not due to a bent or twisted derailleur, you will need a little screwdriver and sometimes a rag — needed if the chain has to be put back on sprocket or chainring. If the chain has got caught, you may have to loosen and retighten the wheel first to free it.

Adjusting procedure:
1. Establish what the cause and nature of the problem is:
   ☐   front or rear;
   ☐   too much travel or too little;
   ☐   on the inside (to the left) or the outside (right).
2. Seek out the appropriate set-stop screw and determine if it has to be screwed in (too much travel) or out (not enough travel).
3. Screw the appropriate set-stop screw in or out about half a turn at a time.
4. Lifting the rear wheel off the ground and pedaling forward while shifting, check operation of the gears in all combinations and if necessary repeat adjustment until all gears work properly.

Generally, the cause of index derailleur problems is either a bent or twisted attachment (see the preceding section for this), or — more typically — cable stretch. However, most of the cables used do not stretch all by themselves: the problem is probably due to the cable or any part being loose, or conversely the cable may have been caught or damaged at some point. First check all those possibilities and proceed to the adjustment process below only when you are sure nothing else is wrong. Generally, no tools are required for this.

Adjusting procedure:
1. If the shifter in question has an F-position for the non-indexed, or friction, mode, set the supplementary lever in this position first.

10.28 and 10.29. Left: Automatic AIR–Shifter. Right: SunTour BEAST, developed by Browning, which shifts the chain in the front by means of hinged chainring sections.

2. Select the highest gear (largest chainring and smallest sprocket) — if it cannot be reached, loosen the cable adjusting mechanism as necessary (if still no luck, also adjust the high range set-stop screw as described above).
3. Adjust the rear derailleur cable in this position so that it is just taut but not under tension.
4. Lifting the rear wheel and turning the cranks, shift into the lowest gear (smallest chainring, largest sprocket) — if necessary, adjust the set-stop screw. If still no luck, also tighten the cable just a little.
5. Shift back into the highest gear and now shift into the index mode (if appropriate).
6. If necessary, adjust the cable tension until the chain runs smoothly and noiselessly in this gear.
7. Shift the rear derailleur's shifter down one step — if the derailleur does not follow perfectly, tighten the cable adjuster half a turn. If it shifts too far, slacken it half a turn. Repeat in quarter-turn steps if necessary.
8. Tighten the adjuster just enough that the chain runs noisily against the next larger sprocket. Then back off again until the noise subsides.
9. Once more check all the gears, paying particular attention to quiet running — repeat the last two steps, if necessary.

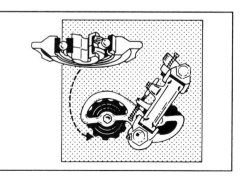

10.30 and 10.31. Left: The derailleur wheels usually run on sleeve bearings. To reduce friction, they can be replaced by models with ball bearings, such as these by Tacx (right).

10.32 and 10.33 Left: SunTour above-the-bar index shifters for mountain bike use. Right: Under-the-bar mountain bike shifters.

Shifter Maintenance

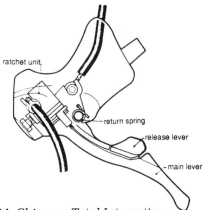

10.34. Shimano Total Integration shifters combined with racing brake levers. Convenient but heavy.

From time to time, the gear shift levers must be tightened, assuming they are also kept clean and very lightly lubricated. To tighten them, there is a screw on top that holds the mechanism together. Index derailleurs can often be salvaged, for the time being, by simply shifting them into the friction mode until you have time to do a proper maintenance or replacement job on them.

Conventional models on which the manufacturer allows for disassembly may be opened up if no satisfaction is obtained by tightening the screw on top. Clean, check, lubricate and reassemble to get it back in working order. If this still does not do the trick, check the cable before resorting to replacement of the shifter mechanism itself.

Chapter 11

Hub Gearing

Although derailleur gearing is used on most bicycles sold these days, the other method of gearing also bears some. Instead of moving the chain sideways between different sprockets and chainrings, this system uses an epicyclic gear built in the rear hub.

The advantages of hub gearing include uncomplicated shifting, fewer external parts to get damaged, and the possibility to enclose the chain. All these add up to enough reasons to choose this system for a wind-and-weather utility bike, as indeed it is in countries like Holland, where the bicycle is to this day seen as a means of transport, as well as in England, where hub gearing remains the choice of many bicycle commuters. Fig. 11.1 shows the typical parts that make up a hub gearing system with — in this case — three speeds. Systems with 2, 4 and 5 speeds are also available. A shifter on the handlebars operates a mechanism connected to the pull rod in the hub via a bowden cable.

Hub gears are available from at least three manufacturers: Sturmey-Archer, Fichtel & Sachs and Shimano. If you ever encounter one that says SunTour, it is in reality a Sturmey-Archer hub. There was a brief period when Sturmey-Archer built 3-speeds with coaster brake for Fichtel & Sachs, which explains the difference with other hubs sold under the same name.

The guts of a typical 3-speed hub are shown in Fig. 11.3. All internal hub gears used these days are based on the epicyclic, or planet, gearing principle illustrated in Fig. 11.4. This section will explain the principle by which these systems operate.

The rear wheel axle holds a fixed central, so-called sun gear. At some distance from this sun gear, on the inside of the hub shell, is an inward facing annular gear. The space between these two gears is bridged by a set of mutually connected small gear wheels, referred to as planet gears. The teeth of the planet gears mesh on the one side with the central sun gear, on the other side with the annular gear.

The axle is hollow and contains a clutch mechanism that is operated by the pull rod and connecting certain parts of the system. The sprocket, or cog (which is the term I shall use throughout this chapter to prevent

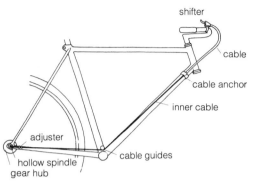

11.1. Hub gearing system components

The Epicyclic Gear Principle

11.2. Fichtel & Sachs Pentasport: five gears spread over a wide range. Available with or without coaster brake.

159

11.3.
Internals of a typical three-speed hub. This is Sturmey-Archer's most popular AW model.

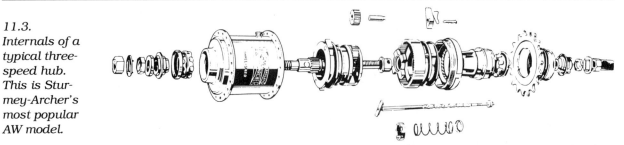

some confusion in the abbreviations used in the formula that follow, even if sprocket is used in the rest of the book) driven by the bicycle's chain can be connected by this same clutch mechanism to particular parts of the system, while a freewheel mechanism sees to it that the wheel can rotate forward while the cog is stationary.

In the normal gear position, the clutch is set so that the entire planet system is by-passed: the cog is connected via the freewheel to the wheel hub. This way, the hub turns just as fast as the cog and there are no mechanical losses — it corresponds to what used to be an overdrive on older cars. Expressed in a formula, the wheel rotation speed in this gear is:

$$V_n = V_c$$

where:
V_n = wheel rotation speed in normal gear
V_c = cog rotation speed.

When the high gear is selected, the clutch mechanism connects the cog with the cage on which the planet gears are mounted, while the hub shell is connected with the annular gear. Consequently, the planet gears turn forward as they move together around the sun wheel and drive the annular gear. The speed with which the annular gear — and consequently the whole wheel — turns can be determined as follows:

$$V_h = V_c \times (T_a + T_s)$$

where:
V_h = wheel rotation speed in high gear
V_c = cog rotation speed
T_a = number of teeth of annular gear
T_s = number of teeth of sun gear.

In the low gear position, the clutch mechanism connects the cog with the annular gear, while the wheel hub shell is connected with the cage holding the planet gears. Consequently, the planet gears turn backwards

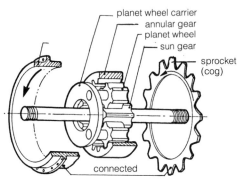

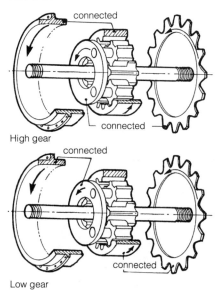

11.4. The epicyclic gearing principle

and drive the hub shell more slowly than the speed of the cog. The wheel rotating speed will be:

$$V_l = V_c \times (T_s / T_a)$$

where:
V_l = wheel rotation speed in low gear
V_c = cog rotation speed
T_a = number of teeth of annular gear
T_s = number of teeth of sun gear

Combining the three formulas for the individual wheel rotation speeds, the ratio between the three gears is:

$$V_l / V_n / V_h = (T_a{-}T_s) / (T_a) / (T_a{-}T_s)$$

Readers familiar with mathematics will recognize the above relationship as a geometric progression. That means that the steps between bigger gears are also bigger than those between lower gears. As was explained in Chapter 10, this contradicts the requirements for an ergonomically correct gearing progression. It is more desirable to have steps that become proportionally smaller as the gears get higher. This is the disadvantage of hub gearing, although it should not be overlooked that few riders actually use hub gears quite so critically that their limitations bother them.

With the gear wheel sizes used on virtually all 3-speed hub gears available today, the sun gear has the same number of teeth as the planet gears, while the annular gear has three times as many. Consequently, the progression is 67%, 100%, 133% — in other words, the low gear is 25% lower than the normal gear, while the high gear is 33.3% higher. The range of gears can be described by the ratio between the extreme gears: the

Gear Progression

11.5. Complete braking and gearing system for touristic bikes from Sturmey-Archer. It includes aluminum hubs, five-speed gearing and a choice of shifters.

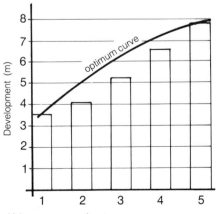

Hub gear progression

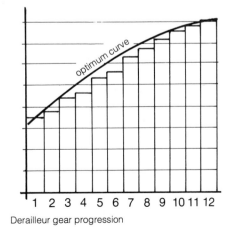

Derailleur gear progression

11.6.
Gear progression compared: The hub gears do not follow the optimum curve as closely as can be achieved with derailleur gears — even though most unsophisticated riders may never notice.

11.7. Sturmey-Archer AW three-speed hub with steel hub shell.

highest is 133 / 75 = 1.78 times as high as the lowest. If we assume a chainring with 48 teeth and a cog with 19 teeth, the normal gear will have a development of 5.40m (a 69-inch gear). The low gear will have a development of 0.75 x 5.40m = 4.10m (a 52-inch gear), while the high gear will have a development of 1.33 x 5.40m = 7.10m (an 89-inch gear). On a 2-speed system, the low gear would be missing, meaning that the available gears have developments of 7.10m and 5.40m (gear numbers of 89 and 69 inches), respectively.

On 5-speed systems, which incorporate a double planet gearing system, the progression is as follows: 67%, 78%, 100%, 122%, 150%. Consequently, the individual gears, assuming the same set- up with 48-tooth chainring and 19-tooth cog, would be as follows: 3.60, 4.20, 5.40, 6.60, 8.10. Thus, these gears do not lie quite as far apart as is the case on the 3-speed, making this a more suitable arrangement with adequate range: the highest gear is 2.24 times as high as the lowest.

Ergonomically, the disadvantage of the geometric progression applies here too, but it should not be overlooked that in reality derailleur gearing usually does not allow perfect progression either. Fig. 11.6 shows a comparison between the two gearing systems, which is clearly not all that unfavorable for the 5-speed hub. On the other hand, the mechanical losses are greater in the extreme gears — on the Sturmey-Archer 5-speed, I actually measured so much more resistance in the lowest gear, that it merely slows you down, without making the load any easier.

The examples listed above were based on a 48-tooth chainring and a 19-tooth cog. Although the ratio between the gears remains the same whatever cog and chainring are selected, the whole range can be made higher or lower to match the user's preference. This is done by installing a cog (or a chainring) with a different number of teeth: either a larger chainring or a smaller cog to increase all gears, a smaller chainring or a bigger cog to reduce them.

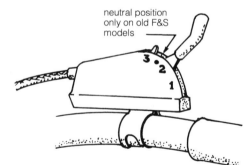

neutral position only on old F&S models

11.8. Three-speed shifter

Hub Gear Controls

Generally, the three-speed hub is operated by means of a handlebar shifter, which operates a little chain or hinge connected with the clutch mechanism in the hub via a flexible cable that runs over rollers or guides. Fig. 11.8 illustrates a typical 3-speed gear shifter. Five-speed hubs may either be controlled by means of a double lever or (less predictable, though more popular) by means of a single lever as illustrated in Fig. 11.9.

The hub axle is hollow and carries the operating rod on

which the clutch mechanism is held. On most models, the clutch rod is attached to a little chain, while other models connect it with a hinge mechanism screwed on in the location of the axle nut. The cable is attached to the little chain or the hinge by means of a cable adjuster which serves to correct the adjustment of the gears. When shifting towards a lower gear, the pull rod is pulled further out of the chain and sets the clutch in the appropriate position. The two-speed gear, used mainly for portable bicycles, works without external controls: it is operated by pedaling back.

The simplest adjusting mechanism is the one used by Fichtel & Sachs. In conjunction with the mechanical superiority of the gears themselves, this is a good reason to choose this make in preference to all others — certainly now that this manufacturer has finally introduced models without a coaster brake.

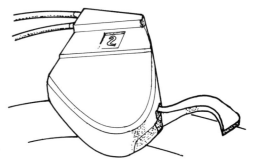

11.9. Single-lever 5-speed shifter

Whenever hub gearing does not work properly, it is generally not due to the mechanism itself, but rather to the controls. Slipped cable guides or pinched cables are the most frequent causes of control problems. Consequently, these points should be checked before attempting to adjust the mechanism.

Most models made by Fichtel & Sachs are lubricated for life and only break down when the hub overheats during prolonged braking with the built-in coaster brake. In that case, the hub should be disassembled and the bearings repacked with the manufacturer's special grease. Most other models are equipped with an oil nipple and should be lubricated with 10 drops of light oil once every three months or whenever the hub appears not to run or shift smoothly. On three-speed models, the coaster brake can simply be eliminated by dismantling the unit and removing the sectioned, cylindrical brake mantle with the brake cone shown in the illustration of the cross section.

Hub Gear Maintenance

To date, Sturmey-Archer's models with built-in drum brakes are not equipped with a seal that separates the brake from the gears. The result is that when the bike lies on its left side, the oil enters the brake drum where it ruins the brake pads. Consequently, the manufacturer delivers them unlubricated — make sure you lubricate such a hub before use. Of course, bikes sometimes do lean over to the left, and during transport the cyclist often has no control over what happens. My value judgment is that this displays a manufacturer's disregard for the consumer's needs (or perhaps it is merely a sign of technical incompetence).

11.10. The heart of a Sturmey-Archer three-speed hub mechanism.

163

But lubrication is not the only aspect of hub gear maintenance. Here is a list of frequent causes of improper shifting with their respective solutions:

☐ Cable (seemingly) stretched: adjust.
☐ Hub, adjusting mechanism, cable or handle does not run freely: lubricate.
☐ Hub defective: overhaul or replace.
☐ Control part (shifter, cable, cable guide, hinge mechanism) defective: repair or replace.

Most often, the cause is one of the first two points, so it can simply be corrected by means of adjustment or lubrication. On the three-speed, the adjustment is generally correct when the cable is taut, but not under tension, when the shift lever is set for the high gear. However, the procedure is slightly different for each of the various makes and models, as will be described individually below. When the system is operated via a little chain protruding from the axle (Sturmey-Archer and Fichtel & Sachs 3-speeds), this chain must be perfectly aligned with the cable — that may mean that it is not fully turned in but backed off a little.

Adjust Sturmey-Archer 3-Speed

On these hubs, the cable is connected to a tiny chain that comes out of the (special) RH axle nut. The correct adjustment can be checked based on the alignment as seen through a viewing port in this nut. Generally, no tools are required, although a pair of pliers may be needed if the adjuster is too tight.

Procedure:
1. Check whether the cable, its guides and stops, and the shifter all operate correctly and the stops and guides are attached properly.
2. If the hub has not been lubricated for more than three months, first lubricate it through the oil hole, then turn the cranks several times in each gear with the wheel lifted off the ground.
3. Place the shift lever in the normal gear position (N or 2), while rotating the cranks at least half a turn.
4. Check the situation through the viewing port in the special RH axle nut. The hub is correctly adjusted if the shoulder on the internal pin to which the chain is connected is exactly aligned with the end of the wheel axle (move the shift lever back and forth a little to check if necessary).
5. If necessary, adjust the cable adjuster: loosen the locknut, turn the internally threaded bushing relative to the threaded pin, then hold in position while tightening the locknut.

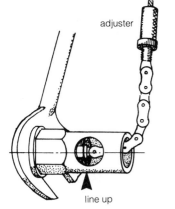

adjuster

line up

11.11. Adjusting detail for Sturmey-Archer three-speed.

6. Check and re-adjust if necessary.

Since about 1975, these hubs no longer have a neutral position because they are usually sold with a built-in coaster brake (braking would then become impossible when the hub is accidentally in neutral). Consequently, the problem here is never evidenced by loss of transmission, but merely by the fact that a different gear than the one selected remains engaged. The adjustment is done in the high gear, and no tools are required.

Procedure:
1. Establish whether the cable, its guides and stops, and the shifter all operate correctly and the stops and guides are not loose. Correct if necessary.
2. Place the shift lever in the high gear position (H or 3), while turning the cranks at least half a revolution.
3. Adjust the special cable adjuster, which is simply clamped on a serrated rod: push the clip in, slide it up or down the serrated rod held in the other hand until the cable is just taut but not under tension, and let go of the clip.
4. Check and re-adjust if necessary.

On this hub, which is available with and without coaster brake, the controls are carried via a 'bell crank' hinge mechanism on the LH side of the hub. This hinge mechanism has an integral locknut and must be positioned so that the pivoting movement is fully aligned with the cable. To achieve this, you may have to loosen the locknut a little, adjust the bell crank in the right position, and then hold it there while tightening the locknut. Generally, no tools will be required for the rest of the work.

Procedure:
1. Check whether the cable, its guides and stops, the bell crank, and the shifter all operate correctly and the stops, guides and bell crank are properly attached. Correct if necessary.
2. Place the shift lever in the high gear position (N or 2), while turning the cranks at least half a revolution.
3. If the gears are correctly adjusted, the letter N (or the number 2) should now be completely visible in the window in the bell crank.
4. Adjust the cable adjuster attached to the bell crank until the number is visible in the window.
5. Check each of the gears in turn, while turning the

Adjust Fichtel & Sachs 3-Speed

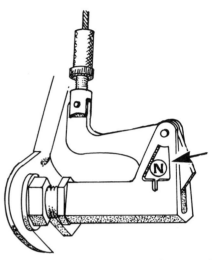

11.12. Shimano 3-speed adjusting detail

Adjust Shimano 3-Speed

11.13. Sachs-Huret gruppo with hub gearing and hub brakes — intended for recreational use.

cranks with the wheel lifted, and re-adjust if necessary.

Five-Speed Hubs

These units, which include a double set of planet gears, each with its own controls, are available from Sturmey-Archer and Fichtel & Sachs. The former exist in versions with and without drum brake, while the latter, though mechanically far superior, only come with a built-in coaster brake which can not be bypassed.

Nowadays, most 5-speeds are not operated by means of separate shift levers, but by a combination lever that controls the two cables used to shift. Although this may seem simpler to use, it is considerably more prone to trouble, and by no means easier to adjust. The main problem is that these shifters are made of a relatively soft fiber-reinforced plastic which deforms too easily, especially at the point where the cable nipple is held. A lot of problems are prevented by taking the unit apart early in its life and applying a generous amount of bearing grease to everything that moves — even though this is not generally considered necessary for the material in question.

Adjust Sturmey-Archer 5-Speed

On most versions of this hub, there is a bell crank mechanism on the LH side, while the RH side has the same nut with viewing port as found on the same manufacturer's three-speed models. Verify whether the cable runs freely, the cable stops are firmly installed, and whether the bell crank and the control chain are exactly aligned with their respective cable sections. If the hub has not been lubricated in the last three months, do that first, after which it should be tried again. Once these points have been corrected, no tools are required as a rule.

Procedure:
A. On models with two separate shifters:
1. Place the LH shifter in the position that releases tension on the LH cable, while turning the cranks at least half a revolution with the wheel lifted off the ground.
2. If necessary, adjust it so that it is just taut but not under tension.
3. Place the RH shifter in the intermediate position, turning the cranks.
4. Shift the LH shifter into the position by which the cable is fully tensioned.
5. Check all gears. If any do not work, adjust the RH adjuster a little looser or tighter.

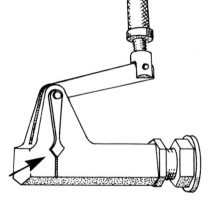

11.14. Sturmey-Archer five-speed adjusting detail.

B. On models with a single shifter:
1. Select the fourth gear.
2. Adjust the RH mechanism as described for the same manufacturer's 3-speed hub.
3. Place the shifter in the position for the fifth gear while turning the cranks half a revolution with the wheel raised off the ground.
4. The LH cable should now be tightened — adjust, if necessary.
5. Try out all the gears and re-adjust, if necessary.

This hub with its built-in coaster brake is always operated by means of a single shifter. No tools are needed for the adjustment, which has to be preceded by the usual check of the cables, shifter, guide and stops.

Procedure:
1. Select the fifth gear while turning the cranks forward with the wheel raised off the ground.
2. Loosen the cable adjusting clips on both sides, so the cables on both sides of the hub are completely loose in this position.
3. Turn the cranks forward by at least one revolution with the wheel raised off the ground.
4. Put the cable adjusting clips on their respective pins so that the cables are just taut but not under tension.
5. Select the first gear, while turning the cranks forward with the wheel raised off the ground.
6. Check whether this gear engages properly.
7. If the first gear does not engage properly, return to the fourth gear and tighten the looser cables one notch, repeating steps 5—7 as necessary until the first gear works properly.
8. Check all the gears, and re-adjust if necessary.

This has to be done if the problem cannot be solved by means of adjustment and lubrication. If the cause is clearly not here either, the hub gear mechanism itself is at fault, which will not be described in detail here. If you are faced with this predicament, it will be easier to replace the entire wheel complete with hub. You can then take your time disassembling the old hub to see whether you can find an obviously defective part.

When replacing shifter or cable, it should be noted that each are basically designed for the same maker's hub. Just the same, there are adaptor pieces that allow the use of one manufacturer's cable with another manufacturer's adjusting mechanism. In the case of the three-speed, it is often possible to use non matching shifters.

Adjust Fichtel & Sachs 5-Speed

11.15. Fichtel & Sachs three-speed hub with built-in coaster brake.

Replace Shifter or Cable

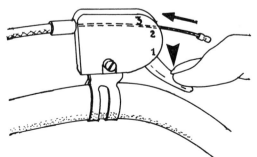

11.16. Freeing cable nipple

11.17. Interesting hybrid solution from Sachs-Huret: A 6-speed rear derailleur is combined with a 2-speed hub to obtain 12 easily shifted gears (the front derailleur is replaced by the hub gear, which is easier to shift).

Five-speeds can be operated with two separate three-speed shifters of any make instead of the original. You will need a screwdriver and a wrench.

Disassembly procedure:
1. Loosen the cable adjuster at the hub.
2. Pull the cable back towards the shifter until there is enough slack.
3. Pull the shift lever in as far as possible as shown in Fig. 11.16 (or, in the case of a 5-speed lever, open it up to gain access) and remove the nipple out of the recess in the shifter.
4. Pull the cable back out of the shifter and off the guides and stops.
5. Remove the part that has to be replaced (cable or shifter).

Installation procedure:
1. When replacing the lever, install it in the right position.
2. Pull the shift lever in as far as possible as shown in Fig. 11.16 (or, in the case of a 5-speed lever, open it up to gain access). Feed the nipple in and hook it in the recess in the shifter.
3. Hold the cable pulled taut and place it over the various guides and stops.
4. At the hub, attach it to the control chain or the bell crank.
5. Adjust the gears as described above.

Adjust Hub Bearings

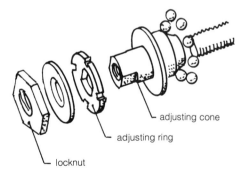

adjusting cone

adjusting ring

locknut

11.18. Bearing adjustment detail

The gear hub's ball bearings must be maintained just like those of other hubs. Actually, the adjustment procedure is quite easy once you have the manufacturer's special hub wrench which is usually supplied with the bike or the hub. Fig. 11.18 shows the relevant parts.

Procedure:
1. Loosen the LH axle nut 2—3 turns (to the left).
2. Loosen the locknut 1—2 turns.
3. First tighten the adjusting nut for the cone fully, then back it off (to the left) by ¼ turn.
4. Hold the adjusting nut in this position and tighten the locknut.
5. Tighten the axle nut, while keeping the wheel centrally positioned.
6. Check the bearing to make sure it is neither too loose or too tight, and re-adjust if necessary.

Chapter 12

Rim Brakes

Although the coaster brake and other forms of hub brake still find a use on simple utility bikes, the overwhelming majority of all bicycles sold for serious use these days are equipped with some kind of rim brake. Even on bikes with a coaster brake on the rear wheel, the rim brake frequently finds application on the front wheel in those countries where two independent brakes are prescribed by law (as it should be everywhere).

All rim brakes are based on one of two principles, which are depicted in Fig. 12.2. By means of a lever and usually a cable (sometimes a pull rod or even a hydraulic system), two brake blocks of a wear-resistant high-friction material are pushed against the wheel rim. In the US, only the type that applies force from the side is used. It is also possible to apply the force radially outward towards the rim, something that is still found on the roller-lever (or stirrup) brakes used on utility bikes in many parts of the world. Neither system is inherently superior to the other: the roller-lever system is just heavier and harder to adjust.

Before getting down to the brass tacks of rim brake maintenance, the next section will be devoted to the subject of braking theory. This theory applies both to the rim brake and to the various types of hub brakes that will be covered in Chapter 13.

In the moving bicycle, a certain amount of so-called *kinetic* energy (the product of mass and the square of the speed) is stored, which is absorbed when the bike is brought to a standstill. This can be done by letting it roll until friction losses have depleted this energy, which may take a long time. Or it can be done by crashing into a fixed object, which will do the job much faster, though with detrimental results to bike and rider.

To stop before an accident happens, the brakes are used. The brakes apply friction between a moving and a fixed part (in the case of rim brakes, between the rim and the brake blocks) to dissipate the energy at a rate controlled by the rider via the force he applies to the brake lever. The energy absorbed by the brakes is converted to heat (rim and brake blocks become hot). The amount of energy to be absorbed is calculated as follows:

12.1. Brake test in rainy weather. With the right choice of rim and brake block, you should not overshoot the mark.

Braking Theory

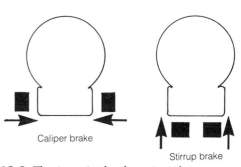

Caliper brake

Stirrup brake

12.2. The two rim brake principles

12.3. Effect of braking on location of mass center.

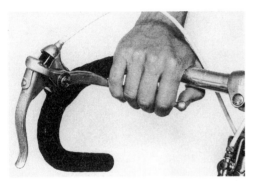

12.4. Auxiliary brake levers flex too much to be used when high braking forces are required.

12.5. Move back and keep the weight low to avoid toppling over.

$$W = 0.5 \times m \times v^2$$

where:

W = energy in kJ (equivalent to N)
m = mass of bike, rider and luggage in kg
v = initial riding speed in m/sec.

The relationship expressed by this formula explains why it is harder to stop a heavily loaded bike, and why it is so much harder to stop it from a higher speed, as evidenced by longer braking distances.

The speed is reduced more or less gradually. Just how gradually is expressed by the deceleration in m/sec^2. A deceleration of $1 m/sec^2$ means that the speed is reduced by one m/sec after each subsequent second of braking. When rolling to a gradual stop, the deceleration is very low (in the order of cm/sec^2), while it is very high (several thousands m/sec^2) when crashing into a fixed object, the damage being roughly proportional to the deceleration.

During controlled braking, decelerations of several m/sec^2 are achieved. If the brakes apply a deceleration of $1 m/sec^2$ (either because they are not more effective or because the rider does not apply more force), it will take 8.3sec to stop from an initial speed of 30km/h (20mph, or 8.3m/sec). The braking distance is then calculated as $v_{O2}/2a = 8.3 2/2 = 34.5m$.

If the deceleration is increased by more powerful braking, the braking time and distance become proportionally less. In practice, decelerations of $1—6m/sec^2$ are typical for the range from gentle speed reduction to hard braking, resulting in braking distances that range from 35 to 6m from an initial speed of 30km/h.

Another situation occurs when riding downhill. In this case, the bike also has a certain amount of *potential* energy, expressed as the product of weight and height (or mass, height and mass constant, or gravitational acceleration, G). Part of this energy is absorbed by the resistance of the air, mechanical friction and rolling of the tires. Any difference that remains between the resulting 'free fall' speed and the desired safe handling speed has to be taken up by the brakes. The steeper the slope, and the heavier the bike, the more energy has to be absorbed (or the more power has to be applied) to maintain the same speed, in addition to any speed reduction that may be required.

While braking, the effective mass center of bike and rider is transferred forward as shown in Fig. 12.3: The front wheel is loaded more, the rear wheel less. Due to the relatively high mass center and short wheel base, this imposes a severe limitation on the deceleration possible as distributed over the wheels, at least on the conventional bicycle. The maximum deceleration that can be reached with the front brake is approx. 6.5m/sec^2, while it is approx. 3.5m/sec^2 with the rear wheel. Anything in excess of those figures would lead to tipping forward and skidding of the rear wheel, respectively, both causing loss of control. To limit this effect as much as possible, the cyclist should place his body weight as low and as far back as possible during sudden braking, as shown in Fig. 12.5.

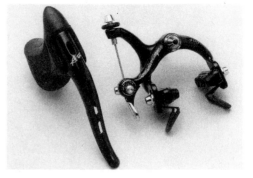

12.6. Gran-Compe lightweight racing sidepull brake. The levers are intended for cable routing along the handlebars.

The braking force required to achieve a certain deceleration can be calculated. The interesting thing is the insight gained that braking, like so many other bicycle phenomena, is not some kind of black magic, but can be rationally determined. Although the average cyclist will rarely feel the desire to figure such things out for himself, the calculation is shown here for reference. Here is the formula to determine the effective braking force that must be applied to the wheel to achieve a given deceleration:

$$F_b = m \times a / G$$

where:

F_b = the effective braking force in N that must be applied to the wheel
m   = the mass of bike and rider in kg
a   = the required acceleration in m/sec^2
G   = the gravitational acceleration (9.8m/sec^2 in most parts of the world)

12.7. Wilderness Trails roller-cam brake. Note the springs connecting the pivots with the rollers.

The force that can be achieved is calculated as follows:

$$F_b = C_f \times F_l \times S_l/S_b$$

where:

F_b = the effective braking force in N that can be achieved under the given circumstances
C_f = the coefficient of friction between brake block and rim
F_l = the force applied to the brake lever
S_l = the amount of travel of the brake lever
S_b = the amount of travel of the brake block

The ratio S_l/S_b is referred to as *mechanical advantage*. This is one of the most unscientific terms used in engineering — *leverage* would be more correct.

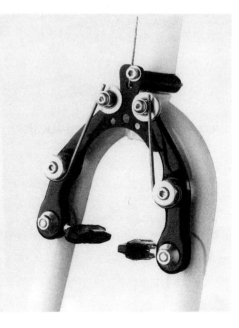

With these two formulas, the unknown factor can be computed. Any manufacturer worth his salt should take the trouble to verify whether the normal human

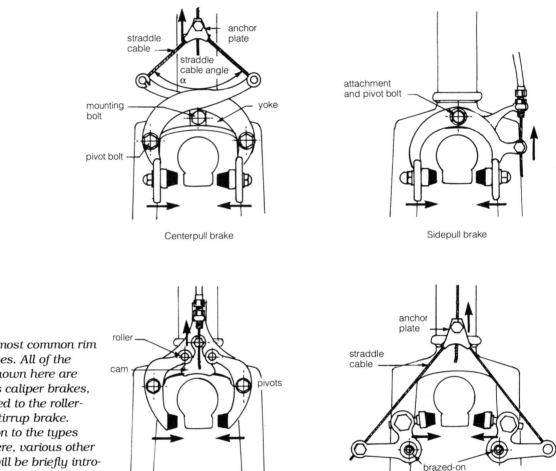

Centerpull brake

Sidepull brake

12.8.
The four most common rim brake types. All of the brakes shown here are known as caliper brakes, as opposed to the roller-lever or stirrup brake.
In addition to the types shown here, various other models will be briefly intro-duced in the sections that follow.

Roller cam brake

Cantilever brake

can apply enough braking force, or conversely to make sure parts are dimensioned correctly.

Brake Design and Construction

As should be clear from the preceding section, in order to brake more forcefully, it does not suffice to pull the brake lever more firmly. In addition, the components must be able to convert the force into friction between rim and brake block. The following factors come into play:

☐ Maximum coefficient of friction between the materials of brake block and rim
☐ Rigid (as opposed to deformable, or 'spungy') construction of brake, lever and braking surface
☐ Favorable relation between brake lever travel and brake caliper travel (mechanical advantage).

The coefficient of friction between natural rubber (as well as most synthetics and composites used for brake blocks) and steel or aluminum used for the rims is quite adequate when dry. However, the harder and smoother the surface of the rim, the more severely the friction is reduced when wet. Smooth hard anodized rims brake poorly when wet, and chrome-plated steel rims are a catastrophe when used with natural rubber or most synthetics. Even unanodized aluminum suffers greatly when wet: with the same applied force, the effective braking force on the wheel is reduced to less than 50%, resulting in half the deceleration or twice the braking distance.

The rigidity of the brake, the lever, the cable and any anchor points is important because all these factors could otherwise limit how much force can be applied. If the components bend, rather than transmitting the force directly to the contact point between rim and brake block, the amount of lever travel may not suffice to apply the force necessary for effective braking (note that neither force nor power gets lost, as is often suggested: it just limits how much force can be applied and consequently how powerful the resulting braking is). The first step to take when brakes feel 'spungy' is to replace the cable with a version that has a thick core and a stiff mantle.

The effective leverage, or mechanical advantage, between lever and brake should be selected with the dimensions of both parts in mind, as well as the size and the power of the rider's hand. Not enough leverage is just as bad as too much: in the first case not enough force is applied; in the latter, the distance of caliper travel is inadequate to apply the available force.

Rim brakes can be divided into two distinct categories: squeezing and pulling. The pulling type, represented by the roller-lever, or stirrup, brake with pull rod operation, is becoming increasingly rare, even in Britain, where it used to be standard equipment on most utility bicycles. All other brakes, referred to as caliper brakes, operate by squeezing against both sides of the rim simultaneously. The four most common types are shown in Fig. 12.8.

On all caliper brakes, the brake arms must return to the unactivated position when the handle is released. This is done by means of one or more springs. As will be explained more fully under *Brake Controls*, these springs are not always powerful enough to overcome the friction in brake, cable and lever. This has something to do with the fact that some manufacturers use

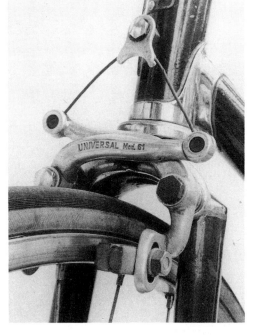

12.9. Universal centerpull brake. Unfortunately this one is no longer available.

Rim Brake Types

12.10. U-Brake with stiffening bracket to prevent twisting of the seat stays.

the method first introduced by Dia-Compe, integrating a spring in the lever as well. In this case, the spring in the brake need not do all of the work — but this brake must be used with the matching lever.

The Sidepull Brake

This is the most common brake on lightweight bicycles. On this model, the two brake arms pivot simultaneously around a common central mounting bolt. This type of brake is illustrated in Fig. 12.12, while Fig. 12.11 defines the critical dimensions that determine whether a particular brake will fit a certain bicycle. The inner cable is attached to one brake arm, while the outer cable is connected to the other. When applied, the cable pulls the lower brake arm up towards the other, causing the lower ends of the brake arms with the brake blocks to push from both sides against the sides of the rim. Generally, a quick-release is installed on one of the brake arms to untension or tension the cable for adjustment or wheel removal.

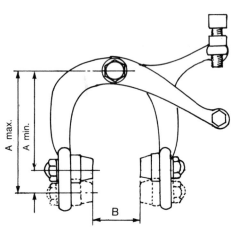

The inherent disadvantages of the sidepull brake are twofold: the distance between pivot and brake block is relatively great (with given overall dimensions), and the brake is hard to center. The first is overcome by building the bike on which this brake is used to such close clearances, using narrow rims and tires, that the dimensions remain small enough to assure adequate rigidity: fine for racing and fitness bikes. But this problem becomes apparent when a big version is used on a bike with fat tires and big clearances, as it is done on cruisers.

12.11, 12.12 and 12.13.
Above: Critical dimensions of sidepull brake.
Below: Off-set pivot type sidepull brake.
Right: Construction of sidepull brake.

Some recently introduced versions of the sidepull brake differ somewhat from traditional models. On these, the pivot point no longer coincides with the mounting bolt, being off-set to one side, while a support pad, off-set to

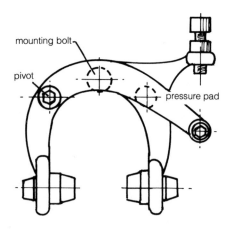

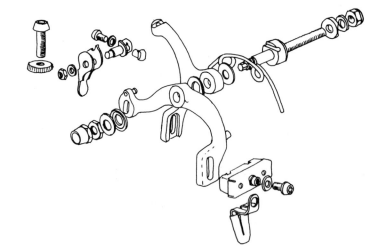

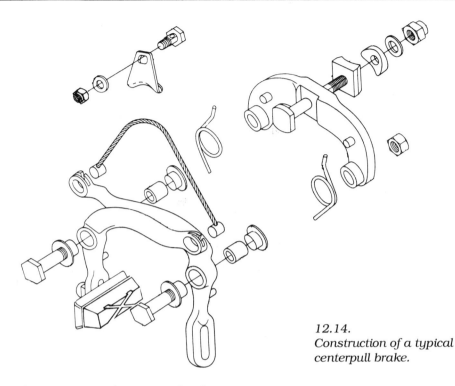

12.14.
Construction of a typical
centerpull brake.

the other side, supports the upper brake arm against the lower one (Fig. 12.14). This reduces the effective brake arm length that is free to flex.

This and some other models are sometimes equipped with ball bearings in the pivot. Although at first this may seem an unlikely location for a ball bearing, it turns out to be quite effective, being an axial bearing. It does not support the brake arm around the pivot bolt but the two brake arms relative to each other, where otherwise high contact forces cause considerable friction when the brakes are applied.

The Centerpull Brake

The centerpull brake, illustrated in Fig. 12.13, is a symmetrical model. Here the brake arms each pivot on their own bushings mounted at opposite ends of a common yoke, which in turn contains the central mounting bolt. The upper ends of the two brake arms are joined by means of a transverse (or straddle) cable to which the inner brake cable attaches, while the outer cable is anchored against an adjustable stop mounted on the frame. When the lever is applied, the upper ends of the brake arms are pulled together, causing the lower ends with the brake blocks to squeeze from both sides against the rim. The adjustment mechanism is contained in the anchor that holds

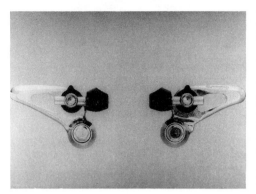

12.15. Shimano cantilever brake

the outer cable, which is generally installed at the headset or the saddle binder bolt, for front and rear brake, respectively. This brake works best if the angle of the straddle cable α is about 120˚.

As in the case of the sidepull brake, the critical dimensions of the centerpull brake are those illustrated in Fig. 12.11. Generally, the centerpull brake is designed for larger clearances and wider rims and tires. This is due to the more favorable (i.e. shorter) distances between the brake block and the pivot for each brake arm. It is important to keep the angle between the two legs of the transverse cable at least 120˚ to achieve adequate leverage. It is unfortunate that in recent years the centerpull brake has been largely ignored: the fashion of using sidepull brakes overlooks the fact that even a cheap centerpull brake offers superior braking and ease of maintenance to what can be achieved with the sidepull brake at the same price.

The Cantilever Brake

This model, formerly only used on cyclocross machines and tandems, has really taken over with the introduction of the mountain bike. Illustrated in Fig. 12.17, this symmetrical brake consists of two separate brake arms that are each mounted on a pivot bushing brazed or welded to the frame. The ends of the brake arms to which the transverse cable is attached reach outward, which makes these brakes protrude laterally beyond the rest of the bike. The critical dimensions are illustrated in Fig. 12.16.

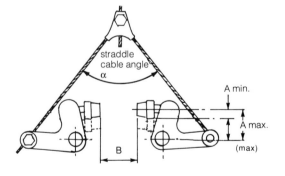

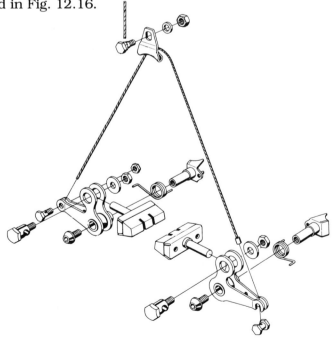

12.16 and 12.17.
Above: Critical dimensions of a cantilever brake.
Right: Construction of typical cantilever brake.

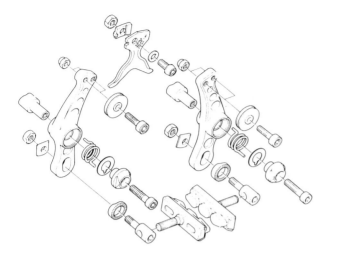

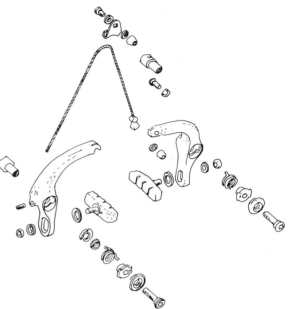

12.18 and 12.19. Construction details of cam-operated brake and U-brake. These two brake types were popular on mountain bikes for some years.

Just about everything said about the centerpull brake applies to this model as well. Once again, the angle between the two ends of the straddle cable must be at least 120° to allow enough leverage. This is particularly critical on some of the newer models that do not protrude outward as much. If a brake like this does not seem to work, just check and correct this feature and you will not believe how much difference it makes.

The adjusting mechanism for the cantilever brake is usually integrated in the brake lever. It is also possible to use an adjuster on the anchor that holds the end of the outer cable, as is the case on the centerpull brake. Most cantilever brakes have no quick-release as such: instead they are released by lifting one of the cable nipples out of the open-ended one of the brake arms, which can be done once the brake blocks are simultaneously pushed against the sides of the rim.

The cam-operated brake is based on an idea that surfaces every so many years: the brake arms are pushed apart by a roughly triangular-shaped cam plate attached to the end of the inner cable. In the late seventies, it was available from Shimano in the form of a self-contained caliper unit and was not exactly a big success in that form. In the mid eighties, another version was introduced by that group of creative California mountain bike engineers that call themselves Wilderness Trails, that has since been licensed to SunTour.

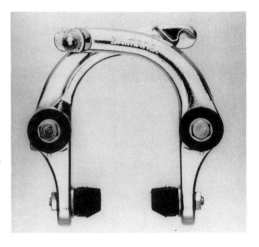

12.20. Shimano U-brake

The Cam-Operated Brake

On this version, the brake arms are mounted on individual bosses, just like the U-brake and the cantilever brake. Illustrated in Fig. 12.18, the critical dimension are the same as those shown in Fig. 12.16 for the cantilever brake. Another version of this brake is the Odyssey, on which the brake arms are installed on a common mounting plate again. It is very suitable for use on BMX-bikes and wherever space is limited, such as on other small-wheeled bicycles (it is the only brake suitable for the Moulton mountain bike with small wheels and suspension).

The U-Brake

The U-brake, illustrated in Fig. 12.19, is essentially a centerpull brake on which the pivots are not installed on a yoke but are brazed or welded to the fork blades or rear stays for front and rear brake, respectively. In many ways, what was said about the cantilever brake applies here too, except that this model does not protrude as far on both sides of the bike. The critical dimensions are as shown in Fig. 12.16. The mounting boss location is different from that for the cantilever, so these brakes are not mutually interchangeable.

The Pivot-Link Brake

Never heard of this? It's the generic term I use to describe the rather rare models operating by means of a complex linkage mechanism as illustrated in Fig. 12.22. Campagnolo's Delta brake, which forms part of that company's top-of-the line C-Record group, is one — very sleek and expensive. Weinmann makes a cheap (and generally unsatisfactory) version based on the same concept. As Fig. 12.21 shows, it's an old idea.

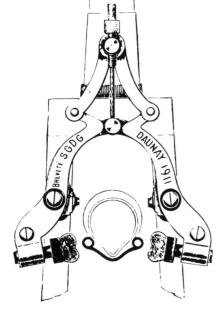

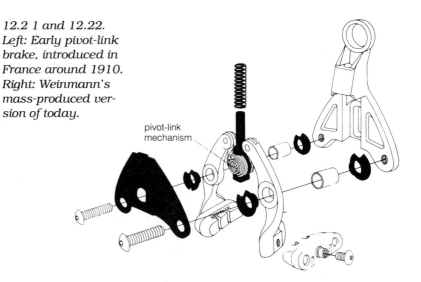

12.2 1 and 12.22.
Left: Early pivot-link brake, introduced in France around 1910. Right: Weinmann's mass-produced version of today.

pivot-link
mechanism

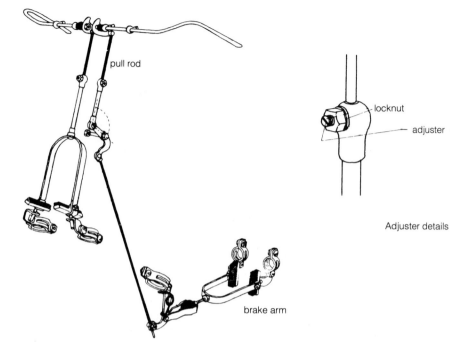

pull rod

brake arm

locknut

adjuster

Adjuster details

12.23 and 12.24.
Left: Roller-lever,
or stirrup, brake
assembly.
Right: Typical ad-
justing details for
this kind of brake.

The Roller-Lever Brake

Instead of cable-operation and two-sided force application against the sides of the rim, this brake, also
known as stirrup brake, is characterized by pull rod
operation and the application of force radially towards
the inside of the rim, as illustrated in Fig. 12.23. The
rigid rods allow very effective force application, and little maintenance is required. On the other hand, the
weight is nearly twice that of typical side-pull brakes,
each including their respective controls. You have to
loosen and readjust the brake controls to adjust the
handlebars — not to mention removing the wheel.

In recent years, both Magura and Mathauser have introduced very satisfactory hydraulic brakes. The
former, made by a renowned German motorcycle brake
specialist and illustrated in Fig. 12.25, is actually
surprisingly affordable. Their recently improved mountain bike version now incorporates a quick-release,
making this a very interesting alternative.

On the hydraulic brake, the force is transmitted by
compressing a liquid. The Mathauser brake uses a
flexible bellows unit contained in an unsealed cylinder,
whereas conventional hydraulic brakes use a hydraulic
cylinder, often leading to leakage. Compared to cable
controls, hydraulics have the advantage of very direct,
rigid and light operation, with negligeable friction. The
argument that damage to the liquid-filled tube connect-

The Hydraulic Brake

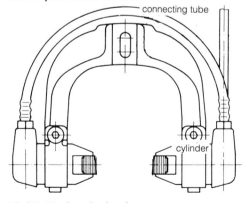

connecting tube

cylinder

12.25. Hydraulic brake

179

12.26 and 12.27. Two modern hydraulic brakes. Left: Mathauser's lightweight brake has an internal bellows, eliminating leak. Right: Magura's affordable mountain bike model.

ing brake lever and brake unit seems far fetched: these tubes are not particularly sensitive and should last a long time with normal use. After all, regular brakes also don't work when the cable brakes. It should not be your choice for a world tour (on a trip like that you only want conventional equipment that can be repaired or replaced anywhere), but it is fine for normal use.

The Spindle Brake

This is another rare item, illustrated in Fig 12.28 and developed by the Swiss-German bicycle brake specialist Weinmann. Here the cable turns a spindle with a helical groove that then pushes the brake blocks against the rim. Since there is not less but more friction in this set-up than in conventional caliper brakes, there is not the slightest technical justification for their use.

Brake Controls

With the exception of the hydraulic brake and the roller-lever type, all rim brakes are operated by means of a bowden cable that connects the lever with the brake mechanism. A typical brake lever is illustrated in Fig. 12.31. The inner cable's end nipple is hooked in a recess in the lever, while the other end is clamped in at a movable part of the brake. The outer cable is anchored against the fixed part of the lever on one end and either a stop on the frame or one on the fixed part of the brake mechanism on the other end. Sometimes the outer cable is not continuous but consists of interrupted sections installed between stops on the frame.

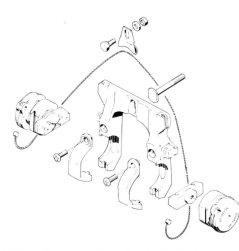

There are several different brake levers, each designed for a particular model of handlebars. The most significant difference is between those made for drop handlebars and those for mountain bikes, the latter being shown in Fig. 12.32. These would be suitable on any kind of straight handlebars, although cruisers, three-speeds and other utility bikes usually come with more primitive and less sturdy versions.

12.28. Construction of spindle brake

There are several variants. In the first place, there are

models with a built-in retraction spring as mentioned before, intended for use with matching brakes with weaker return springs. Secondly, it has become fashionable to use so-called aero levers, on which the cables don't project from the front but are run along the handlebars under the handlebar tape.

Then there are those with extension levers, shown in Fig. 12.33 and often incorrectly referred to as safety levers. Although they are not inherently dangerous, they are not particularly safe either. The auxiliary lever can be reached from the top of drop handlebars, a position frequently used by inexperienced cyclists. Unfortunately, these auxiliary levers are not rigid enough to allow the application of full force: they simply bend. Their other disadvantage is that they interfere with another, more suitable, hand position, namely 'on the hoods' — i.e. on top of the brake lever mounts. A better solution for those who want to reach their brakes from the tops of the bars are the French *guidonnet* levers, shown in Fig. 12.35.

Finally on this subject, a few words about the roller-lever brake. Operated by pull rods, it relies on a number of pivots mounted on the frame and several adjusting connectors between rods. The attachment of the pivot mechanisms to the handlebars, the frame and the front fork must be checked occasionally. These brakes are adjusted by means of the rod connectors.

A distinction should be made between brake blocks and brake shoes: the former is essentially only the piece of friction material, the latter includes mounting hardware. Nowadays, one rarely finds replaceable brake blocks, so that the entire shoe usually has to be replaced when the brake block is worn. Not all brake shoes fit all brakes. Some manufacturers cleverly design them to match, often precluding replacement by other makes and models. In addition, there are essentially two types, respectively adjustable in one and mul-

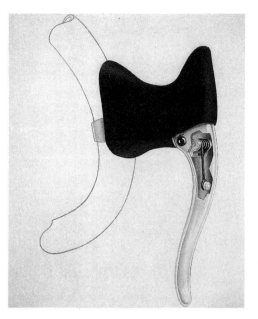

12.29 Dia Compe racing brake lever with return spring for light action.

Brake Shoes

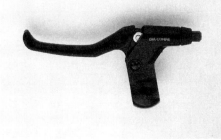

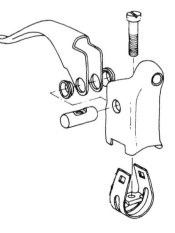

12.30 and 12.31. Left: Dia-Compe mountain bike brake lever. Right: Assembly of typical brake lever for drop handlebar bike

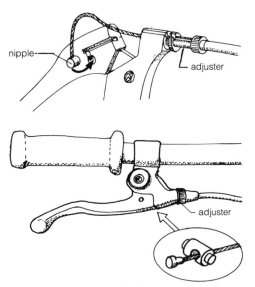

12.32. Mountain bike lever with cable nipple and adjuster detail.

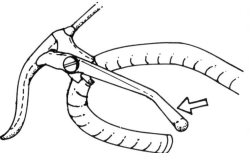

12.33. Extension lever

12.34. Magura lever for hydraulically operated mountain bike brake.

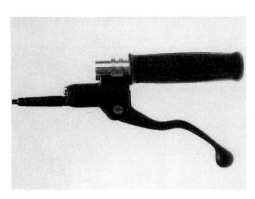

tiple planes, referred to as directly and indirectly mounted, respectively, and illustrated in Fig. 12.41.

On the directly mounted brake shoe, the mounting stud is screw threaded and is held in the brake arm by a nut (or, alternately, the brake shoe has a threaded hole and is mounted by means of a bolt). On the indirectly mounted version, the stud is plain and is held in a kind of eye bolt that is in turn mounted in the brake arm. Although the latter design allows more flexibility of adjustment, the use of concave and convex washers in combination with direct mounting can achieve similar flexibility and is used on many mountain bike brakes.

The material used for the brake blocks is either natural rubber, a synthetic material, or a composite of several materials. Natural rubber is quite poor, especially in wet weather, as pointed out before. Some of the synthetics give higher friction coefficients, but those that work better in wet weather operate poorly when it is dry. The only universally satisfactory material for use on aluminum rims seems to be the sintered material first introduced by Modolo, which is being picked up by some other manufacturers as well now.

Some of the other supposed improvements are mere farces. Brake shoes with cooling fins are a typical example. While braking, the heat is mainly absorbed by the rim, which gives it off to the air. Although the brake blocks get hot too, the measured effect of external fins is just about zero: the heat transfer from the brake block surface to the metal of the shoe is so poor that this does not provide effective cooling.

Another fallacy is the assumption that longer brake blocks, or any other design that offers more contact area, would be more effective. The friction is a function of the force and the coefficient of friction, and the area has no effect. Although the larger brake block may wear better, the braking may even be worse, since the contact pressure is inversely proportional to the area, which may lead to vibrations and to the build-up of water between rim and brake block in wet weather.

Braking a bike with steel rims is a different kettle of fish altogether. When dry, this material works as well as aluminum, except that some of the homogeneous synthetics tend to leave deposits on it and are therefore not recommended. But when it gets wet, trying to brake such a bike becomes a true adventure: the coefficient of friction is reduced to about 25% of its dry weather value, resulting in dramatically increased braking distances. Although Fibrax and Altenburger offer special materials for use on steel rims (which may never be used on aluminum because they are extremely abrasive), the use of hub brakes, described in Chapter 13, is a better solution for bikes with steel rims.

From a maintenance standpoint, the brakes should be considered as complete systems, each incorporating the levers, the control cables and the various pieces of mounting hardware, as well as the brake itself. In fact, brake problems are most often due to inadequacies of some component in the control system. Consequently, it will be necessary to approach the problem systematically, trying to isolate the fault by checking off one component after the other.

When the brakes work inconsistently, often associated with vibrations or squealing, the cause is frequently found either in dirt and grease on the rims, or in loose mounting hardware. First check the condition of the rims, then the attachments of brake blocks, brake arms, brake units, cables, anchors and levers. If the rim is dented, there is usually no other solution than to replace it, while all other causes can usually be eliminated quite easily.

This simple job is often not only the solution to squealing, rumbling or vibrating noises, but may also solve inadequate braking performance and prevent serious mishaps. As it wears, the brake block's position relative to the rim changes. On a cantilever brake the brake block moves radially inward, further away from the tire towards the spokes, while it moves up towards the tires on all other brakes. If left unchecked, chances are the brake blocks will hit the spokes or the tire.

To prevent this, it is not enough to follow the systematic brake test described below regularly: you also have to check the position of the brake blocks as they contact the rim, and readjust them when they don't align as shown in Fig. 12.40. In addition, it is preferable if the front end of the brake block is about 1—2mm closer to the rim than the rear. This is to compensate for the deformation of the brake arm as brake force is applied, which tends to twist the back of the brake shoe in. Only when you adjust them this way, called *toed in*, will the brake force be equally distributed over the entire length of the brake block.

In order to verify their condition and effectiveness, test the brakes according to the following systematic procedure at regular intervals — about once a month under normal conditions. The idea is to establish whether the

Brake Maintenance

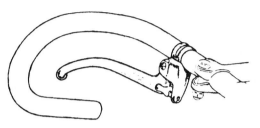

12.35. 'Guidonnet' lever

Adjust Brake Shoes

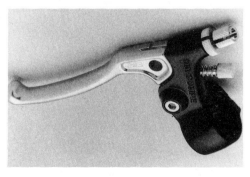

12.36. BMX freestyle brake lever. The adjusting screw allows the rider to limit the brake force by reducing the lever travel.

Brake Test

12.37. *Aztec composite brake blocks*

Brake Check

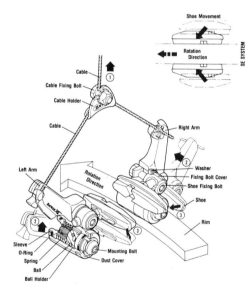

12.38. *SunTour's Petersen self-energizing brake. Wheel rotation energy queezes the brake against the rim.*

Adjust Brake

deceleration achieved with each brake is as high as the physical constraints of the bicycle's geometry will allow. Tools are not needed for this test.

Procedure:
1. Ride the bike at a brisk walking speed (about 8km/h, or 5MPH) on a straight, level surface without traffic.
2. Apply the rear brake hard. If the rear wheel skids, you have all the braking you can use in the rear, reaching a deceleration of $3.5m/sec^2$.
3   Repeat the procedure with the front brake. If the rear wheel starts to lift off, a deceleration of $6.5m/sec^2$ has been reached. Let go of the front brake again.

If one brake or the other flunks the test described above, check the entire brake system and adjust or correct as necessary. Usually, no tools are needed for this inspection, but you may have to use a variety of items to solve individual problems uncovered this way.

Procedure:
1. Check to make sure the rim and the brake blocks are clean. The presence of wet or greasy dirt plays havoc. Wipe clean or degrease the rim or scrape the brake block with steel wire wool.
2. Check whether the cables move freely and are not pinched or damaged. In the case of special controls, such as hydraulics or pull rods, check them for correct operation and installation. Clean, free and lubricate or replace cables that don't move freely. Repair or replace anything else found wanting.
3. Inspect the levers — they must be firmly installed and there must be at least 2cm (¾") clearance between lever and handlebars when the brake is applied fully. If necessary, tighten, lubricate, adjust.
4. Make sure the brake arms themselves are free to move without resistance, and that they are returned to clear the wheel fully by the spring tension when the lever is released. If necessary, loosen, adjust, lubricate, overhaul or replace.

Roughly the same operation is followed for all caliper brakes, although the adjustment mechanisms may be installed in different positions. By way of tools, it is handy to have a pair of needle nose pliers to adjust a centerpull brake, while you may need a wrench to fit the cable clamping nut on all models.

Procedure:
1. If the brake does not perform adequately, the cable tension has to be increased. Do that initially by tightening the cable adjuster by two turns (it may be easier to first release tension with the quick-release or by removing the nipple of the transverse cable, not forgetting to tension the cable again afterwards).
2. Verify whether the brake now engages fully when 2cm (¾") clearance remains between lever and handlebars. Repeat point 1 if necessary.
3. If the correct adjustment cannot be achieved within the adjusting range of the cable adjuster, first screw it in all the way, then pull the cable further in the clamping bolt and tighten it again. On the centerpull brake this can be done by wrapping the cable around the needle nose pliers and twisting it further as illustrated in the photograph. Now fine-tune with the adjuster.
4. If after all this adjusting the brake finally applies enough tension but does not clear the rim adequately when disengaged, check all parts of the system and replace or overhaul as necessary.

12.39. Holding centerpull brake cable

One of the most frustrating problems can be the off-centered position of a brake, always dragging the rim on one side while clearing it on the other. Depending on the kind of brake, this problem is solved differently.

Centerpull Brake:
1. First make sure the brake is firmly attached, tightening the mounting bolt if necessary, while holding the brake centered.
2. If the brake is properly fastened and still off-set, take a big screwdriver and a hammer. Place the screwdriver on the pivot point that is too high and hit it with the hammer.
3. Repeat or correct until the brake is centered.

Sidepull Brake:

Here the problem is due to the stubbornness of the mounting bolt, always twisting back into a rotational orientation by which the brake is not centered. Straightening is easier said than done: it will find its way back to this wrong position the next time the brake is applied. Some brake models come with a special adjusting tool with which the mounting bolt is repositioned, each of them with its own instructions.

On simpler models, no tool is provided, and the proce-

Center Rim Brake

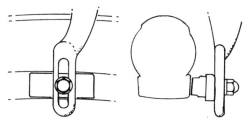

12.40. Brake block alignment detail

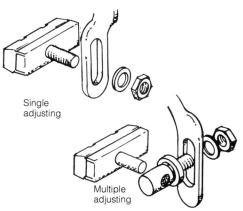

Single adjusting

Multiple adjusting

12.41. Brake block attachment details

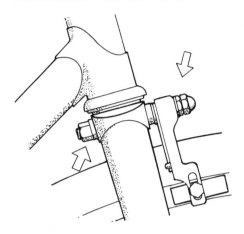

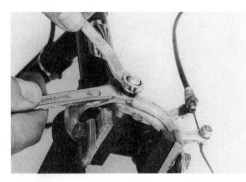

12.42 and 12.43. Left: Details (left) and method (right) used to center simple sidepull brake.

dure illustrated in Figures 12.42 and 12.43 may do the trick, always turning two nuts simultaneously. To twist the brake clockwise (seen from the top of the brake), turn the top nut and the one in the back. To twist it counterclockwise, use the second nut in the front and the one in the back. There is also a universal tool called Take-a-Brake that may work on brakes without their own specific centering tool: place each of the pins inside a loop of the spring and twist in the appropriate direction.

If after all this the problem remains or returns, install a flat, thin steel washer between the brake body and the fork or rear stay bridge (or the shaped spacer installed there). This will provide a smooth 'unbiased' surface that can be twisted into the desired position, rather than getting stuck in existing incorrect indentations.

Cantilever Brake:

On this kind of brake, the solution is usually rather primitive: simply bend one of the springs that spread the brake levers in or out a little using needle nose pliers. In other cases, there is a hexagonal recess in one of the pivots that is turned one way or the other, tensioning a spring that is hidden inside the bushing.

U-Brake:

This type usually has a small adjusting screw in one of the brake arms that can be turned in a little to bring that arm in, or out to bring the opposite brake arm in towards the rim.

Roller-Cam Brake:

This is the most popular form of what I generically refer to as a cam-operated brake. These usually have a similar adjusting screw on one of the brake arms that is turned in or out to center the brake arms.

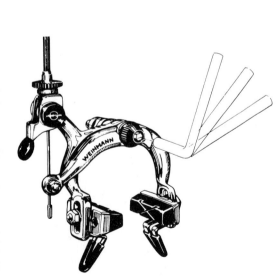

12.43. Use of Weinmann centering tool

Chapter 13

Hub Brakes

Although not used very much on quality bicycles these days, the alternative way of stopping a moving vehicle by means of brakes contained in the wheel hubs remains of considerable technical interest. Used on virtually all other vehicles in some form or another, hub brakes can't be all wrong. Besides the coaster brake, which is operated by pedaling backward, there are several other brakes that are built into the wheel. All these will be covered in the present chapter: drum brake, disk brake, roller brake, band brake and expansion-contraction brake. Except for the former two, which are popular mainly in Europe, the others are primarily known as Japanese products.

The advantage of any hub brake is its insensitivity to rain, sleet and snow: being tucked away nicely inside, these banes to the conventional rim brake don't have a negative effect on their performance. Their disadvantage is mainly in the mind: it's not considered *cool* to have anything except what is in fashion, and clearly rim brakes are *in*. Technically, they all have minor problems, but they remain interesting alternatives, as was recently demonstrated in a decent from one of Europe's steepest and longest mountain roads, where Sachs-Huret's drum brakes performed superbly.

The common technical disadvantage of all these brakes is that the braking force is applied far from the most effective point (the circumference of the wheel), so it has to overcome the leverage of the distance between the hub and the outside. Furthermore, the braking force must be transmitted via the spokes, while the countereffect is taken up via a restraint that works on an inherently weak point of the bike — the fork blades or the rear stays. All these problems can be solved through the correct selection of dimensions and components. And let's not forget: all other components on the bike also have some problems.

Except for the coaster brake and the roller brake, all these brakes are operated just like rim brakes by means of cables, although pull rod systems are available for some drum brakes. The simplicity of pedaling back to stop with the coaster brake and the roller brake may be very appealing, in reality these are a real nuisance, since they make it impossible for the rider to pedal backward to place the pedals in the right position

13.1. Sturmey-Archer Elite aluminum drum brake for the front wheel. Matching units are available for the rear.

13.2. Fichtel &Sachs coaster brake with built-in automatic two-speed gearing mechanism.

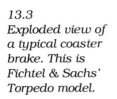

13.3
*Exploded view of
a typical coaster
brake. This is
Fichtel & Sachs'
Torpedo model.*

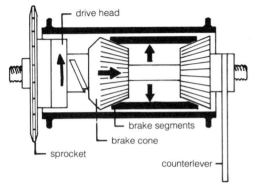

13.4. Coaster brake operating principle

The Coaster Brake

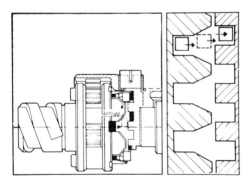

*13.5. This clutch on the Fichtel & Sachs
coaster brakes with gearing assures
that the brake remains functional even
with the gears out of adjustment.*

Coaster Brake Maintenance

to start off. In practice, this is a more serious problem than the often stated fact that the cranks have to be rotated into the correct position before you can brake.

Generalizing, it can be said that the bigger the brake, the more satisfactory it will be. Bigger brakes have large cooling surfaces. On the rim brake, it is the wheel rim that acts as cooling surface, while it is the outside of the hub on most hub brakes. Checking the size of some coaster brakes and particularly the roller brake, one appreciates that these things, designed for rear wheel use, cannot be suitable for longer descents. So they should always be used in combination with another brake on the front wheel.

Fig. 13.4 illustrates the principle of the world's most popular coaster brake. Although some models work differently, none are as simple, powerful and reliable as Fichtel & Sachs' Torpedo brake, which is shown in an exploded view in Fig 13.3 in its simplest form — other models have built-in 3- or 5-speed gear mechanisms. Modern versions of the Bendix brakes, the traditional US make, work on the same principle.

The Torpedo brake incorporates an interesting frictionless freewheel mechanism illustrated in Fig. 13.6. When you stop pedaling forward, the rollers of the freewheel drop down into the lower position, disengaging the interior from the forward rotating hub shell. When pedaling back, this position of the freewheel rollers allows continued wheel rotation, but at the same time the backward rotation forces the brake cone up a helical groove towards the right, pushing out the segmented brake mantle against the inner braking surface of the hub shell. The resulting friction absorbs the energy and decelerates the wheel. The resulting forces are countered by means of a brake counterlever that connects the fixed center with the LH chain stay.

The major maintenance described here will be adjustment of the wheel bearings and other bearing work. Coaster brakes tend to run hot when used vigorously over longer distances. In extreme cases, the lubricant burns out of the bearings. If this happens, it is usually sufficient to partly disassemble the bearings and repack them, using the manufacturer's recommended special hight-temperature grease.

From time to time, check the bearings as described for the regular hub. If they are too loose or tight, adjust them without removing the wheel from the bike. Use the special wrench supplied with the bike or the brake hub (or order it through a bike shop). Refer to Fig. 13.7.

Procedure:
1. Loosen the LH axle nut 2—3 turns.
2. Loosen the round locknut with recesses about one turn.
3. If the hub is equipped with a square end on the RH axle end, turn it clockwise to loosen the axle, counterclockwise to tighten it.
4. On models without a square axle end, such as those with built-in gearing, remove the locknut altogether and loosen the underlying shaped plate that engages the cone: to the left to loosen, the right to tighten the bearing.
5. Tighten first the locknut, countering at the axle or the shaped plate, then the axle nut.

This type of brake is available for both the front wheel and the rear wheel, the latter in versions with built-in hub gearing or with screw thread for the installation of a regular freewheel block with multiple sprockets for derailleur gearing.

Fig. 13.10 shows how this thing works, while an exploded view of a typical one is depicted in Fig. 13.12. When the brake lever is applied, the attached cam pushes the brake segments apart against the interior of the drum on the hub shell. The resulting friction absorbs the energy, slowing the bike, while the counterlever fixes the interior against the fork or rear stays. This counterlever must be quite substantial, as disastrous experiences with early models have proven: they tended to crumple up, as did some of the frames that were not designed for the high local forces.

The material of the brake segment linings should not come in contact with lubricants, since that reduces friction dramatically. This is often a problem on Sturmey-Archer's models with built in hub gearing, since they lack a seal between the two parts. If this happens, get the brake segments relined (or exchanged) by an automotive brake specialist.

Adjust Hub Bearings

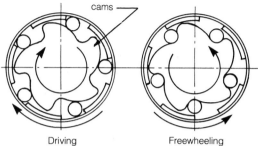

cams

Driving   Freewheeling

13.6. Frictionless freewheel on Fichtel & Sachs coaster brake.

The Drum Brake

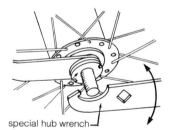

special hub wrench

13.7. Loosening or tightening the lockring on a coaster brake bearing.

13.8. Torpedo coaster brake by Fichtel & Sachs.

Fading

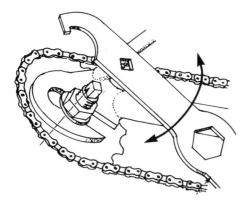

13.9. Adjust bearing play

Drum Brake Maintenance

Adjust Drum Brake

The drum brake, whether used on bikes, cars or motor cycles, is quite sensitive to a phenomenon called fading. During long descents, the brake heats up and causes the drum to expand away from the brake liner. As the diameter increases, the surfaces of the two don't match anymore, leading to a drastically reduced braking effect. The problem is minimized by intermittent front and rear wheel braking, allowing the other one to cool off after every half minute of application.

A related problem that applies to all commercially available drum brakes is the fact that the liners wear asymmetrically, due to the one-sided pivoted arrangement. Since one of the segments spreads in the direction of rotation, the other one in the opposite direction, unfavorable wear results, and the brakes not only become less effective during long descents, but gradually become less effective over their lifespan as well.

The brake's effectiveness is verified as was described for the rim brake in Chapter 12. Other maintenance operations include adjustment of the cable (or in a control rod on models so operated) and bearing adjustment and maintenance, as well as exchanging the segments when the liners are worn or contaminated. In the latter case, disassemble and remove the old segments which can be exchanged by a brake specialist.

Essentially, this is done as on any other hand-operated brake. The cable adjuster is used to increase the cable tension if the brake does not engage properly, and is loosened if it does not clear when the lever is released. As with the rim brake, the cable, the lever, the guides and the anchors must be checked first, since these points are the most frequent causes of improper operation. If necessary they must be cleaned, freed, lubricated or replaced when adjustment does not have the desired effect.

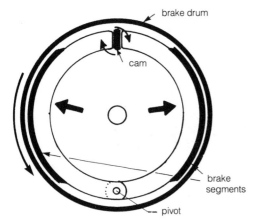

13.10 and 13.11.
Left: Operating
principle of drum
brake.
Right: Sachs-Huret
drum brake for
mountain bike use.
On bikes with
front suspension,
this is a good
brake to use.

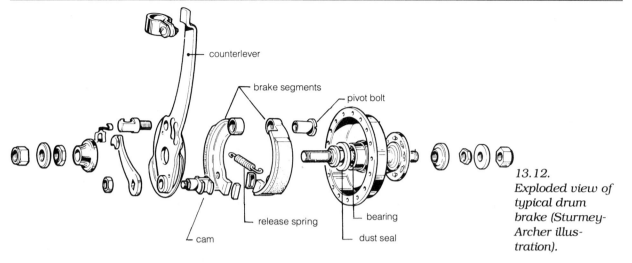

13.12.
Exploded view of typical drum brake (Sturmey-Archer illustration).

The need for this is established as described in Chapter 8 for the regular hub. All you need is a wrench and the special hub wrench that may be available for the particular model. Fig. 13.14 shows the parts that are affected, while the wheel may be left on the bike.

Procedure:
1. Loosen the axle nut on the control side by 3—4 turns.
2. Loosen the locknut by 1—2 turns, and lift the lock washer.
3. The adjusting plate, which engages the bearing cone, can now be turned to the right to tighten the bearings, or to the left to loosen them.
4. Hold the adjusting plate while tightening the locknut.
5. Tighten the axle nut, making sure the wheel is properly centered.
6. Check and repeat the adjustment if necessary.

This can become necessary when the bearings or brake liners are so far worn or damaged that adjusting does not solve the problem. The wheel must be removed from the bike, also disengaging the control cable and removing the bolt that holds the counterlever to the fork or the chain stay. Refer to Fig. 13.12 for the way the hub is assembled.

Disassembly procedure:
1. Loosen the locknut completely and remove the lock washer.
2. Loosen the cone by means of the adjusting plate (or, after removing the latter, by means of a wrench), and remove it.

Adjust Hub Bearings

13.13. Sturmey-Archer rear wheel drum brake for use with derailleur gearing (a standard six-speed freewheel block can be installed).

Overhaul Drum Brake

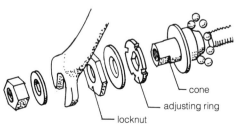

13.14. Bearing adjustment detail

13.14. Coupled pull-rod operation of both drum brakes from either brake lever, as used on a Dutch utility bike.

3. Remove the mounting plate on which the entire mechanism is installed, while catching the bearing balls, which are usually contained in a retainer.

Maintenance and reassembly:
1. Clean and inspect all components:
   ☐ Replace the brake segments if they are worn down to less than 3mm (⅛") in any location or when they are contaminated with oil and simply roughing them with steel wire wool does not restore them;
   ☐ Replace the ball bearings with their retainer and any other bearing components that are damaged (pitted, grooved, corroded);
2. Fill the bearing cups with bearing grease and push the bearing balls into the cups.
3. Apply just a little grease to the pivot and the cam on which the brake segments sit.
4. Wipe excess grease away to make sure it cannot reach the brake liners or brake mantle.
5. Install the mounting plate with the installed brake segments.
6. Screw the cone in and tighten it with the aid of the adjusting plate.
7. Install the lock washer and the locknut, while holding the adjusting plate so it does not turn.
8. Check the bearing and adjust as necessary.
9. Once the wheel is installed, check brake operation and adjust the cable tension if necessary.

Other Hub Brakes

All other types of hub brakes will be covered only for interest's sake. Due to their variety, no detailed maintenance instructions can be given here. Even so, with a

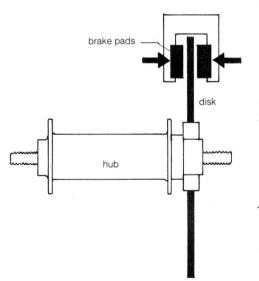

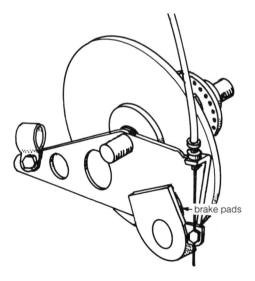

13.15 and 13.16. Left: Operating principle of disk brake (basically, it works like a caliper rim brake, except that the braking surface is flat and rigid and closer to the center of the wheel). Right: Overall view of a typical disk brake.

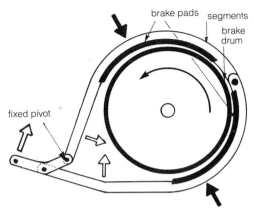

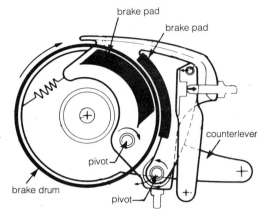

13.17 and 13.18. Two unconventional hub brakes. Left: Operating principle of simple band brake. Right: Operating principle of contraction-expansion brake (essentially a drum brake and a band brake in one).

little imagination and experience, gained on other bike maintenance operations, it will generally be possible to figure out what to do and how to go about it.

Separate Drum Brake

This is a variant of the drum brake that is not an integral part of the hub but is screwed on the threaded end of a special hub by the same maker — usually Araya. It is intended only for use on the rear wheel, and its most common application is on tandems. Everything said about the conventional drum brake applies here too.

The Disk Brake

Fig. 13.15 shows the principle of the disk brake, while Fig. 13.16 illustrates a typical model made for bicycle use. These too are generally of Oriental origin, although some American manufacturers, such as Phil Wood, also offer them. Basically, the rim brake works on the same principle, except that on the real disk brake the disk is smaller and more solid. Since the disk and the brake pads are designed to run hot, this brake can be quite effective, although it does have a tendency to grab, unless used very gingerly. If you clean the disk occasionally, it will work a long time before the pads have to be replaced. Pad wear is checked by means of a reference mark visible from a viewing port. Any brake specialist can replace the pads when they are worn.

The Band Brake

Seen mainly in the Far East, this is essentially a drum brake turned inside-out. As shown in Fig 13.17, a strap wiath brake shoes is pulled inward against the exterior of a brake drum. Although it is a remarkably powerful brake, it suffers from overheating on longer descents because the surface that heats up is not directly exposed to the cooling air. This feature makes it inferior to the contracting drum brakes and most other rim and hub brakes.

13.19 and 13.20. Left: Bridgestone Dynex contraction-expansion brake. Right: Band brake on Japanese utility bicycle.

The Contraction-Expansion Brake

This rare bird is sold by Bridgestone under the designation Dynex. As illustrated in Fig. 13.18, it combines the principles of the drum brake and the band brake, simultaneously pushing and pulling brake shoes against both the inside and the outside of a heavy brake drum directly connected to a mounting plate with cooling fins. It works very well, due largely to the fact that the effect of fading in the one mode is compensated by increased braking force in the other.

The Roller Brake

A little rear brake that is found primarily on Formula-1 kid's bikes. Its operating principle is shown in Fig. 13.21 and corresponds to that of the unique freewheel used in Fichtel & Sachs' coaster brakes. When pedaling back, the rollers travel up the inclined recesses and contact the brake mantle. It works very well for short-time braking but is unsafe for longer descents due to overheating on account of the brake's miniscule cooling surface.

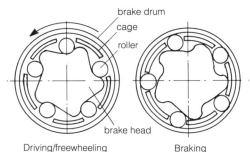

13.21. Operating principle of roller brake

Chapter 14

Accessories

This chapter is devoted to the equipment that can be used on the bicycle but is not essential for its operation at all times. Some machines are devoid of all such accessories, while others are generously equipped with items ranging from luggage racks to lights, water bottles, fenders and computers. Although there is little doubt that the naked bike is the more enjoyable one to ride, circumstances often dictate a need for one accessory or another.

As regards selection and maintenance of accessories, the most important advice is to select only items that can be firmly attached to the bike and are in themselves structurally sound. Racks that swing back and forth, bend under the load or slip down the frame are dangerous and frustrating. Other items only work well if they are themselves properly designed and constructed. Basically, everything that is not attached in at least two points will tend to come loose, although very light items may be clamped less firmly — but only if they are held very close to the member they are attached to.

Simply clamped items are likely to slip down along the tubes of the frame if they are not specially secured. This problem can be eliminated by first sticking a patch from the tire patch kit around the location where the accessory will be mounted, as shown in Fig. 14.2. Use rubber solution on the tube just as though you were patching a tube. It will prevent not only slip, but also damage to the frame. The same effect cannot be achieved by means of self-adhesive tape (e.g. handlebar tape), since this tends to slip because the adhesive never hardens enough to form a permanent bond.

For accessories that should be easily removed from the bike, be it because they are not usually needed or to avoid theft, it is often possible to make some kind of quick-release attachment. In cases where this is not practical, it is still possible to ease installation or removal by means of e.g. wing bolts, which may be made by soldering a sizeable washer in the slot of a screw bolt per Fig. 14.1, if not commercially available in the right size.

Of all the accessories, lighting equipment is probably the most important: lighting defects (or missing lights)

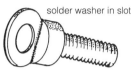

solder washer in slot

14.1. Home-made wing bolt for removable accessory installation.

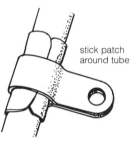

stick patch around tube

14.2. Installation of provisional clamp around frame tube or stay.

14.3. The author at work testing lighting systems. — during a lighthearted interlude. No better use could be found for the two leg lights at the side of his head.

Lighting Systems

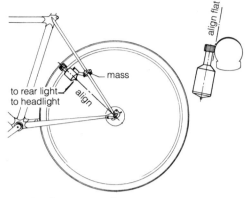

14.4. Alignment of generator

Generator Lighting

14.5. Connecting details of generator

are the only technical defects that cause a significant percentage of all serious bicycle accidents. The major problem is that many cyclists are so scared of riding in the dark that they swear never to do it, and consequently feel no need to install lights. Invariably, they get caught in situations where lights are necessary — and risk it anyway. Others use their lights so rarely that they fail to maintain them properly.

Basically, there are two different types of lighting systems: generator (or dynamo) and battery powered. In addition, there are hybrid systems that combine elements of the two systems, as well as different battery-operated variants, namely with the battery either built in the individual lights or centrally located and connected to the lights by means of wiring. Finally, reflectors can fulfill certain lighting functions and can be considered as secondary lighting systems. Below, each of these systems will be treated separately.

Fig. 14.3 shows a typical generator lighting system. It consists of an electric generator, or dynamo, which generates electricity when it contacts a moving part of the wheel, connected to a headlight and a tail light. One pole of the electric circuit is connected by means of insulated electric wires, while the metal of the bike acts as the second pole via mass contacts between the frame and the mounting hardware of generator and lights. The bulbs in headlight and tail light have a rather limited life expectancy (on the order of 50—100 hours of operation) and are usually simple to replace.

Most generators work by means of a roller that contacts the side of the tire. To minimize slip, wear and

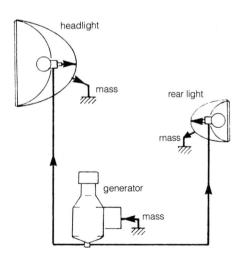

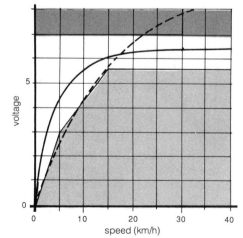

14.6 and 14.7.
Left: Wiring diagram for typical generator lighting system.
Right: Electrical criteria for generator performance (see text for explanation).

resistance, it is critically important to align the center-line through the generator perfectly with the wheel axle. In the other plane, the roller should lie flat on the tire sidewall when engaged and retract about 1cm (⅜") when disengaged. These criteria are illustrated in Fig. 14.7.

The best place to mount the conventional generator is on the LH side of the rear wheel, pointing forward from the LH seat stay. In this position, it is not likely to get caught in the spokes if it should come loose, nor does it get in the way or obstruct the rider's view of the rear derailleur. The attachment by means of a lug brazed on to the frame tube is far preferable to the usual clamping method — something to keep in mind when specifying a custom-built frame. An alternative is the so-called block generator which forms one unit with the headlight. It is installed on the front fork and has the advantage of easy removability, especially if it is not connected with a rear light (use either a battery light in the rear or rely on a really big amber or red rear reflector wherever that is legal (it *is* adequate, as will be explained in the section devoted to reflectors)

The generator converts mechanical energy into electrical energy. Unfortunately, it usually does this rather inefficiently. Whereas an efficiency of 70% should be easy to achieve, most dynamos do not surpass 20—30%, meaning that 10—15 watts of mechanical output has to be produced by the rider to keep a 3 watt system operating. To put it into perspective, that is about 20—30% of the output required to keep a bike moving at 16km/h (10mph).

A few special generators are somewhat more efficient than the conventional model, although even these waste more energy than they should. The best conventional dynamo appears to be the Swiss Nordlicht generator with a rubber roller that runs on the rim rather than the tire. Even more efficient are some roller dynamos that are installed under the bottom bracket to run off the top (rather than the side) of the tire, as shown in Fig. 14.8. Amongst these, the German Union model was tested most favorably. Unfortunately, many roller generators do not fit on a racing frame with short chainstays.

The mechanical efficiency is not the only critical factor. Equally important is the voltage and power curve, which defines the relationship between speed on the one hand and voltage and (electrical) power output on the other. Ideally, the output should increase rapidly at low speeds to achieve adequate lighting even at a

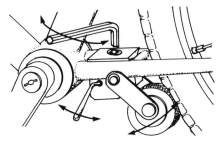

14.8. Roller generator

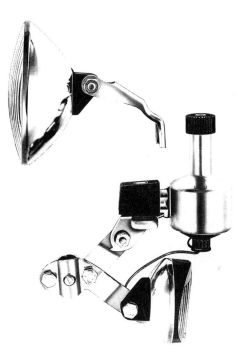

14.9. Union rear-wheel-drive generator system.

14.10. Sanyo Dynapower roller generator

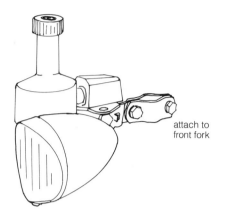

14.11. Block generator for front wheel

attach to
front fork

Bulb, Headlight and Rear Light

14.12. Designer dream: This integrated unit of head light, generator and front brake is not very practical.

modest riding speed, after which it should level off and remain relatively constant so the bulbs do not burn out due to excess voltage at higher speeds. The optimal curve is shown in Fig. 14.7. In this graph, the non-shaded area defines the range within which the output voltage should remain. The graph is based on a 6-volt system.

Although there are a few 12-volt systems on the market, all of them are characterized by such a disastrous output curve that bulbs burn through at the drop of a hat when cycling at speeds exceeding 16km/h (10mph). These 12-volt systems usually produce a nominal 6watt of output, compared to the 3 watt generated by most 6-volt systems. Generally, they have separate contacts for a 12-volt headlight and a 6-volt rear light.

The most efficient light bulbs are those filled with a halogen gas (usually krypton). These not only produce up to 50% more light than conventional bulbs, they don't dim over time, when regular bulbs rapidly get black as the filament material sublimates and condenses on the inside of the glass. Halogen bulbs require different fittings, so the headlight in which they are used must be designed differently. They also burn hotter and are more sensitive to excess voltage. The bulb should not be touched with bare hands since that would etch the special glass — replace these bulbs with the aid of a tissue.

Amongst the headlights, the best models are those that bundle the light most accurately and evenly over an area wide enough to light up the width of the traffic lane when aimed about 6—10m (20—33 feet) ahead of the bike. An additional narrow beam, aimed further ahead, may be useful as an early warning system, but a brightly lit area close to the bike is more critical under most circumstances. Large headlights tend to be more satisfactory, with the additional advantage that they make the bike more visible to others coming towards the bike or approaching from a side road. For the same reasons, a relatively high mounting position (on the handlebars in preference to lower down) lights up the road better, throws less confusing shadows, and maximizes visibility. Although on a road bike, narrow beam lights should turn with the handlebars, cycling off-road calls for a wide-beam light that does not move with the handlebars — preferably supplemented by an additional light mounted on the handlebars.

The rear light should preferably be mounted relatively high. If a luggage rack is used, the best location is just underneath the luggage platform. On a bike without luggage rack, the optimum position is just under the seat. If you use a saddlebag, which would obstruct it there, you have to mount the light on one of the rear stays, again making sure it does not get obstructed. One location that is not recommended is on a plastic or aluminum fender, since vibrations causes fatigue cracking. Sooner or later, the attachment bolt simply breaks out of the fender.

There is a dramatic difference between the light output and visibility of various rear lights. Invariably, the larger ones are much more visible than smaller models. Those that contain a built-in parabolic reflector behind the bulb are more visible than those without, and amber lights are more visible than red ones, and flashing lights are both more visible and much more economic in terms of battery life. Recently, very compact rear lights have been introduced that use flashing LED's instead of bulbs.

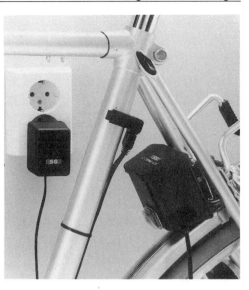

14.13. ESGE rechargeable system

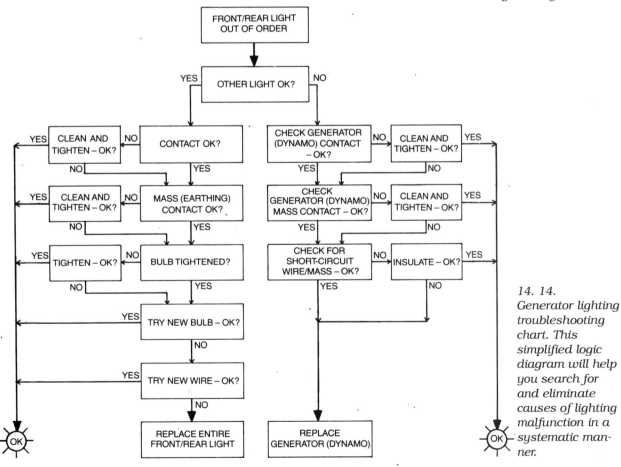

14. 14. Generator lighting troubleshooting chart. This simplified logic diagram will help you search for and eliminate causes of lighting malfunction in a systematic manner.

Generator Lighting Defects

When a generator system fails, it is only possible to establish what went wrong if you follow a very systematic approach. After all, this system comprises a large number of mutually connected components. Fig. 14.14 shows a simplified logic diagram for this. But don't let system rule over logic: ask yourself what is the most likely cause under the given circumstances. Thus, when it is raining or snowing, generator slip is more likely the cause than in dry weather — so that is the point to start: make sure the generator is aligned properly and increase contact pressure by bending in the attachment.

Reflectors

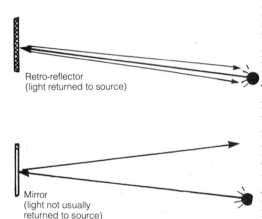

14.15. Retro-reflection compared to mirroring principle.

In the US, and a rapidly increasing number of other countries, a whole plethora of reflectors is currently prescribed — in some countries only when the bike is sold, in others when the bike is operated. Although the latter approach seems more logical, it is by no means favorable, because the assumption on which this legislation is based is totally unscientific.

The only reflector that is of any use is the one mounted in the rear facing straight back (although pedal reflectors may be a useful supplement, on account of their movement). All other reflectors do not serve any purpose that is not better met by other forms of lighting equipment. The two things to keep in mind with reflectors — more correctly called *retro-reflectors* (Fig 14.15) — is that they are only visible to those whose headlights are directly aimed at them, and that they do not help the cyclist see any better, whereas lights are visible from a wide arc, and help the cyclist see his way and anything in his path.

Only a headlight can protect the cyclist to the front from running into obstacles and make him visible to approaching or crossing drivers and pedestrians. An additional white reflector does not help one bit (if the headlight does not work, the cyclist should not be riding in the dark).

To traffic approaching from side roads ahead, again only the headlight is visible. Spoke reflectors and reflecting tire sidewalls remain invisible to those who could endanger the cyclist, since the crossing driver's headlight is not aimed at them until it is too late.

From the rear, either a rear light or a reflector aimed straight back gives adequate protection. All drivers approaching the cyclist have headlights that are aimed straight at the reflector, which lights up brightly.

Totally inept is the concept of dividing the rear reflector into three smaller panels aimed under angles offset to

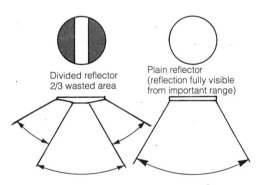

14.16. Loss of reflective surface due to angled reflector surfaces.

the left and the right, as shown in Fig 14.16. Drivers whose lights are aimed at the bike under this angle are not on a collision course with the cyclist, so do not need to see him: they will cross the point where the cyclist is now — but the cyclist will be gone by then.

There are a few points to consider in the selection and maintenance of reflectors. In the first place, bigger is better: larger reflectors are more visible than smaller ones, all else being equal. Secondly, lighter colored reflectors are more visible than darker ones. Amber reflects about twice as much of the light as red. Consequently, amber reflectors should be selected for the rear wherever it is legal to do so (the argument that it might be confused for a side-reflector is invalid, because lateral movement distinguishes side reflectors unambiguously from those mounted in the front or the rear).

As for maintenance, reflectors only do their job properly when they are kept clean: wash them regularly with plenty of water. However, if water should leak inside the reflector, it condenses on the inside, making the reflector virtually blind. For this reason, a cracked or broken reflector should be replaced immediately. To check a reflector's operation, aim a light at it from a distance of 10m (33ft), observing from a point close to the light source whether the reflector appears to light up brightly. But if your eye is too far from the straight path between the light source and the reflector, you will not notice the retro-reflection.

Although most of what was said above under *Bulb, Headlight and Rear Light* applies to battery lighting as much as it does to generator lights, there are a number of considerations that are specific to battery lighting systems. All of them have the advantages of being independent from the rider's efforts: it's no more work to cycle with than without light and the light stays equally bright at any speed. They are all rather expensive to operate and require regular attention to make sure the batteries are adequately charged for the riding ahead.

The simplest form of battery lighting consists of separate units for headlight and rear light, each containing its own batteries. This type is used almost universally for bicycle lighting in Great Britain (whereas the rest of Europe uses mainly generator lighting). Nothing wrong with this relatively simple type of light, except that it rarely has quite enough output. Its advantages include easy removability and relatively low purchase and operating cost.

14.17 and 14.18. Above: Ever-Ready battery rear light. Below: Grün rechargeable frame-mounted light.

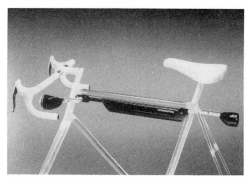

Battery Lighting

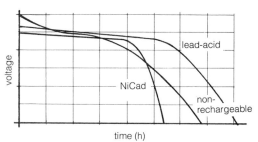

14.19. Comparison of battery characteristics.

14.20. Flash light attached to the front fork. Although it shines a long way, the beam is not wide enough for safe cycling under most circumstances.

The best lights of this kind are those made by Chloride, sold under the name Ever-Ready in Britain and Berec in the US. These units run on two large D-cell batteries each and are designed to light up a rather narrow spot quite far away, while still being highly visible due to their large lens. Although even this best of regular battery lights is marginal for the front, the rear light is brighter than anything else I've ever seen. Unfortunately, the mounting hardware supplied with these lights, does not keep the lights aimed properly.

The other form of battery lighting is a central battery wired up to a separate head light and rear light. These tend to be very expensive and not all of them give either more light or better service than the simpler and cheaper integrated battery lights. Designed correctly, they can have a bright light that is optimally selected to put the light where it is needed, possibly even with an option of high and low beam for different situations.

Batteries

The batteries are a special problem for all forms of battery lighting. Regular dry cell batteries have an output characteristic that is highly life-dependent: when new, the output is about 1.5V per cell, which gradually falls to an average of 1.2V, eventually dwindling to nothing. Consequently, the light is bright at first, settles at an average value for some time and then drops off further.

The output of a new battery provides a light that is twice as bright as the average value, while in the end it gives off only a tiny fraction of the average. Bulbs are selected to give the rated output at the average value of 1.2V per cell (thus, a bulb for a two-cell unit should be rated at 2.4V, rather than 3V, although the cells are nominally quoted at 1.5V each).

Rechargeable batteries are available in the form of nickel-cadmium (NiCad) cells that are fully interchangeable with regular dry cells, or as lead-acid gel batteries suitable only for separate mounting. Both models have entirely different characteristics, as is apparent from Fig. 14.19. The output of a NiCad cell stays relatively constant at 1.2V and the light remains almost equally bright up to the (shorter) overall charge life, but suddenly dims without warning. This is one

14.21 and 14.22.
Top: Eclipse rack.
Right: Jim
Blackburn's
stability test for
distribution of lug-
gage.

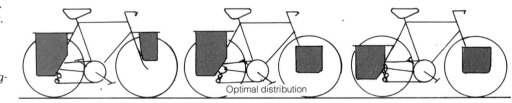

Optimal distribution

reason to carry fully charged spares if you use NiCads. The correct way to maintain NiCad batteries is to run them down completely before recharging them. If they are recharged before they are fully drained, they will soon lose their ability to hold a charge. If this happens, they can usually be revitalized by fully charging and discharging them five times. They have a limited shelf life and should be depleted and recharged at least once a month — and discarded when they don't hold a charge.

The other form of relatively common rechargeable battery is the lead-acid gel type. Unlike NiCads, these are not available in sizes and shapes that are interchangeable with regular dry cells, usually being rectangular. They do hold more charge and can be recharged before they are fully run down — in fact, they should never be completely discharged. This type lends itself best as a central battery wired to separate light units.

These accessories should be regarded as load-carrying components of the bicycle. Consequently, they should be designed, constructed and attached with the same considerations in mind as the major components of the bike. The support stays should run straight to their mounting points and must be firmly attached. Additional stays should be arranged so that the load is distributed and the design is triangulated in such a way that lateral rigidity is achieved. The illustrations show satisfactory racks for front and rear and a stay arrangement that achieves adequate lateral rigidity.

As important as the construction of the racks themselves is their arrangement on the bike. From a stability standpoint, the most favorable load distribution is as shown in Fig. 14.22. Thus, the front rack should be designed so that the load can be carried low and in line with the steering axis (i.e. just behind the front wheel axle). The rear rack should carry the load as far forward as possible — attempts to lower the load invariably also require it to be placed further back for heel clearance, which deteriorates the bike's handling.

Probably the finest material for racks is tubular steel with a diameter of at least 8mm. Since this kind of construction is rather work-intensive, with lots of brazed joints, most racks are made of aluminum alloy rod. It should have a diameter of at least 6mm, while racks made of steel rod may use material that is about 4.5mm in diameter. Important details are a restraint on the top platform to stop the load from pushing against the rear brake, and stays that are arranged so that the pannier bags cannot move sideways against the wheel.

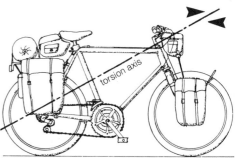

14.23. Checking for stability of loading

Luggage Racks

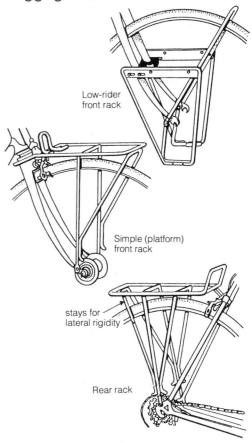

14.24. Luggage rack types

Fenders

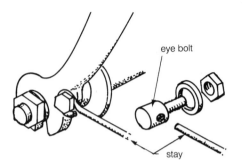

14.25. Attachment of stay to fork

Chain Guard

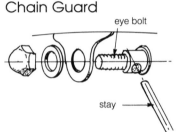

14.26. Attachment of stay to fender

Kick Stand

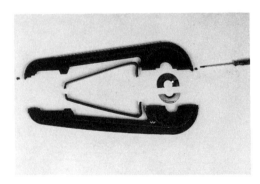

14.27. Fully enclosing ABS chain guard as used on most Dutch utility bikes.

Child Seat

Fenders, or mud guards, are useful items in most climates. Though it may not be as much fun to ride in the rain as it is in sunshine, it is a lot more endurable on a bike with fenders. After all, you cannot dictate the weather, but you can prepare for it. Suitable fenders for lightweight bikes are made of plastic or aluminum, each attached to the bike with stays made of steel rod and clips as shown in Fig. 14.25 and 14.26.

To make easily removable fenders, it is possible to attach the stays to the drop-outs and fork-ends by means of wing bolts and with the clips with which they are attached to the brake mounting bolts held between double nuts. Use two (thin) locknuts instead of the single nut provided, and tighten both nuts even when the rack is not installed, so the brake is held adequately, which could not be done with only one thin nut.

Chain guards are not *in*. And even those that are used, generally don't serve their purpose. However, good chainguards that protect both the chain and the rider's clothing do exist and are installed on just about every utility bicycle in some countries. They usually limit you to the use of bikes without derailleur gearing, although the Dutch importer of the Japanese Miyata bicycles and Shimano components has dug out some components that actually make it possible to use derailleur gearing with a fully enclosed chain guard.

More correctly known as prop stand outside the US, this device is typically only used on simple bicycles. Although few are any good, some models work better than the others. The Japanese model that is attached on the rear stays close to the rear wheel axle is much more effective than the more common type that is attached just behind the bottom bracket. Besides, it does not get in the way while wheeling the bike backwards, as the conventional kick stand does.

Another interesting model is the two-legged version. Its advantage is that the bicycle can be balanced on it so that it does not lean over. With this model, either the rear wheel or the front wheel can be raised off the ground to work on the bike. The same maintenance purpose can be achieved by means of a $15 shop stand — nothing to install on the bike, but handy at home.

Not your everyday accessory perhaps, but a rather important one if you have a young child. They exist for installation in the front and the rear. The former type is only suitable for mountain bikes and other machines with flat handlebars and a rather long top tube, since on other models the child would interfere with handling and balancing the bike (or the other way round). These must be attached to the top tube, not to any part connected with the steering system. Children above the age of 4 are generally too big to be carried in the front. Bigger children are better carried in the rear than in the front.

The type for installation in the rear comes in two versions: for independent installation and for attachment to a luggage rack. Only the very strongest and rigid racks lend themselves to the installation of a seat. Models for direct attachment to the bike are more common in the US, while luggage-rack mounted models are often seen in Europe. Any child seat should meet the following criteria:

☐ Very sturdy, rigid construction and attachment to the bike
☐ Integral support for the child's back and sides
☐ Seat belt to tie the child in
☐ Adequate support and protection for the feet to stop them from getting caught in the spokes, a frequent cause of bicycle-related child injury.

A final word of warning on the subject: don't ever leave a child in the seat when you are not holding the bike — always take the child out of the seat first, before you do anything else.

14.28. Rear-wheel-mounted kickstand

Bicycle Computer

Today, this is about the most common bicycle accessory, and these things are getting both cleverer and smaller every year. Select one that has the minimum number of knobs consistent with the functions you desire. Follow the manufacturer's instructions for installation, calibration and maintenance. Generally, it must be calibrated for the wheel size, measured accurately between the road and the center of the loaded bike. It pays to look for a model that is advertised as being waterproof and comes with a guarantee to back up this claim. If it is not, put a plastic bag over it in the rain and always take it off the bike when transporting it.

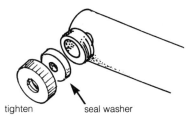

tighten   seal washer

14.29. Pump head and seal washer

Pump

There are two types of bicycle pump. For workshop use, I suggest using a big floor pump with an integrated pressure gauge, making sure it has an connector for the kind of valves on your bike (Schrader and Presta valves each require a different nipple, while Woods, or Dunlop, valves can be inflated with the same connector as the one designed for Presta valves). For on-the-road use, get a frame-mounted pump that can be installed along one of the bikes's frame tubes, again

14.30.
Detail of pump showing the plunger with its cup-shaped end.

keep plunger greased

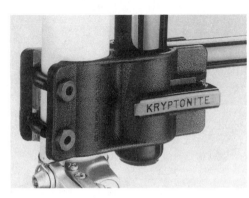

14.31. Kryptonite lock mounting bracket (photo Robert Dickson/Kryptonite).

Lock

Other Accessories

with the appropriate connection for the valves on your bike. With their relatively small volume, frame pumps should be of the kind without connector hose, since too much air gets trapped in the hose to allow adequate inflation of high-pressure tires.

If the pump does not work, it is due to a leak at either the washer in the head of the pump or the plunger. First try to close up the washer in the head by turning the end cap a little tighter. If it is a leak in the plunger, disassemble the pump, grease, soften and knead the plunger and reassemble it again. It may be necessary to install a new washer or plunger.

In recent years, the pump is being edged out by devices with CO_2 cartridges. Though small and handy, they are rather wasteful, especially considering that a typical mountain bike tire can't be fully inflated with one.

Unfortunately, this is one of the most essential accessories. And even the best are inadequate to keep pace with the developing means to crack them. As a minimum, lock the frame and both wheels together with a fixed object big enough so it cannot be lifted off. The familiar U-locks, though not completely fool-proof, are generally quite satisfactory. Use a bracket to attach it to the top tube or the seat tube of the frame.

By way of maintenance, it may occasionally be necessary to lubricate the lock. Do that very sparingly, using one or two drops of light oil on the key and on each of the points where the shackle or bracket disappears into the lock housing. Then open and close the lock a few times and wipe off any excess lubricant.

In addition to the ones listed above, other items are introduced from time to time, some of which hardly warrant mention due to their simplicity. Most of the newly introduced gadgets are taken off the market as quickly as they are introduced, since few are really as practical or well conceived as may at first appear.

Chapter 15
__ Bicycles for the Short and the Tall

The chapters of this last part of the book are devoted to the perhaps 1% of all bicycles on the road that differ from the run of the mill. Here we shall cover the special bicycles, machines that are technically different for one or more reasons. In the present chapter, we shall cover machines for riders whose physical size makes off-the-peg bikes uncomfortable. In the remaining chapters, we shall first look at the tandem, and then at the various other uncommon bicycle designs, followed in the last chapter by a tongue-in-cheek evaluation of the bike of the future.

The most common reason for choosing a bike that differs from the norm is that no standard design comfortably fits the particular rider. Long ignored by the industry and large segments of the bike trade, some riders just can't find standard bikes to fit them. Often, the answer to the need for such a machine has simply been either to modify an existing bike somewhat, or at best to build a version that is either scaled up or down a little. Many women have problems finding a bike to fit. That is not only due to their overall size, but also to the fact that most bikes are still made with the typical male proportions in mind. Fig. 15.2 shows in what respects even an average female physique differs from that of an average male of the same size.

Tall riders typically not only need seat and handlebars that are higher, they also need a frame that achieves these positions without requiring excessively long (and therefore flexible) extensions of seat post and handlebar stem. The length of the top tube should probably be longer than on an average bike. In addition to the frame, crank length (and consequently bottom bracket height) and quite a number of other items should also be adapted to the rider's proportions. Achieving all this while maintaining proper steering and handling is no mean feat.

For short riders — be they small adults or children — the problems are at least as severe. Only too often, the

15.1. The biggest and smallest bikes that can be considered 'normal': A youth's bike with 24-inch wheels and a 45cm frame and a 28-inch frame on 700mm wheels.

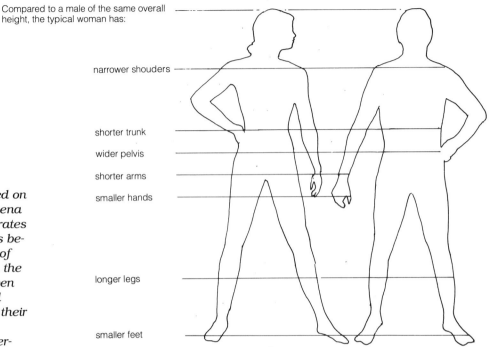

Compared to a male of the same overall height, the typical woman has:

narrower shouders

shorter trunk

wider pelvis

shorter arms

smaller hands

longer legs

smaller feet

15.2.
This illustration, based on one taken from Georgena Terry's catalog, illustrates the typical differences between the physiques of the average man and the average women — even with the same overall body height. Clearly, their bicycles should be adapted to these differences.

15.3. One way of making it big: This Gazelle fitness cycling frame has a long head tube for maximum stability and a slightly lowered top tube. Suitable for riders who are both tall and relatively heavy.

height of the frame is all that is reduced, and that just isn't enough: they need a shorter top tube while maintaining adequate steering tube length, shorter cranks (and consequently a lower bottom bracket) and quite a few other modifications.

Even the best intended attempts to accommodate short or tall riders often go amiss. To give an example, merely scaling down a regular bike to achieve a design with smaller wheels will likely results in insufficient trail for proper steering stability. In recent years, some manufacturers have taken these problems a little more seriously, with the result that more choices are available today — at least among high priced machines. Even when ordering a custom-built frame, it is good to consider the points that will be explained in this chapter, because not all frame builders have a thorough enough grasp of the ergonomic needs of small and big riders.

Often quite minor points may matter a lot. Take the brake cables for example: it is common to run them over the top of the top tube. But that adds about 6mm (¼") to the effective top tube height when trying to straddle the frame. That does not seem like much, but a few minor points like that soon add up to a difference of 2.5cm — a whole inch, which is a lot when you are trying to minimize frame size for a short rider.

Obviously the frame should be small for short riders. Yet that usually can't be achieved by either shortening only the seat tube or by scaling all dimensions down. The first solution does not achieve the required shorter top tube length, nor does it address the need for an adequate head tube length — the most important criterion for overall frame rigidity and steering predictability. The second solution can't be carried out within the constraints of the required minimum clearances around parts such as the wheels.

One solution for a small bicycle is the design pioneered by frame builder Bill Boston, later successfully implemented and perfected by Georgena Terry in her production bicycles for women. This design uses a smaller front wheel, providing adequate head tube length even in the smallest frame sizes, as shown in Fig 15.10. Other methods that can be successfully used include using a steeper seat angle and a shallower head tube angle (providing the other steering dimensions are adjusted to suit).

For most tall riders, another problem should be addressed as well: not only must the frame be bigger overall, it also needs to be stronger. There are two reasons for this: in the first place, the longer tubes of the bigger frame (assuming top tube and down tube are also longer) tend to flex more under the same load; in the second place, the taller rider is likely to be heavier and stronger.

All this has to be achieved using standard wheel sizes, since larger ones are just not available. In addition, the distribution of weight and the correct steering geometry must be maintained. No mean feat, and numerous frame builders have had to disappoint their tall customers, some of whom got nearly unridable machines as a result of the vagaries of oversize frame design.

The Frame

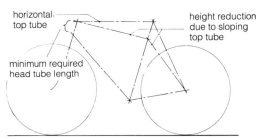

15.4. The effective frame size can be decreased by means of a sloping top tube.

15.5. One good way to make a woman's frame with a low top tube without sacrificing rigidity. This is achieved with additional bracing tubes between the rear axle and the point where the top tube meets the seat tube.

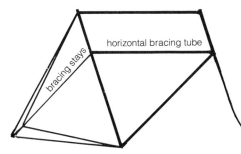

15.6 and 15.7. Two examples of suitable bracing of a large frame, using horizontal and diagonal bracing tubes for torsional rigidity.

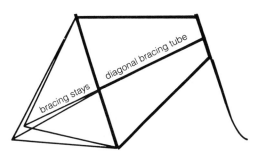

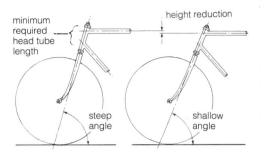

15.8. Lowered effective frame height due to use of shallower head tube angle.

The longer frame length that may be required for a tall rider has to be compensated by means of an additional stiffening member. Fig. 15.6 and 15.7 show common solutions, which seems to be required when frames exceed a size of 65 cm (26"). On the other hand, this adds more strength than stiffness, while both problems may be adequately addressed by running the seat stays in such a way that they cross the seat tube and tie into the top tube at a point forward of the seat lug, as shown in Fig. 15.9.

Other methods to achieve increased frame strength and rigidity include the use of thick-wall and oversize tubing. Obviously, bikes for large riders should not be made with the lightest tubes, and there may be good reasons to choose mountain bike tubing with its greater diameters and wall thicknesses for such frames if they will be subjected to hard use.

Whether big or small, different size frames often involve different angles between the various tubes. Thus, the use of precision cast steel lugs is often not possible for such frames. Stamped plate lugs, though not as accurately dimensioned and often not as pretty, at least allow some bending without doing damage. If the difference becomes more than 3°, a lugless construction should be used instead, so as not to stress the lugs excessively.

The Steering System

To steer a bike with a big frame properly, it has to be long enough so the rider is not too close to the steering axis. On small bikes, sufficient trail must be provided, even if the front wheel is smaller than usual, or if the head tube angle is different. This means that the fork rake should not be the same on bikes with different wheel sizes or with different head tube angles. A small front wheel requires less rake, as does a steeper head tube angle, to achieve the same trail. The effect of wheel size on steering stability was discussed in Chapter 6.

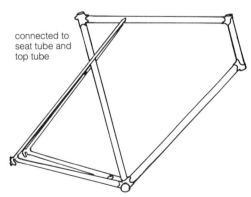

15.9. Frame with seat stays crossing the seat tube for increased rigidity.

Racing type handlebars appear to be readily available to fit any male gorilla, but to find one that matches a small rider with relatively narrow body build may be next to impossible. The correct posture keeps the arms parallel if the bars are held at the drops. There are some children's size bars that may do the trick, but very few of them seem to be available in the quality that is justified in the price category where one lands when getting a custom built bike. Mountain bike handlebars can at least be cut short, assuming they are not bent too far from the center. Even the handlebar diameter should be reduced for riders with small hands.

Very small or big riders often differ in that part of the anatomy that contacts the seat. Although there are now quite a number of reasonably comfortable women's seats available, people who are both heavy and broadly built may have difficulty finding something to match. Although it looks weird on an otherwise fine racing bike, the kind of leather saddle with spiral springs in the (very wide) back seems to be the only comfortable solution for many women and quite a few males.

For big riders, the seatpost may have to be rather long if the frame is not perfectly matched to the leg length. In recent years, very long seatposts have become available — but only in diameters to match the typical inside diameters of mountain bike seat tubes, which are slightly smaller than those on most racing and touring bikes. It is possible to install a shim around the seatpost in the seat lug, but this had better be quite long: at least 10cm (4") are required for adequately secure clamping.

Normal wheel sizes for adult bikes are nominally 26, 27 and 28 inch (again nominally: 650, 675 and 700mm). In reality, these usually do not differ very much from each other, due to the fact that the nominally smaller wheels are frequently equipped with wider tires, the larger ones with very narrow tires. As we've seen in Chapter 8, wheels called 700mm (28") actually have smaller rims than those referred to as 675mm (27").

For small riders, there are some 26" wheels available with narrow 1¼" tires. This size is still readily available in France, Italy and to a lesser extent in Britain, while the are virtually impossible to find in the US. The next step down is the 24" wheel, available both with relatively wide tires, as used on so-called dirt bikes and some mountain bike rear wheels, and with moderate tire widths.

Even more serious than the tire situation is that of the rims. In the US, it is often very hard to obtain strong aluminium rims in any size other than those that fit 27" and 700mm ten-speed or 26" mountain bike tires. When my children were so small that their bikes required 22, 24 and 26" tires, I stocked up on those rims and tires on a trip to Italy, but I can't seriously suggest you go there to buy rims and tires on a regular basis. Most of these smaller rims come with fewer than the standard number of 36 spoke holes: anything from 24 to 32. That means you also need matching hubs, which are hard to find, although they are now more readily

The Seat

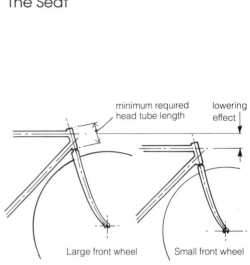

15.10. *Lowered top tube on account of small front wheel.*

The Wheels

15.11. *Small riders probably also need smaller handlebar grips, such as Gary Fisher's design (top).*

15.12. Terry's advertising is as original as her special bikes.

Drivetrain and Gearing

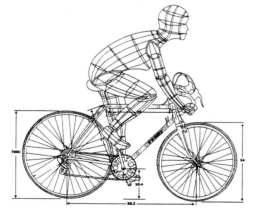

15.13. Design basis for Terry's small-wheel woman's bike design.

available — at a price — thanks to the recent craze for light and supposedly aerodynamic equipment.

Tall cyclist can't count on finding bigger wheels, but their wheels still need special attention. Heavy riders require particularly strong wheels, calling for relatively heavy rims and more than the usual number of spokes. This also affects the need for special hubs, which are available (usually intended for tandem use) but again hard to find.

The spoking pattern should be selected to match the number of spokes. On wheels with 36 spokes, 3- and 4-cross patterns are optimally strong, while fewer crossings are required for (smaller) wheels with fewer spokes, more crossings for wheels with more spokes.

Even small cyclists generally want to keep up with others as much as possible. Consequently, the drivetrain had better be adjusted to their special needs, especially if smaller wheels are installed. The biggest problem occurs on small bikes, especially those for children. Manufacturers often overlook the fact that the smaller wheel already provides a lower gear. This effect is illustrated in Fig. 15.14. Instead of equipping the bike with the right gearing to compensate for this, they tend to install scaled-down versions of the chainring, with fewer teeth, aggravating the problem even more.

True, a tiny bike with small wheels looks weird if it has a big chainring, but it is technically required to obtain useful gearing. Another solution is to choose a freewheel block with smaller sprockets. Sprockets with 12 teeth are readily available these days, and even smaller ones (all the way down to 9 teeth) can be found. In that case, it will be quite essential to make sure the chain wraps as far as possible around the smallest sprockets, by selecting the chain length and the derailleur orientation appropriately.

Cranks must match the rider's leg length as well as possible. Expensive cranksets are available in a variety of crank lengths ranging from 165mm to 180 or even from 160 to 185mm. This may be satisfactory for most big and small adults, but it still does not satisfy the needs of children, who may require even shorter ones. It also leaves those on a budget without consolation, because the more modest quality found on affordable bikes is just not available in enough different sizes to satisfy all. Really small children's cranks are usually of very inferior quality.

Pedals are available in a limited number of sizes, but most high quality pedals in only one size. Actually, this

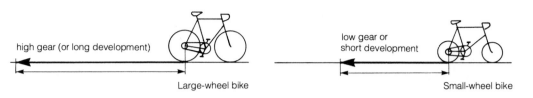

high gear (or long development)

Large-wheel bike

low gear or
short development

Small-wheel bike

*15.12.
Comparison
of gearing ef-
fect with
large and
small wheels.*

is often not a problem on racing bikes, since most modern pedals for use on the drop handlebar derailleur bike are of the clipless design, and are not so much influenced by the size of the foot as was the case for conventional pedals with toeclips. The problem is really most severe on touring and utility bikes for large riders, where few pedals will prove wide enough. One solution may be to install mountain bike pedals, which tend to be rather wide. Toeclips for conventional pedals also are available in a number of different sizes, although they rarely match children's or small women's feet. If it suits your kind of riding, the use of clipless pedals will solve most problems — but only if you don't plan on getting off the bike to walk.

The Brakes

Nowadays, brakes are not really a problem even on bikes of quite extreme sizes. Brake levers have been introduced that are readily adjustable with respect to the hand's reach. Other models, such as those intended for BMX bikes, can often be used successfully on mountain bikes for small riders. Fig. 15.15 shows the critical dimension for reach of the lever.

Another recently introduced improvement is the brake with return springs both in the lever and in the brake calipers. This feature makes brake operation very light and accurate, even for riders with relatively weak hands.

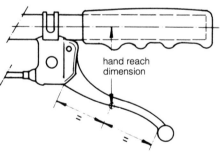

hand reach
dimension

Finally, in this respect, the modern hydraulic brakes should be mentioned. Their operation is really an experience to behold, requiring absolutely minimal force. Unfortunately, there is not a suitable range of brake levers for these brakes available to date: either a small or an adjustable version is sorely needed.

15.15. Brake lever reach definition

Accessories

Whereas the lock and lighting are no different on a small or big bike than on any other machine, some other accessories may pose particular problems, especially for small bikes. Finding a good small frame pump, light fenders or a sturdy luggage rack to fit a small bike, can be very hard, since many of such items are not available off-the-shelf.

15.16. The wrong way to make a small frame: The continuous twin tubes don't provide adequate rigidity. Interesting detail: the ergonomic 'guidonnet' bar-end brake levers.

If you are willing and able to pay the price, the problem may be less severe. Anyone who is prepared to buy himself, his children or his spouse a custom-built bike should also investigate the possibility of matching accessories, which many frame builders will gladly design and produce. It does leave those on a budget out on a limb, but being different always costs a little more, it seems.

Chapter 16

The Tandem

Tandem is the Latin term for *at length*, and it is used to describe bicycles for two or more riders sitting in line, each contributing to the propulsion. Although just about every tandem you see these days is designed for two, machines for three or more riders can be built and were in fact used extensively around the turn of the century. The longest tandem on record accommodates 36 riders — who have so far not managed to cover the distance of the machine's own length. The modern two-man tandem, by contrast, is a highly efficient bicycle.

Interest in the tandem has increased significantly in recent years, so that it is now relatively easy to buy quality machines of this kind in a wide range of sizes. And just as important, tandem parts and accessories are becoming more readily available. That is one essential factor for keeping a tandem on the road, since many of the parts used differ from those installed on other bicycles.

Although tandems are efficient, enabling two riders to cover greater distances at higher speeds than they could individually, they are a bit of a nuisance in other respects. Shear size makes it hard to live with them. Transporting one is at least as difficult as finding a convenient place to store it, and when it does break down, the second rider is stranded as much as the first, making it hard to get help.

All these are mere sober, practical drawbacks, that don't weigh up against the pure delight of riding such a machine in unison at high speeds and over long distances in perfect cadence. A properly designed and constructed tandem is indeed so reliable that it does not break down more frequently than any other bike — practically never if properly maintained.

The reason why tandems do present a special challenge to their designers and manufacturers lies in the fact that a higher load has to be carried on a longer structure, at the same time propelled by a greater output applied in two different locations. Combining two bottom brackets, two saddles and two handlebars together so that the whole can be balanced and steered safely and predictably is no mean feat, but it can be done when it is designed properly.

Unlike the riders of single bikes, those on a tandem are

16.1. *Excellent lightweight European touring tandem by Mittendorf.*

16.2 and 16.3.
American challengers: Burley's crude but well-engineered Bossa Nova (top) and Samba Mixte. Rear seat stays and chain stays are made of one continuous tube, wrapped around on both sides.

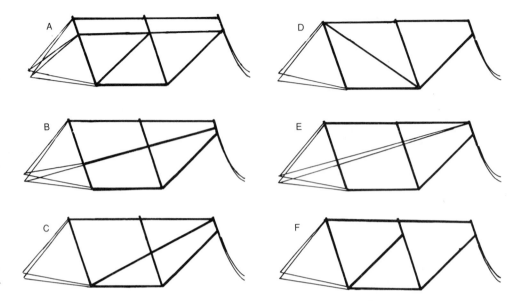

16.4.
A number of different tandem frame variants. The ones in the LH column are those with high torsional rigidity — the thing that matters most on a tandem.

usually unable to relieve the load when riding over bumps in the road. This often gives the tandem the feel of having lots of dead weight. Actually, the machine itself is not all that heavy: typically 1.6 times the weight of a single bike of comparable quality — or 0.8 times the weight of the two single machines it replaces. What gives the feeling of dead weight is the fact that the wheels are so far apart that the riders' weight can't be shifted. Consequently, any jolts really give the bike a beating, requiring an even more sturdy construction of bike and components.

Tandem Frames

The tandem frame is some 60cm (24") longer than that of a single bike. Since longer members are basically more flexible than shorter ones, it should be obvious that the tandem frame, which also has to carry double the load, must be specially constructed if it is not to flex excessively, which would lead to unpredictable steering and balancing characteristics. Fig. 16.5 shows how the various static and dynamic forces act upon the tandem frame.

The dynamic, or variable, forces generate a torsional effect along the axis that runs from the rear wheel axle to the bottom of the headset, as shown in the same illustration. In addition to being strong enough to carry the vertically applied static load, the frame has to be so rigidly constructed that the resulting torsional deformation is minimized. Ideally, this is achieved with a very large diameter tube that runs along the torsion

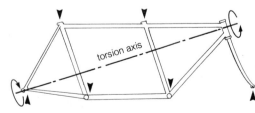

16.5. Loading sketch of tandem frame during riding, showing reaction forces at wheels and the torque axis.

axis. In practice, several different methods have been tried, as shown in Fig. 16.4.

Of the various details represented in Fig. 16.4, the ones on the LH side tend to be the better solutions, since they reinforce with the more rigid member close to the torsional axis. The details shown on the right, on the other hand, are obviously designed with at best the static loads in mind (including the recently popular design per detail g). In fact, some of these designs are not even adequate from the static standpoint: none of the designs that provides a low instep, be it in the front, in the rear or for both riders, is statically or dynamically adequate unless extremely heavy walled and large diameter tubing is used. A hight top tube has to be used on tandems — even for those women who would prefer a lower instep (fortunately a rapidly receding demand in the US, though still very common elsewhere).

A relatively popular solution is the one with two small diameter diagonal bracing tubes, referred to as *twin laterals* or *mixte tubes*. This design is inherently inadequate, especially for a lightweight machine used for touring. Some of the problems of tandem design are lessened by using special tandem tubing, made by at least three of the major tubing manufacturers (Reynolds, Columbus and Ishiwata) and by most of the others on special order in some minimum quantity. Obviously, tandem tubing must be of greater diameter and greater wall thickness. Besides, some special tubes are not found on other bikes, such as the tube connecting the two bottom brackets (referred to as bottom tube or 'drainpipe') and the diagonal reinforcing tube. Those two tubes are particularly critical, as are the down tube and the head tube. All these tubes, being both long and heavily loaded, should have greater diameter than what is found even on mountain bikes.

To be at all comfortable in the long run, the distance between the two seats is quite critical. Racing tandems are kept rigid by minimizing this distance, and they are a royal pain in the neck for the rider in the rear, referred to as the *stoker* in tandem parlance, while the one in front is known as the *captain*. For non-competitive purposes, the length of the rear top tube should be at least 65 cm (26") — preferably up to 75cm (30").

Because tandem frames have some rather complicated joints that differ from those that are standard elsewhere, it is quite common to build tandem frames without lugs. Often fillet brazed joints are used instead, although the large tube wall thicknesses justify the use of TIG welded joints, leading to considerable cost

16.6. Dutch recreational tandem. Insufficiently rigid , despite relatively high weight.

Tandem Frame Geometry

16.7. French recreational tandem. Little rigidity due to low rear top tube.

savings. In fact, Cannondale builds its unique aluminium tandem frame this way, which is extremely light despite its very large diameter tubing.

Tandem Steering

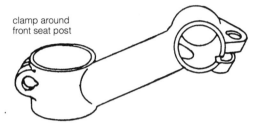

clamp around
front seat post

16.8. Tandem rear handlebar stem for installation on front seat post.

It took a long time for tandem builders to give up on trying to do the impossible: the earliest tandems and other multi-rider bicycles were invariably designed in such a way that both riders could influence the steering. Although that may seem socially responsible, it did make tandem riding extremely dangerous until this idea was given up. For the last hundred years now, tandem riders seem to accept that only the captain can steer the bike, while the stoker just has to trust him (although I don't understand why, it is an almost universal custom today that the man of a 'mixed' couple rides in the front, while the woman takes the back seat).

To achieve a reliable tandem steering system, the fork should be made of thicker tubing than usual and the oversize headsets with matching steerer tubes recently introduced for mountain bikes are the answer to a maiden's prayer for tandem builders and riders as well. These are so much more rigid that they provide an entirely new sensation of control over the bike's steering, especially on less than perfect road surfaces.

The front handlebars can be normal, like on any single bike of the same kind, although a slightly wider and perhaps heavier version may be justified to overcome the greater steering forces. For the rear handlebars, I recommend choosing flat but curved bars installed with the ends pointing forward. This shape allows the rider in the rear to reach forward for a low position or hold the bars near the center to relax. As will be pointed out below, these forward pointing bar ends provide an excellent location for the gear shifters. The rear handlebars can either be installed with a special stem clamped around the front seat tube, or with a special clamp that is attached directly to the frame.

16.9. Special tandem rear handlebars with stem.

Tandem Seats

Since most tandems are used as touring bikes, typical touring or mountain bike seats are usually installed. Certainly for the stoker, who usually cannot anticipate road shocks, finishing up fully exposed to them, a sprung leather saddle is recommended. The forward seat post must be clamped in very firmly, since the rear handlebars are usually attached to it: you don't want panic reactions of the stoker to twist the captain's seat.

Tandem Wheels

Tandem problem number one is the fact that the wheels are so heavily loaded, especially dynamically.

Bent or dented rims and lots of broken spokes are typical headaches on the tandem. With the advent of the mountain bike and the hybrid, these problems should have receded, providing the wheels are treated properly.

More than any other part of the tandem, the wheels suffer anytime the bike takes an obstacle in the road surface. High tire pressures and properly tightened spokes are the clues to making tandem wheels last, providing they are sturdy enough in the first place. That means they should not be selected for low weight: considering you only have two wheels for two riders, even the strongest wheels will weigh less than the equivalent on two single bikes, so the effect of the rotating mass is not so serious as might seem at first.

The tires should be relatively wide and must withstand a high pressure, since the double weight will tend to push them in more than on a single bike. For touring use on regular roads, I prefer 32mm wide tires inflated to 6bar (85psi) or more, although 28mm is adequate for continuously smooth road surfaces. Unloaded tandems may be used with 25mm wide tires on smooth roads. On rough surfaces on or off road, only mountain bike wheels with matching highly inflated tires should be considered. Aramid (Kevlar) belted, puncture-resistant designs are of little additional help, since tandems don't puncture in the tread area but by pinching between rim and road, against which no reinforcing helps, high tire pressure being the only answer.

Also the (aluminium) rims should be pretty strong — that means heavy. The introduction of the hybrid bike is a real boon to the road tandem, since it has popularized wheel components that are superbly suited to tandem use as well. Installing mountain bike wheels with their smaller diameter wheels, on the other hand, does not work on a tandem even if clearances are adequate, since the brakes will not reach the rims.

It has long been customary to install wheels with more than the standard number of 36 spokes, requiring special rims and hubs with the appropriate number of spoke holes. If you use 44 or even 48 spokes per wheel, these should be spoked in at least a 5-cross pattern, while a 4-cross pattern is the best you can do for 36- and 40-spoke wheels. The use of thicker spokes does not seem to lead to reduced wheel problems, but one simple trick does: place a small washer under the head of every spoke to fill the distance between it and the hub flange, as shown in Fig. 16.12. This reduces the movement of the spoke bend relative to the flange, thus

16.10. Jesper Søling's Copenhagen Pederson tandem. A unique feature of this tandem is that the frame can be folded up like an umbrella for easy transportability and storage.

Rims and Spokes

16.11. Something different: Simultaneous hand and foot cranking for the captain on a unique American design (photo Steven Kodish).

greatly reducing the likelihood of fatigue-induced spoke breakages.

Wide hubs with solid axles are recommended, rather than models with quick-release. Once more, the mountain bike has provided new sources for tandem components, since there are now suitable solid-axle hubs that are wider as well as stronger. These solid axle hubs should be used with axle nuts with integral washers to reduce the friction resistance against the fork-ends and drop-outs when tightening them.

The Tandem Drivetrain

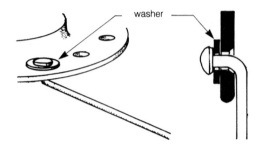

washer

16.12. *Place a washer under the spoke head to minimize spoke breakages due to fatigue on all but the thickest hub flanges.*

Two bottom brackets, two cranksets, four pedals and two chains are needed to transfer the riders' effort to the rear wheel. That allows a number of different configurations, the most common of which are shown in Fig. 16.14. At a time when it seems the only thing most cyclists think of is more gears, the call for 18- and 21-speed tandem gearing is not unreasonable. In part, this is due to the more pronounced difference between easy going and hard riding on a tandem: the extremes are more noticeable than on a regular bike: climbing is harder, and cruising is easier.

To maximize the number of available gears, the connecting chain between the two cranksets should be run on the LH side, since no more than two chainrings are effectively available for the derailleur gearing when one of those on the right is sacrificed for this purpose. On the other hand, if you can live with 10-, 12- or 14-speed gearing (e.g. in level terrain), the latter solution offers the advantage of simplicity and easily available standard bicycle parts. Real tandem cranksets designed for the connecting chain on the LH side are harder to find and quite expensive. For touristic purposes, TA is the only manufacturer whose range is reasonably widely distributed. Campagnolo's excellent tandem cranksets are only intended for racing use and are not available with three chainrings on the RH side.

There are other solutions. As can be seen from Fig. 16.14, it is not necessary to connect the rear crankset

16.13.
Gary Fisher's Gemini mountain bike tandem. The rearward oriented rear diagonal bracing tube provides more vertical than torsional rigidity.

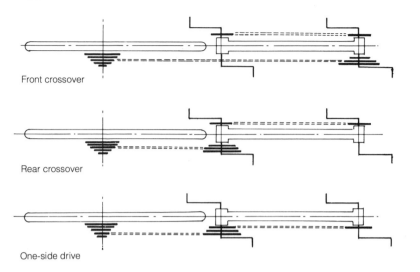

Front crossover

Rear crossover

One-side drive

16.14.
Tandem drivetrain options. The most common one is the cross-over drive in the middle. Easiest shifting is the one shown at the top. The one-side drive shown at the bottom is least demanding in terms of loading, but limits the number of available gears.

directly to the rear wheel: when the front one is used, it is easier to shift gears and many experienced touring tandem riders prefer this configuration. Whatever way they are connected, the chainrings over which the connecting chain runs should be relatively large, preferably 36 teeth, which minimizes wear and offers smooth running. That's not to say it can't be done differently: the German framebuilder Günther Sattler actually runs a small-pitch connecting chain over tiny chainwheels inside the very large diameter horizontal bottom tube that connects the two cranksets.

The connecting chain should be kept adequately tightened, allowing no more than 12mm (½") vertical movement. Although this can be achieved by means of a sprung chain tensioner, the preferred method is to adjust the crankset locations so that their distance tensions the chain. This is done by means of an eccentrically held bottom bracket bearing for one of the cranksets, allowing about 2 cm of forward adjustment.

It is not necessary to keep the cranks of front and rear cranksets in line. Many touring tandem riders prefer to offset them relative to one another by 90°, as shown in Fig. 16.20. The advantage of this configuration lies in the fact that both riders' cranks are not in the dead center position at the same time, resulting in an overall smoother flow of output. This is achieved simply by undoing one of the pairs of cranks and installing them on the square axle of the cotterless spindle 90° offset. On one-piece and cottered cranks, the same can be achieved by undoing the connecting chain and installing it again when the cranks are in the desired orientation relative to each other. In fact, when the latter

16.15. Probably the first off-road tandem. This Mountain Goat by Jeff Lindsey dates back to 1982.

221

method is followed, you are not even stuck with 90° offset but can choose almost any angle.

To accommodate a child stoker on a standard tandem, the rear crankset has to be installed higher. This can be done by means of a special adaptor known as Kiddy Cranks, shown in Fig. 16.21. Although the traditional manufacturer of these items, Andrew Hague, has gone out of business, something similar can be made by any slightly inventive bicycle mechanic using the bottom bracket shell of an old bike and a welded or brazed-on bracket. A custom-built tandem frame could even be ordered with a perfectly aligned adjustable bracket.

In a pinch, one can use standard components to make a tandem drivetrain with triple derailleur chainrings. To do this, use RH cranks on the left as well as on the right. Then the pedal hole of the one installed on the left must be drilled out and a Helicoil insert for a LH pedal installed there. Don't do what seems obvious, namely use RH pedals on both sides, keeping the threaded pedal hole the way it is, since the RH pedal with its RH screw thread will most likely come undone if installed on the left. Besides, pedals are sold in pairs, while cranks can be bought singly and Helicoil inserts are cheap.

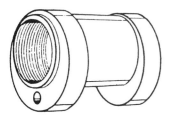

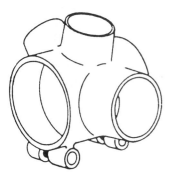

16.16. Eccentric front bottom bracket

Tandem Gearing

For serious tandem use, only derailleur gearing is suitable, certainly if loaded touring in hard terrain is involved. Three- and five speed hubs have hollow axles which are just not strong enough for this kind of use, regardless of their relative merits from a gearing standpoint.

The need for 18- and 21-speed gearing systems is by no means unjustified. Yet that does not mean that conventional mountain bike systems with the same number of gears are suitable for tandem use. Unlike the mountain bike, the tandem also needs very high gears, with developments of 8.80m or more (110-inch gear), due to the phenomenal speeds that can be reached on level ground.

16.17. Typical rear bottom bracket detail. Shows crossover drive and oval bottom tube (also referred to as 'drain pipe').

However, those restrictions really only apply to the choice of chainrings and sprockets. The derailleurs and shifters developed for the mountain bike, on the other hand, lend themselves very well for tandem use. The modern index shifters, unfortunately, only work well with their pre-cut cables, which may not have the right length for tandem use. The one way to get around this is to install the shifters on the front of the stoker's handlebars, where they are accessible to both riders and work with the normal cable lengths.

Trying to stop or slow down a machine weighing 150kg (330 lbs) with standard bicycle brakes is a risky affair, especially if one considers the fact that this machine is likely to travel faster in the first place. Downhill, the problem is an even bigger one. Yet tandem brakes can be quite adequate if a combination of measures are taken to make the most out of their properties.

One advantage from a braking standpoint is that the tandem's weight distribution over the long wheel base does not lead to the tipping forward effect that limits braking on regular bikes. You can brake in the rear and in the front with about equal effect and with very little risk — assuming the brakes themselves are powerful enough.

Probably the most suitable brake arrangement for the tandem is to use cantilever brakes in combination with an additional drum or disk brake on the rear wheel. Amongst suitable tandem drum brakes, the Maxicar is the finest available. With its large drum, it offers superb brake mantle cooling, and its construction is so superior that it assures light rolling as a hub and reliable stopping power as a brake, combined with a 'buttonhole' spoke hole design assuring easy spoke replacement. Some tandems are actually used with hub brakes both front and rear, doing without the usual rim brakes altogether. This solution is not recommended, since it places a very high strain on the front fork when braking.

For the normal configuration with two rim brakes and one drum brake, the accepted standard operation is by means of one special lever with double cables that control both rim brakes together and a second lever that controls only the drum brake. Another method is to use the drum brake only as a drag brake and connect each rim brake to its own lever, installing a little ratchet lever (from a derailleur gearing system) for the drum brake.

Due mainly to their heavy use, tandems do require a little more attention to maintenance than most regular bicycles. Consequently, here is a brief list of tandem-specific maintenance suggestions, most of which apply to normal bikes as well, but are more critical in this case.

Tire pressure:

Check and inflate if necessary before every ride. The pressure should be at least 1 bar (15psi) higher than for the same tires used on a single bike.

Tandem Brakes

16.18 and 16.19.
Above: Eccentric bottom bracket
Below: Drum brake on rear wheel.

Tandem Maintenance

16.20.
Aligned and
off-set tan-
dem crank
sets. The off-
set method
evens out the
flow of power.

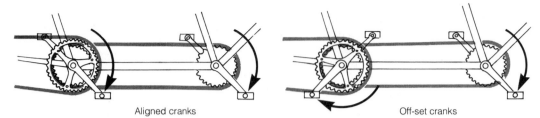

Aligned cranks   Off-set cranks

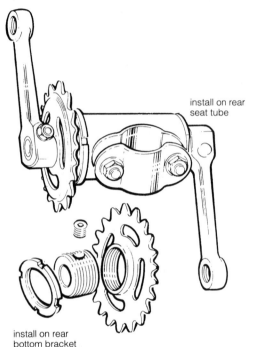

install on rear
seat tube

install on rear
bottom bracket

16.21. Kiddy crank for child stoker

Brake adjustment:

Check the brake performance before every ride, adjusting if necessary, to make sure the full braking force can be applied with at least 2cm (¾") clearance between the brake lever and the handlebars.

Spoke tension:

Check and tension the spokes at least once a month, to make sure they are really tight and all equally tensioned, which avoids both wheel warp and spoke breakages.

Crank attachment:

Check, and if necessary tighten, the crank attachment bolts once a month — before every ride during the first 100 miles.

Chain tension:

Check and adjust (by reorienting the eccentric bottom bracket) once every three months. If the eccentric does not allow tightening the chain any further, it is better to replace the chain than to remove two links, since the worn (and consequently seemingly 'stretched') chain links run less smoothly and cause wear of the chainrings.

Chapter 17
__ Unconventional Bicycle Designs

It is not unreasonable to say that the bicycle has essentially remained unchanged since the safety bicycle was introduced in the 1880's. Although the overwhelming majority of all bicycles on the road are based on this same familiar concept, using the same standard parts and built to the same set of standard specifications, different designs are introduced from time to time.

Two reactions are common when people discover how old the bicycle's design is: They either consider it time for some drastic changes, or take it for granted that it must be the optimum solution that simply could not be improved upon. Both reactions are partly incorrect: on the one hand, materials and construction methods, as well as insights in the physics and mechanics of cycling, have not stood still during the last 100 years. On the other hand, the bicycle is so close to the limit of what can be achieved with human power, that at best only marginal improvements can be expected from even the most thorough redesign.

In discussing this subject, it is often claimed that the restrictive rules of the UCI, the international sanctioning organization for bicycle racing, which applied until the fall of 1990, should be blamed for the lack of innovation and development in the industry. I find that hard to believe, just as the rules of Formula 1 motor racing haven't stopped the manufacturers of road cars from improving them. In fact, most don't even feel a need to participate in the expensive and irrelevant business of racing. Similarly, it is not likely that any major manufacturer would hesitate introducing a different machine just because it could not be used in sanctioned races. After all, the overwhelming majority of bicycles are neither used nor intended for racing.

Although you wouldn't think so looking at the bicycles on the road today, many different concepts have been introduced at times — both for the bike as a whole and for individual components. That most of these innovations never became universally accepted is not in itself proof of the conventional bike's superiority. Quite likely, some were basically sound ideas whose time had not come — or perhaps they just did not get enough publicity to become commercial successes. With recent developments in materials and production techniques,

17.1. This 1922 Jarray recumbent bicycle not only features an unconventional rider's position, but also a cable-operated treadle drive.

17.2. The most unconventional bicycle that keeps the rider sitting the way God meant him to is the Moulton. This is the City version with two-speed hub.

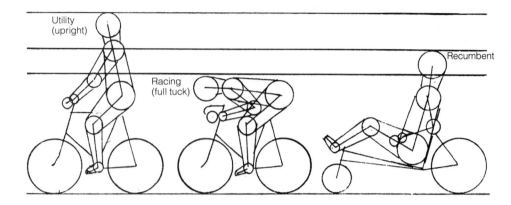

17.3.
Different bicycle designs allow different postures. But the recumbent does not really allow a lower profile if the rider is to see where he is going.

some of the earlier ideas may now be easier to realize. Just don't expect any miracles.

In the remaining sections of this chapter, the various real or presumed problems that most designers of alternative bikes and systems seem to address are presented, referring to the solutions that have been offered so far. It should be noted that many of the problems addressed only exist in the eyes of non-cyclists. Others find non-solutions to real problems — such things as bent cranks have been seriously suggested in the past, although they don't solve the problem of the rider's limited force which they supposedly set out to correct, and equally absurd designs are sometimes proposed today.

Seating and Riding Position

Leaning back lazily is the ideal in seating comfort in most modern cars, so to those not used to cycling, this seems desirable on bicycles too. Ever since the early 1920's, recliner and recumbent designs have been proposed and sometimes even marketed in the hopes of making life more comfortable for the cyclist.

Fig. 17.3 compares the posture for a normal bicycle with that for a recumbent. The most frequently quoted reasons for the leaning-back posture are better aerodynamics and the ability to apply more force. One argument is as fallacious as the other. Let's look at the supposedly increased force first.

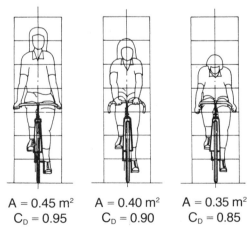

| A = 0.45 m² | A = 0.40 m² | A = 0.35 m² |
| C_D = 0.95 | C_D = 0.90 | C_D = 0.85 |

17.4. Comparison of frontal area and drag coefficients on regular bicycle.

True, sitting on the floor with your back against the wall, it is easier to apply the available force of the legs, so that is the way to move a heavy cabinet. The force that can be applied with the legs is not determined by the position but by the presence or absence of a restraint in the back. But on the bike your output is not limited by how much *force* can be applied, but by how much *power* can be delivered. Pushing a heavy cabinet slowly along the floor does not really prove you have more power than you have in another position. In fact, without a restraint, the bicycle's gearing takes care of this.

Actually, the normal position is the more effective. Here, the legs are hanging down naturally, while isometric work has to be performed in order to keep the legs in the horizontal position dictated by the recumbent pose. Although this problem can be largely overcome with the use of clipless pedals, the fact that the legs have to be forced into a position that is not natural reduces long-term comfort as well as output.

Let's look at the aerodynamic advantage next. On a racing bike, and in fact even on most other conventional machines, the body can be lowered considerably when battling a headwind, effectively reducing the wind resistance. On recumbents, the rider is stuck with the position forced on him by the bike, and that is rarely so low as to provide less wind resistance than in the full tuck, or racing, position on a regular bike. Except for designs that are so extreme as to be dangerous or impractical, none of the recumbent designs on the market allows a lower or more aerodynamic posture than a standard racing bike.

The other related argument for the recumbent is the possibility to enclose machine and rider so as to reduce air drag even more dramatically. An additional advantage of this enclosure would be weather protection — a curious argument, considering the number of people who claim being out in the fresh air as one of the major attractions of cycling. But even if you accept it, there have been enclosures for normal bicycles and in races between enclosed recumbents and normal bikes, the normal machines often enough run away from the recumbents.

Officially sponsored international races between aerodynamically enclosed bicycles have been held since 1914 (that's right: aerodynamics have been around longer than most people realize), when the Dutch rider Piet Dickentman defeated the German Arthur Stelbrink in Berlin. They used regular bicycles with torpedo-shaped enclosures. In recent times, both recumbents and regular bikes have been used in such races, and although the recumbent position seems to allow better aerodynamics, the regular shape has the advantages of more convenient dimensions and better long-term comfort.

A serious drawback of the recumbent posture is that

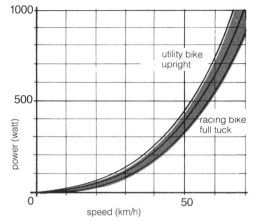

17.5. Wind resistance as a function of speed and posture.

17.6. Unconventional alright, if not very aerodynamic. This is a modern version of the Dursley Pederson bicycle with its unique triangulated frame design. It is ridden here by its builder Jesper Søling.

the rider cannot unload the seat by shifting his weight when riding over unevennesses in the road surface, as can be done on any conventional bike. Consequently, the only way to make a recumbent comfortable is by integrating a rather sophisticated suspension, adding both weight and complications. Sure, it can be done, but then most of the bicycle's inherent advantages are lost. Just the same, I hope developers keep working on the concept of the recumbent, because having the choice between really different bicycles makes cycling more interesting.

Suspension

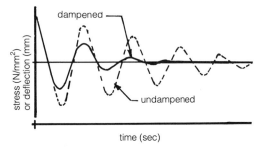

17.7. The effect of dampening

Even though the introduction of the pneumatic tire brought hitherto unknown comfort to cycling, most cyclists agree that a little more suspension would be nice. The real need for suspension is not so much in road riding and for comfort, but rather in off-road cycling for traction: an effective suspension keeps the wheels on the ground. Actually, the pneumatic tire, perhaps unbeknown to its inventor John Boyd Dunlop, put the suspension in exactly the right place. The theory of suspension, which was largely developed since that time, recognizes that the unsprung mass should be minimized. That's another way of saying the closer to the road, the more effective the suspension. You can't get any closer to the road than the tires.

Most other suspension systems ever proposed or realized have been mere compromises compared to the pneumatic tire, which can even be adjusted by regulating the inflation pressure to match the road conditions. Not only do all of those other systems leave some portion of the mass unsprung (namely whatever is between the spring and the road), most of them also affect dimensions that should remain constant for effective cycling. Although the tire's problem is the very limited depth by which it can deform without negatively affecting rolling resistance on a smooth road, most of the other suspension devices have other disadvantages that are at least as serious.

17.8. Allsop mountain bike with dampened, sprung saddle mount. This is purely a downhill bike, since the suspension is in the wrong place to keep the distance between pedals and seat constant for efficient pedaling.

For the efficient transfer of power to the pedals, the distance between the rider's seat and the crank axle should remain constant. Any suspension system in the seat, the seat post or the seat tube completely ignores this requirement. Oddly enough, such designs recur on a regular basis. Three other dimensions that should remain constant are the wheelbase, the amount of trail, and the head tube angle. That rules out all but the cleverest suspension systems in the front end. Finally, the suspension must be dampened to be satisfactory. That means that after contracting, it should come to

rest in the original position with a minimum number of occilations, as shown graphically in Fig. 17.7. Off-road, the need for a well dampened suspension becomes most apparent, even if it is bought at the price of more weight. It vastly increases wheel contact in rough terrain, improving both traction and steering accuracy, while still allowing the high tire pressures that keeps rolling resistance down on smooth surfaces.

Fortunately, sometimes people with more insight and fewer illusions tackle the problem, and then interesting designs result. But that clearly involves doing more than adding a spring to a conventional design. The most prominent and successful approach has been that of Alex Moulton, the ingenious British engineering consultant whose small-wheeled bicycle designs have toppled conventional thinking twice in the last thirty years, because he looked at the machine as a whole, drawing the conclusions that were necessary to make his suspension work.

Moulton's bicycles, the current design of which is shown in Fig. 17.2, have small wheels to provide room to take the displacement of the suspension and to minimize the unsprung mass. The 17" wheels have only about 65% of the mass of regular size wheels. The front suspension is designed in such a way that it does not noticeably affect the bicycle's trail, head angle and wheel base. The rear suspension is arranged around the bottom bracket in such a way that it does not change the distance between seat and crank spindle, nor does it affect the wheel base. Besides, both suspensions are adequately dampened to avoid the see-saw effect of many other sprung components.

The bicycle's inventor Von Drais propelled his machine by intermittently pushing off with the legs on the road. That turned the intermittent motion of walking into the continuous one of rolling, which represented a milestone in transport efficiency. It took until about 1860 before pedal-drive bicycles gained acceptance and this was another step forward due to the continuity maintained in propulsion. Another twenty years went by before the chain-driven bicycle was introduced, which has remained the standard for well over a hundred years now. Not surprisingly, some inventors feel it is time for a change.

Although the chain transmission has a high efficiency (about 95% in clean, well maintained and lubricated condition), it is by no means without drawbacks. In the first place, its efficiency suffers dramatically from neglect, soon reaching a mere 80% if allowed to run

17.9. Offroad Flexstem. This is probably the lightest method of suspension, but it merely keeps vibrations off the hands — rather than stabilizing the bike.

Drivetrain Alternatives

17.10. Toothed belt drive. Although it is a lot cleaner than the familiar chain, it precludes the use of derailleur gearing.

17.11. Crankset with an internal mechanism that increases the gearing during the downstroke. This one dates back to 1924. The same idea is reintroduced under different names from time to time, most recently as the Bio-Cam drive.

17.12. Allenax drive system. Instead of a circular leg motion, it relies on a reciprocating one — without any noticeable benefit to the rider.

dry, dirty and rusty. The other disadvantage is the fact that it is an inherently messy system that cannot easily be protected, nor can the rider's clothes be protected against this moving, greasy, dirty component, certainly not on a bicycle with derailleur gearing. On the other hand, the alternative transmission systems don't allow the use of derailleur gearing.

The various alternative concepts for bicycle transmission that have been proposed and sometimes actually used in the past fall into three categories: belt drive, shaft drive and treadle drive. All of them are old hat. Shaft-driven, so called *acatane*, or chainless, bicycles have been introduced at intervals ever since the 1890's. In fact, the famous Black American bicycle racer Major Taylor set some of his early time trial records on such machines. Obviously, this system can work — until you realize that the chain has been improved more than the shaft and bevel gearing systems used for the chainless bicycles since those days, not to mention price and weight: the chain drive method is incomparably cheaper and lighter. Most recently, the German manufacturer Fendt introduced a shaft-driven bicycle in the early 1980's, but this model had relatively crude bevel gears that are noisier and less efficient than they should be.

Belt-drive designs have certain advantages, especially if one considers the recent perfection of the toothed belt designs, using high-tech materials such as aramid (Kevlar) and synthetic rubber that make them both light, flexible and unstretching. The Japanese Bridgestone company, though now fully independent from the company that makes such belts by the same name, successfully uses belt drives on their folding bicycles. Their replacement requires the frame to be separated (except on frames with raised chainstays) and they cannot be used with derailleur gearing, but for the utility bike without gearing, belt drives may well provide a workable alternative.

The third method of transmission is by means of treadles that rock back and forth. In fact, this design was the major characteristic of the bicycle by Gavin Dalzell, probably built around 1860 (based on unsubstantiated records, this design is often claimed to be the work of Kirkpatrick Macmillan and to date back even further). More recent attempts to make this kind of mechanism work include Jarray's revolutionary recumbent introduced in 1921, and the Allenax introduced in the 1980's. This recent version replaces parts of the rods with cables and chains, allowing the use of derailleur gearing. It appears at one bicycle trade exposition after

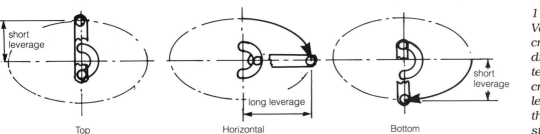

short leverage

Top

long leverage

Horizontal

short leverage

Bottom

17.13. Variable crank length drive systems increase the leverage on the downstroke.

the other without ever having caught on. Perhaps it just doesn't work as well as it is claimed to.

One concept that never seems to die, despite all proof of its inadequacy, is the use of cranks that are either longer or vary in length depending on their orientation in the pedaling cycle. The underlying assumption is that long cranks offer more leverage, allowing more power to be done with the same force, or the same power with less force. How silly: the bicycle's transmission ratio can take care of that and the rider's output can't be increased over what his physical abilities determine.

Sure, long cranks are probably more effective for riders with long upper legs, but so are short cranks for those whose legs are shorter. The 170—175mm crank length used on most bikes is an excellent choice for the vast majority of riders, and the option to replace them is there for those who feel they need it. Ideally, the bicycle should be designed for the crank length actually used: the bottom bracket should be slightly higher if very long cranks are installed to keep the pedals from hitting the ground.

More subtly wrong is the concept of variable length cranks shown in Fig. 17.13, which is the underlying principle of a number of special drive units introduced from time to time. Here the crank effectively gets longer on the down stroke, increasing the leverage, to shorten again on the rest of the pedaling cycle. It's all in vain: the supposed advantage of the longer leverage on the downstroke is not real, because the total distance between top and bottom position of the pedals stays the same — and on designs where it does not, anything said above for longer cranks applies.

Oval and other non-round chainrings are all based on the same erroneous kind of reasoning as the concept of longer or variable length cranks. In the 80's, Shimano spent a fortune on (successfully) advertising its egg-shaped BioPace chainrings to convince the public there

Long Cranks and Other Tricks

17.14. A recent attempt to revolutionize the drivetrain with variable length cranks. This is the Canadian-German STS Power-Pedal.

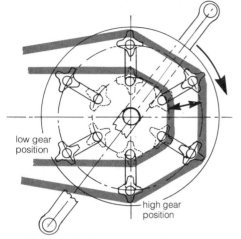

17.15. Most infinitely variable transmissions for bicycles rely on this principle.

17.16. Deal Drive automatic transmission.

Automatic and Infinitely Variable Gears

would be an advantage to this shape due to the distribution of forces during the pedal cycle. They put up a smoke screen of highly scientific looking graphs and formulas — and other companies followed suit with their own non-round designs the public started demanding.

It took Shimano five years to come out with a new, more efficient form of chainring that was nearly round, finally followed by the ultimate High Power BioPace, which turned out to be perfectly round. But I suppose millions will be fooled again the next time a big company tries to sell them such a bill of goods.

Other developments based on the same fallacy as the variable length crank and the oval chainring include cam-assisted devices that reduce the length of the power stroke and increase that of the recovery phase in each crank revolution. This is based on the physiological fact that short powerful muscle contractions, followed by long recovery phases, allow a higher output to be maintained. Other manufacturers, who have heard something about the concept but don't even understand the theory behind it, have done similar things to achieve the opposite effect. Sure, if you believe in the benefits, the placebo effect will be enough to give you the feeling of greater efficiency, but self-hypnosis would provide the same benefit.

One concept that is perhaps more promising than any of the tricks covered so far is pedaling backward. After all why should we have to pedal in such a way that the leg is extended forward and withdrawn in an almost vertical position. Doing it the other way round is not particularly difficult, and some tests indicate that it is perhaps marginally more efficient. It remains a mystery that this simple trick, which any handyman can teach his own bike by running the chain differently, has not been pursued more extensively.

This is another dream of most non-cyclists: gears that adjust themselves automatically to the conditions, or at least allow easy selection without having to shift in distinct steps. Actually, since the introduction of indexed gearing, which takes most of the guesswork out of gear shifting, especially in conjunction with Shimano's Hyperglide tooth design, which allows shifting under load, this demand should become less prevalent. Even so, attempts to provide an automatic transmission still continue to be pursued.

The wonderful thing about modern-day index gearing is that it works with otherwise normal components:

you need neither a different frame, nor a different crankset, nor anything else beyond a special shifter and matching cable. And it seems even the novice can handle most systems without problems, which is not always the case with the more complex automatic or infinitely variable gearing systems that have been introduced from time to time.

All such systems require major modifications to the bike, meaning that they can't succeed unless several bicycle manufacturers agree to design their production models around them. The problem with most automatic systems is that the human factor is overlooked: the cyclist feels differently one day than another, even from one minute to the other. While an engine is fully predictable and can work well with an automatic transmission, the cyclist may want to go uphill in one gear today, in another tomorrow, while the automatic system would force him to ride in the same gear each time.

The most recent, and probably most perfected, automatic transmission introduced so far was the model known as Deal Drive, invented in the 1980's by a French engineer working in Britain (see Fig. 17.16). Like all other such devices, it was rather heavy, but it worked like a charm and its efficiency was about as high as that of normal gearing systems.

Most infinitely variable gearing systems are based on a system by which the individual chainrings in the front are replaced by concentrically arranged separate smaller toothed wheels that can be moved equally far in or out, as shown in Fig. 17.15. In the retracted position, they form what is effectively a small chainring; when extended out, they provide the high gearing achieved with a large chainring. Excel's patented Cambio Gear of the mid eighties and the Tokheim design of the early seventies were both based on this principle, and neither of them ever made it commercially.

17.17. The first Moulton of around 1962 — with small wheels and suspension both front and rear.

Alternate Frame Designs and Materials

Bicycle frames don't have to be made with steel tubing joined together in the familiar shape. Although it is hard to understand what is wrong with the familiar frame, I can sympathize with those who want to travel different paths. Different materials and different joining methods have been introduced or at least suggested at times, and recently there has been a veritable influx of revolutionary designs using other materials and construction techniques.

The idea of a plastic bike has been around for a long time, early versions dating back to the fifties. A com-

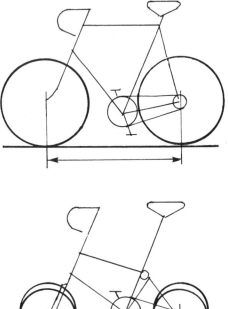

17.18. Comparison between dimensions of regular bike and Moulton's small-wheeled machine.

17.19. Probably the best folding bike available: This Montague bicycle is based on conventional bicycle geometry and hinges around the seat tube.

mercially produced plastic bike was introduced in the 80's under the name Itera. Like most of the earlier ones, it was not a success, probably because it did not address the whole concept of the bicycle, but merely replaced the frame with something that looked more like a motor scooter than a bicycle. Although this provided slightly better protection to the rider's clothing, the use of plastic did not really solve any problem that was inherent in the conventional design.

The argument that plastic does not rust is rather insignificant, because the frame is about the last part of a bike that will rust — long after rims, spokes, hubs and cranks, chains, chainrings and handlebars have become corroded. Add to that the fact that the plastic frame reverberates, amplifying any sounds generated as the bike bounces along the road, as well as the increased weight combined with reduced rigidity, and you have a concept that is sure to fail, as the Swedish state, which had financed the whole idea, learned the hard way.

Recent years have brought both aluminum and titanium tubing, followed by carbon fiber reinforced composites and magnesium. The latter materials are no longer restricted to the conventional tubular shapes joined together by conventional methods. One-piece frame designs using these materials have not only been shown, they are now commercially available. Some of them may have certain virtues for certain applications, but none have so far hinted at being competitive with the conventional frame construction method on all counts.

An entirely different way is still open: the use of thinner tubing in a fully triangulated design. This method can achieve a lighter and very rigid structure if done right. Take a look at many modern structures such as tall building site cranes, and you get an idea of the concept. Moulton's present generation of small-wheeled bicycles is built this way: expensive, but beautiful and sound from an engineering standpoint.

The first bike built with thin tubes was the Dursley Pederson, designed around the turn of the century by a Danish engineer working in Britain. This design is characterized by more than the thin tubes: it also uses cables instead of rigid members to take up the tension forces that result in certain members due to the fully triangulated design. The problem of this design was its inadequate lateral stability, largely due to the fact that the cables were only tensioned by the rider's weight.

A more recent and more satisfactory design on the

same basis is one introduced by the Dutch industrial designer Frans de la Haye in 1979. This design, recently adapted in essence by California mountain bike frame builder Joe Breeze, uses a cross-shaped frame held under tension by tie cables. Unlike Breezes design with its continuous cables, the original was fully collapsible and was perfectly rigid under all kinds of static and dynamic loads.

Bicycles are often too big to transport easily, as anyone arriving at an airport with his machine will soon find out. Most US airlines now punish the cyclist with such exorbitant excess luggage charges that it may seem cheaper to buy another bike at the destination. This reasoning led to the development of folding bicycles.

Folding bicycle designs have been around a long time: I have found patents dating back to the last century. The first practical folders were developed during the first twenty years of the twentieth century with military use in mind. Not until the 1950's did the idea surface again seriously. This time, the manufacturers used smaller wheels, the prototype of most of these designs being the Japanese Star bicycle.

The first generation of Moulton bicycles picked up on the idea of the small wheels but distinguished itself from the others by including all the details that were needed to turn this into a fully satisfactory bicycle. It was unfortunate that this concept was eventually killed by its own popularity: Moulton sold out to Raleigh who stripped it bare of its virtues and retained only the name and the small wheels. During most of the sixties, the small-wheel bicycle, despite its discomfort, dominated a large part of the European market — setting bicycle technology back by at least as many years.

More recently, interesting compact designs have been introduced. Not only did Moulton return with a second generation, as was mentioned earlier in this chapter, but a number of other manufacturers also came up with more or less satisfactory designs. On the one hand, most of these are easier to disassemble or fold than the Moulton, which does require rather extensive nuts-and-bolts work to separate or join the two parts. On the other hand, they are compromises, few of which are really rigid, light and adjustable enough for serious use, especially by tall cyclists. The very light Bickerton and the extremely compact DaHon do deserve special mention under the compact machines, while the Montague should not be overlooked because it is essentially a full size bicycle when it comes to riding, even though it does not fold down to quite such a small package.

Folding and Parting Bicycles

17.20. Bickerton folder with lightweight aluminum frame and tiny wheels. Collapsed, it is small and light enough to be carried as luggage on just about any bus, train or plane.

17.21.
Simple coasting
test set-up. Use
this method to
evaluate the rela-
tive efficiency of
bikes and compo-
nents.

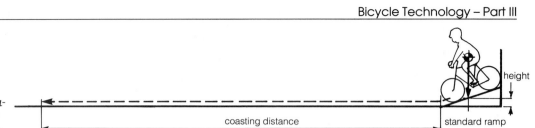

coasting distance   standard ramp

Home Testing

The relative virtues of different bicycle or component designs can often be tested objectively by the interested cyclist. This has the advantage that it is possible to test for those properties that seem personally relevant. In this section a few simple testing techniques will be suggested.

Many properties can be established by a simple rolling test, using a set-up as illustrated in Fig. 17.21. Make sure the bike starts with the rider's center of gravity at the same point each time and let it roll down a known ramp over a standard surface. The bike that rolls over the longest distance has the best rolling properties. Even more accurate would be a similar test using an accelerometer, a $400 device that measures how much the bike is retarded.

17.22. Weird and wonderful: Designer's answers, such as this Strida bicycle from England, are rarely efficient — or even comfortable.

Another interesting method allows testing the drive-train components, but also such factors as riding position, seat height and crank length for any particular rider. To do this, use a heart rate monitor and a cyclo-simulator, which is a turbo trainer equipped with a wattmeter to measure the output. Realizing that the cyclist's pulse is a pretty reliable indicator of relative effort, the combination of this device with a pulse rate monitor gives you the closest thing possible to a work physiology laboratory on a reasonable budget. You can compare the pulse rate that results from reaching the same output under different conditions — different bikes, different components, different gears, or the same bike adjusted differently. Whatever combination requires the lowest heart rate is the most efficient.

Chapter 18
The Bicycle of the Future?

This last chapter will be a somewhat more personal interpretation of the bicycle and its role in the future. To be quite honest, I doubt whether future bicycles will look very different from those of the present time. Similarly, I would answer the question about the future of the bicycle less wildly enthusiastic than some of my environmentally hopeful friends. Of course, I may be badly mistaken in these predictions — and indeed it would make life more interesting if I were. But most of what is being projected had as fair a chance in the past as it ever will in the future; if they didn't make it then, why should they make it now?

Most of what I call the *Bicycle Fiction* images that are conjured up by those who see a golden future for two-wheeled self-propelled transportation are totally unrealistic. They present visions of a world with roads dominated by sleek pedal-driven cars, with overhead monorails in which the passengers sit merrily pedaling away, while fully enclosed recumbents dart by on separate bicycle paths. From the air, the whole pedal-driven mess is being controlled by police in human-powered helicopters.

The underlying assumptions are so unrealistic as to make this vision a sure loser. In fact, nowhere today are we any closer to realizing any of this in practice than we were when such concepts were first drawn up in the 1950's. In this chapter, I will present my own expectations for the future, comparing them, as well as the premises on which they are based, with those of my more optimistic or imaginative colleagues.

Such visions are all based on unrealistic assumptions. One of these assumptions is the total collapse of external energy sources, combined with a sudden desire on the part of the populace to maintain their mobility on the one hand, while accepting the need to provide the requisite propulsive power themselves. The alternative, and more popular vision, is the one by which bicycles and other human powered vehicles become so much more attractive that those who now drive around in cars will be converted to the cause of self-propulsion. The one is as unlikely as the other.

Let us first take a closer look at the presumed prototype of tomorrow's vehicle, the HPV, or human powered

18.1. He was going to revolutionize the bicycle industry: European designer Colani. Other than some balsa wood models, nothing remains of these grandiose plans. If you have read this book, it will not be difficult to appreciate why, looking at this photo.

18.2. Fully enclosed recumbent on three wheels. This Euro-Vector is still one of the world's fastest HPV's. Interestingly enough, the aerodynamic shape of this one was not computer-generated, as was the original US Vector, but 'eyeballed' by the German physicist-framebuilder Hans-Christian Smolik.

Human Powered Vehicles

18.3. This HPV was raced successfully as early as 1914.

18.4. Four-wheeled cruiser. Although it offers weather protection and looks sleek, it is sluggish and clumsy — hardly the transport of the future.

The Cycling Power Equation

vehicle. Although most interest in these sleek machines was generated since the 1970's, similar concepts have been around since record attempts were first made on streamlined bicycles by renowned bicycle racers before the outbreak of the First World War.

In addition to the things said in the preceding chapter about the concepts on which these machines are based, we should take a look at their actual form and use as developed until now. Whether another 10, or even 100 years of development will lead to such improvement that they will lend themselves to mass use can perhaps best be judged by extrapolating their development to date.

In the HPV races that are held regularly under the auspices of the IHPVA (International Human Powered Vehicle Association), some impressive speeds have been reached by such machines — sometimes exceeding 100 km/h (62mph). That's in an all out sprint with a flying start over a distance of 200m (650ft). Not really all that impressive when you realize that regular bicycles in competition reach speeds of 80km/h (50mph) over similar distances.

Although the speed reached over such a short sprint may say something about the vehicle's aerodynamic properties, a more practical measure is the speed reached continuously over a longer distance. Under such conditions, as established in the one hour time trial, the HPV's performance is less impressive. So far they have not improved on the records established on regular machines by more than 10%, even when ridden by highly trained racing cyclists.

That's after nearly eighty years of development, of which the last twenty were quite intensive, with international cooperation and commercial sponsoring. In fact, the hour record on regular bicycles (presently more than 52km) has been improved more during that time than that on HPV's.

All work on HPV's aimed at optimizing the speed reached on them is based on a comparison between the available propulsive power and the power required to overcome the resistances of the bicycle. The ultimate speed can be determined by equating the two. The total resistance that must be overcome when cycling is comprised of the following components:

☐ Rolling resistance of the tires on the road surface
☐ Air resistance, or drag, of bike and rider relative to the surrounding air (with or without wind)

☐ Friction resistance of the bicycle's various moving parts
☐ Resistance against acceleration, determined by the inertia of the moving mass of bike and rider
☐ The effect of gravity when going up (or down) hill.

When all these factors are considered, the required power output can be determined from the following (simplified) formula as a function of speed and acceleration:

$$P = v \left(F_r + F_d + F_g + 0.5\, a^2\, m\right)/\eta$$

where:

P	= required power output in watt
v	= speed in m/sec
F_r	= rolling resistance, which is essentially proportional to the speed (given tire pressure and road surface quality) in N (Newton)
F_d	= air drag in N, which is essentially proportional to the square of the speed relative to the surrounding air
F_g	= weight factor, calculated by multiplying the weight of bike and rider in N with the incline expressed as a decimal (or one hundredth this value expressed as a percentage)
a	= acceleration in m/sec^2
m	= mass of bike and rider in kg
η	= the efficiency, which is a function of the resistances in the bicycle's drive train.

For conditions of steady speed and level road, the acceleration and gravity factors can be left unconsidered, leading to the following simpler steady-state, level road formula:

$$P = v \left(F_r + F_d\right)/\eta$$

HPV's have to get their improvement over the regular bicycle out of a reduction of the air drag value, F_d in these formulas. Everything else can be improved at least as easily on a regular bike as on an HPV. Take weight and mass, which are invariably lower, or more favorable, for the regular bicycle than for the HPV. The other factor is rolling resistance, which is easier to minimize without undue discomfort on a road bike than lying flat in an HPV. Fig. 18.6 summarizes the results on a level road at steady speed for a number of different machines: regular bike in upright position, racing bike in low crouched position, and HPV.

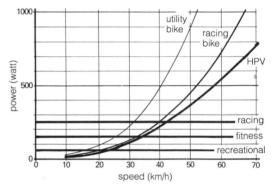

18.5. Colani's dream HPV. Although it is optimistically marked with the inscription '100km/h,' it never got to be more than a scale model.

18.6. Relationship between output and speed as a function of bicycle type.

18.7. Today's track racer still looks remarkably much like a conventional bicycle, despite disk wheels.

18.8 .Three years of work went into this experimental HPV at Oldenburg University's Applied Physics Department.

18.9. Prof. Schöndorf (left) of Cologne Technical University has developed some interesting human powered vehicles.

Comfort and Suspension

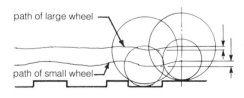

18.10. Wheel size and its effect on uneven surfaces: Smaller wheels have more 'ups and downs.'

The cyclist's output, here referred to as P_c followed by a number, must be equated to the value for P to calculate the speed v. It has been found that cyclists can be divided into three categories, each with particular riding habits and power output level:

☐   The casual and utility cyclist: P_{C1} =   60W
☐   The fitness or fast recreational cyclist: P_{C2} = 150W
☐   The racing cyclist P_{C3} = 250W

These values are represented in Fig. 18.6 as horizontal lines. Wherever such a line intersects the curves for the required output, the speed reached by that cyclist with that bike can be read off. The HPV brings an advantage only to the racer, while the casual or utility cyclist does not reach a noticeably higher speed on the HPV than he does on the racing bike — in fact, this person would benefit considerably more by replacing his utility bike by a racing machine. Thus, the UCI regulations, which until 1990 prescribed the limits of design dimensions for bikes used in sanctioned races, can not be blamed for stagnating development.

Curiously enough, this is exactly the public the propagators of the future bicycle millennium have in mind: the non-cyclist or hitherto casual cyclist who has to be dragged from behind the steering wheel of his car to appreciate the virtues of self-propulsion. Fitness and racing cyclist ride bicycles anyway, they are quite satisfied but are too small in overall numbers to make much of an impact on the overall situation. In addition, HPV would need more development than they have undergone to date if they are to be made roadworthy and practical. So far, none of them are much good when ridden on public roads — and even less so when faced with the non-riding situations bicycles are exposed to, including storage and transportation.

As described in Chapter 17, most of the concepts for tomorrow's dream bike include the wish to sit back the way you do in a Porche. If you've ever driven any distance in that kind of car, you may know that it is not as comfortable in the long run as it is exhilarating at first. On a bicycle, it makes even less sense than in a car, because you have to move your legs around and around.

Whatever else one tries to achieve, two goals remain essential: minimizing rolling resistance and keeping the whole structure as light as possible. Leaning back, there is no way you can be comfortable without additional suspension. Adding any kind of suspension negatively affects at least one, if not both of these criteria.

Thicker tires add weight, and if inflated less to increase their cushioning effect, the rolling resistance goes up too. For road use, all other kinds of suspension, though less effective, tend to have the same effects of increased weight. The one place to use suspension is off-road, because on very rough surfaces, traction can be improved by means of a suspension, and the tires can be inflated harder, resulting in a greater overall efficiency.

Of course, futurists also expect their utopian road bicycles to have more, rather than less, comfort compared to the conventional bike of yesterday. In the low-slung design that is taken for granted in most of these concepts, small wheels and a low body position are required. Both increase the need for an effective suspension, even to get the same comfort — much more so if a higher degree of comfort is required. All this adds weight and further complicates the machine. The effect of small wheels on comfort and energy recovery is illustrated in Fig. 18.10. You may also refer to the comments about this subject in Chapter 17. Another example would be the fact that the low slung body position only works well if a restraint holds the rider's back in place. But that then has to be designed in such a way that it allows the perspiration generated at the physical output level of cycling to evaporate.

The point I am trying to make with this example is that, to be practically suitable, any bike design that differs drastically from that of the conventional model requires so much in the way of other tricks as to become hopelessly complicated and often harder to handle.

Very similar to the arguments for the other aspects of the HPV and similar special designs are those in favor of enclosures. Since people drive around in cars that are covered, it is assumed they will be more easily converted to riding bikes if they are covered too. Except if one considers that cycling is hard work, generating enough heat to make any enclosure unbearable. Air conditioning cannot be the answer: to remove the heat generated by the cyclist, approximately ten times the cyclist's output has to be made available to the air conditioner.

There are other problems with this idea. Whereas a conventional bicycle is relatively insensitive to cross winds, the enclosed model is easily swept aside by a strong wind or passing trucks. Handling the machine, easy enough on the conventional bicycle, is a veritable nightmare with anything enclosed. The materials used must be very light, so are quite prone to damage

18.11. A futuristic utility bicycle that is supposed to be practical — but not ridable, as the author found out when requesting a closer look at it.

Cycling Under Cover

18.12. Dream bike of the fifties. This American designed plastic-framed bike never did go into production.

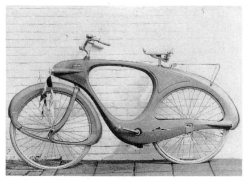

18.13. A recent attempt at designing a plastic utility bicycle. This pedal-driven motor scooter weighs nearly as much as its motorized counterpart.

18.14. Despite heavy funding from Volvo and the Swedish state, this Itera plastic bike didn't live up to the expectations.

caused either accidentally or by vandalism. And while today's bike can be transported or parked relatively painlessly, anything enclosed resists any attempts in that direction.

At least one experiment with the presumably practical use of fully enclosed bicycles — roadworthy versions of HPV's — for commuting was carried out in 1980 with more publicity than the results warranted. Two such vehicles were ridden between Davis and Sacramento in California on a closed-off freeway section during the otherwise praiseworthy though short reign of the environmentally conscious Adriana Gianturco as head of Caltrans, the California state transportation authority.

The route and the time were selected to avoid significant hills and wind, curves and other nuisances or obstacles. The riders were both skilled bicycle racers, experienced handling HPV's. An entire infrastructure was provided, with changing facilities at the end of the freeway section, transport into the city, reporters and medics, traffic police and others standing guard. The result was proclaimed a great success and promptly buried in the files: the cyclists had managed to complete the trip in about five minutes less than they would have done on normal racing bikes.

So, a success after all? Not really. Unless the state can be counted on to provide every commuter with enough training to bring up his speed to the point where an HPV is of any speed advantage. Unless whole freeways are permanently blocked to other traffic to allow HPV's to do their thing. Unless changing facilities and showers, taxi service and police protection are provided at the end of every trip. Unless California summer weather can be guaranteed everywhere all the time. In short, it's all of no use whatsoever.

Don't take my skeptical approach too seriously, though. There may be sound reasons for some people to believe in, or at least dream of, a golden age for self-propelled transportation. There are good, or at least understandable, reasons to have faith in man's perfection, which should also increase his appreciation of the bicycle and concern about the environment. Even if most of tomorrow's bikes will look just like today's machines, even if most people riding them will do so because they are a little different from the rest, there is nothing wrong with hoping some will choose different machines and some who prefer to drive their cars today may someday voluntarily choose to cycle. Just don't expect either a social or a technical bicycle revolution — either now or in the future.

Table 1. Metric gear table: development in meters _____ ## Appendix

	Number of teeth on sprocket																		
	12	13	14	15	16	17	18	19	20	21	22	23	24	25	26	27	28	29	30
28	4.98	4.59	4.27	3.98	3.75	3.51	3.32	3.14	2.99	2.84	2.71	2.60	2.48	2.39	2.30	2.21	2.13	2.06	1.99
29	5.14	4.76	4.42	4.12	3.88	3.64	3.44	3.25	3.09	2.94	2.81	2.68	2.57	2.47	2.38	2.29	2.21	2.13	2.06
30	5.34	4.92	4.58	4.27	4.01	3.77	3.56	3.36	3.20	3.05	2.91	2.76	2.68	2.55	2.46	2.36	2.29	2.20	2.13
31	5.51	5.08	4.73	4.41	4.14	3.89	3.68	3.48	3.31	3.15	3.01	2.84	2.75	2.64	2.54	2.44	2.36	2.28	2.21
32	5.69	5.24	4.89	4.55	4.27	4.02	3.80	3.59	3.41	3.25	3.10	2.92	2.84	2.72	2.62	2.52	2.44	2.35	2.28
33	5.87	5.41	5.04	4.69	4.40	4.14	3.92	3.71	3.52	3.35	3.20	3.00	2.93	2.81	2.71	2.60	2.52	2.42	2.35
34	6.04	5.57	5.19	4.84	4.53	4.27	4.04	3.83	3.63	3.45	3.29	3.09	3.02	2.90	2.79	2.69	2.60	2.49	2.42
35	6.22	5.74	5.34	4.98	4.67	4.40	4.16	3.94	3.75	3.56	3.39	3.17	3.11	2.99	2.87	2.76	2.68	2.75	2.48
36	6.40	5.90	5.49	5.12	4.80	4.53	4.27	4.05	3.85	3.66	3.49	3.25	3.20	3.08	2.95	2.84	2.75	2.64	2.56
37	6.58	6.07	5.75	5.27	4.93	4.65	4.38	4.16	3.95	3.76	3.59	3.34	3.29	3.17	3.03	2.92	2.83	2.72	2.63
38	6.77	6.23	5.80	5.41	5.07	4.78	4.50	4.72	4.06	3.86	3.70	3.24	3.38	3.25	3.11	3.00	2.90	2.79	2.70
39	6.94	6.40	5.94	5.55	5.21	4.90	4.62	4.38	4.16	3.96	3.79	3.62	3.47	3.33	3.20	3.08	2.97	2.86	2.77
40	7.12	6.57	6.10	5.69	5.34	5.02	4.74	4.50	4.27	4.07	3.88	3.71	3.56	3.42	3.28	3.16	3.05	2.94	2.84
41	7.30	6.73	6.25	5.84	5.47	5.15	4.86	4.61	4.37	4.17	3.98	3.80	3.64	3.50	3.36	3.24	3.13	3.01	2.92
42	7.47	6.90	6.40	5.98	5.60	5.27	4.98	4.72	4.48	4.27	4.07	3.90	3.75	3.58	3.45	3.32	3.20	3.08	2.99
43	7.65	7.06	6.56	6.12	5.74	5.40	5.10	4.83	4.59	4.37	4.17	3.98	3.82	3.67	3.53	3.40	3.28	3.16	3.06
44	7.83	7.23	6.71	6.26	5.87	5.52	5.22	4.94	4.70	4.47	4.28	4.08	3.91	3.76	3.61	3.48	3.36	3.24	3.13
45	8.01	7.39	6.86	6.40	6.00	5.65	5.34	5.05	4.80	4.57	4.37	4.18	4.00	3.84	3.69	3.56	3.43	3.31	3.20
46	8.18	7.55	7.01	6.55	6.14	5.78	5.45	5.17	4.91	4.67	4.46	4.27	4.09	3.93	3.78	3.64	3.51	3.39	3.28
47	8.36	7.72	7.17	6.69	6.27	5.90	5.57	5.28	5.02	4.78	4.56	4.36	4.18	4.01	3.86	3.72	3.59	3.46	3.35
48	8.54	7.88	7.32	6.83	6.40	6.03	5.69	5.39	5.12	4.88	4.66	4.45	4.27	4.10	3.94	3.80	3.66	3.53	3.42
49	8.72	8.05	7.47	6.97	6.54	6.15	5.81	5.50	5.23	4.98	4.75	4.55	4.36	4.18	4.02	3.87	3.75	3.60	3.49
50	8.90	8.21	7.63	7.12	6.67	6.28	5.93	5.62	5.34	5.08	4.85	4.64	4.45	4.27	4.10	3.95	3.82	3.68	3.56
51	9.07	8.38	7.78	7.26	6.81	6.40	6.05	5.73	5.44	5.18	4.95	4.73	4.54	4.35	4.19	4.03	3.89	3.75	3.63
52	9.25	8.54	7.93	7.40	6.94	6.53	6.17	5.84	5.55	5,29	5.04	4.83	4.62	4.44	4.27	4.11	3.97	3.82	3.70
53	9.43	8.70	8.08	7.54	7.07	6.66	6.29	5.95	5.66	5.39	5.14	4.92	4.71	4.52	4.35	4.19	4.04	3.90	3.77
54	9.61	8.87	8.23	7.69	7.20	6.78	6.40	6.07	5.76	5.49	5.24	5.01	4.80	4.61	4.43	4.27	4.12	3.97	3.85
55	9.78	9.03	8.39	7.83	7.33	6.90	6.52	6.16	5.87	5.59	5.34	5.10	4.89	4.70	4.51	4.34	4.19	4.04	3.92
56	9.97	9.20	8.54	7.97	7.47	7.03	6.64	6.29	5.98	5.69	5.43	5.20	4.98	4.78	4.58	4.42	4.27	4.12	3.98

number of teeth on chainring

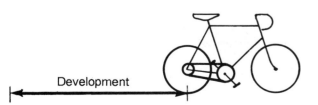

Development

Table 2. English gear table: gear size in inches

number of teeth on chainring	\ Number of teeth on sprocket																		
	12	13	14	15	16	17	18	19	20	21	22	23	24	25	26	27	28	29	30
28	63	58	54	50	47	44	42	40	38	36	34	33	31	30	29	28	27	26	25
29	65	60	56	52	49	46	43	42	39	38	35	34	33	31	30	29	28	27	26
30	67	62	58	54	51	48	45	43	41	39	37	35	34	32	31	30	29	28	27
31	70	65	60	56	52	50	47	44	42	40	38	37	36	34	32	31	30	29	28
32	72	67	62	58	54	51	48	45	43	41	39	38	36	35	33	32	31	30	29
33	74	69	64	60	56	53	50	47	45	43	41	39	37	36	34	33	32	31	30
34	76	71	66	61	57	54	51	48	46	44	42	40	38	37	35	34	33	32	31
35	78	73	68	63	59	56	53	50	48	45	43	41	39	38	36	35	34	33	33
36	81	75	69	65	61	57	54	51	49	46	44	42	40	39	37	36	35	34	32
37	84	77	71	67	63	59	56	53	50	48	46	44	41	40	39	37	36	35	33
38	86	79	73	68	64	60	57	54	51	49	47	45	42	41	40	38	37	35	34
39	87	81	75	70	65	62	58	55	53	50	47	46	43	42	41	39	38	36	35
40	90	83	77	72	68	64	60	57	54	51	49	47	45	43	42	40	39	37	36
41	93	85	79	74	70	65	62	59	56	53	51	48	46	44	43	41	40	38	37
42	95	87	81	76	71	67	63	60	57	54	52	49	47	45	44	42	41	39	38
43	97	89	83	77	73	68	65	61	58	55	53	50	48	46	45	43	41	40	39
44	99	91	85	79	74	70	66	63	59	57	54	52	50	48	46	44	42	44	48
45	101	93	87	81	76	72	68	64	61	58	55	53	51	49	47	45	43	42	41
46	104	96	88	83	78	73	69	65	62	59	57	54	52	50	48	46	44	43	41
47	106	98	91	85	79	75	71	67	63	60	58	55	53	51	49	47	45	44	42
48	108	100	93	86	81	76	72	68	65	62	59	56	54	52	50	48	46	45	43
49	110	102	95	88	83	78	74	70	66	63	60	58	55	53	51	49	47	46	44
50	113	104	96	90	84	79	75	71	68	64	61	59	56	54	52	50	48	47	45
51	115	106	98	92	86	81	77	72	69	66	63	60	58	55	53	51	49	48	46
52	117	108	100	94	88	83	78	74	70	67	64	61	59	56	54	52	50	48	47
53	119	110	102	95	89	84	80	75	72	68	65	62	60	57	55	53	51	49	48
54	122	112	104	97	91	86	81	77	73	69	66	63	61	58	56	54	52	50	49
55	124	114	106	99	93	87	83	78	75	71	68	65	62	59	57	55	53	51	50
56	126	116	108	100	95	89	84	80	76	72	69	66	63	60	58	56	54	52	50

Table 3. Conversion between metric and English gearing designations

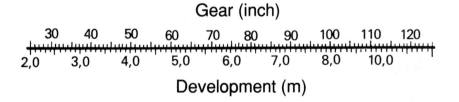

Gear (inch)

Development (m)

Table 4. Bicycle screw threading standards

Location	BCI standard (British)	ISO standard (French)	Italian standard	Swiss standard
bottom bracket fixed (RH) side	1.370 x 24tpi (L)	35 x 1mm (R)	1.370 x 24tpi 55°(R)	35 x 24 tpi (R)
bottom bracket adj. (LH) side	1.370 x 24tpi (R)	35 x 1mm (R)	1.370 x 24tpi 55°(R)	35 x 24 tpi (R)
pedal LH side	9/16 x 20tpi (L)	14 x 1.25mm (L)	(BCI)	(BCI)
pedal RH side	9/16 x 20tpi (R)	14 x 1.25mm (R)	(BCI)	(BCI)
headset (standard)	1.000 x 24 tpi	25 x 1mm	1.000 x 24 tpi 55°	(BCI)
headset (oversize)	not standardized in any system			
freewheel	1.370 x 24 tpi	34.7 x 1 mm	35 x 1mm	(BCI)
derailleur eye	(ISO)	10 x 1mm	10 mm x 26 tpi	(ISO)

Table 5. Typical bearing ball sizes for bicyce applications

Bearing location	ball size inch	mm (approx)	to measure 8 balls (mm)
bottom bracket	1/4	6.4	51
rear hub	1/4	6.4	51
front hub	3/16	4.8	37
	7/32	5.0	40
headset	5/32	4.0	32
	3/16	4.8	37
pedals	5/32	4.0	32
freewheel	1/8	3.2	25

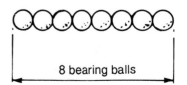

8 bearing balls

Table 6. Tire sizes and matching rims

Nominal wheel dia inch (mm)	Rim shoulder circumference (mm)	ETRTO designation (mm)	British/Dutch designation (inch)	French designation (mm)	US designation (inch)
14 (350)	939	32–299	14 x 1⅜		
	911	37 –290		350A	
16 (400)	1096	32–349	16 x 1⅜		
	1068	37–340'		400A	
	996				16 x 1¾
18 (450)	1253	32–399	18 x 1⅜	450 x 32A	
	1225	37–390		450A	
20 (500)	1417	32–450	20 x 1⅜	500 x 32A	20 x 1⅜
	1382	37–440		500A	
	1327	47–406			20 x 1.75
22 (550)	1574	32–501	22 x 1⅜	550 x 32A	
	1539	37–490		550A	
24 (600)	1728	32–550	24 x 1⅜	600 x 32A	
	1700	37–541		600A	
	1646				24 x 1.75
					24 x 2.125
26 (650)	1876	32–597	26 x 1⅜	650 x 32A	
	1854	37–590		650A	
	1835	40–584		650B	
	1805	47–559			26 x 1.750
		54–559			26 x 2.125
	1794	47–571	26 x 1¾		
27 (675)	1979	32–630	27 x 1¼		27 x 1¼
		28–630	27 x 1⅛		27 x 1⅛
		25–630	27 x 1		27 x 1
28 (700)	1954	32–622	28 x 1⅝ x 1⅜	700C	
		28–622	28 x1⅝ x 1⅛	700 x 28C	
		25–622		700 x 25C	
	2017	37–642	28 x 1⅜	700A	28 x 1⅜
	1995	40–635	28 x 1½	700B Std	

Table 7. Spoke thickness designations in gauge numbers and mm

Thickness mm	British gauge no.	French gauge no.	Application
1.4	17	10	time trial records
1.6	16	11	light road racing
1.8	15	12	racing and fitness
2.0	14	13	touring and mountain bike
2.3	13	14	heavy duty and tandem
2.6	12	15	expeditions

Table 8. Frame sizing in cm and inches

leg length — max. frame size (center bottom bracket to center top tube) (dimension Y; add 1.5 cm or 0.5 in for dimension X)

inseam size inch (cm)	road bike cm	road bike inch	mountain bike cm	mountain bike inch	touring bike cm	touring bike inch
28 (69—70)	45	17	42	16	46	18
29 (71—72)	46	17.5	44	16.5	48	19
(73—74)	48	19	46	17	50	20
30 (75—76)	50	19	48	19	52	21
31 (77—78)	52	21	54	22	50	20
32 (79—80)	54	21.5	56	22	51	20.5
(81—82)	56	22	58	23	53	21
33 (83—84)	58	23	60	24	55	22
34 (85—86)	60	24	62	25	57	22.5
35 (87—89)	62	25	63	25.5	58	23
36 (90—92)	64	26	65	26	60	24

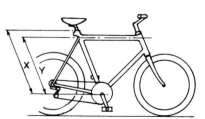

Table 9. Typical frame tubing outside diameters (in mm)

Tube	top tube	seat tube	down tube	head tube	chain stays	seat stays
Road bikes:						
English	25.4	28.6	28.6	31.7	22.0	14.0
French	26.0	28.0	28.0	32.0	22.0	14.0
Mountain bikes:						
regular	28.6	28.6	31.7	33.2	25.4	16.0
oversize	31.7	31.7	33.2	35.0	25.4	16.0

Table 10. Conversion factors between metric and English/US units

Multiply	by	to obtain
Length and distance:		
mm	0.039	inch
cm	0.394	inch
m	3.28	ft
km	0.621	mile
inch	25.4	mm
ft	0.305	m
mile	1.61	km
Mass, force and weight:		
gm	0.035	oz
kg	2.20	lb
N (Newton)	0.225	lbf
lbf (force)	4.45	N
lbm (mass)	0.454	kg
Volume:		
cm^3	0.061	cu in
l	611.0	cu in
l	0.220	gal Imp
l	0.258	gal US
cu in	16.4	cm^3
l	1.76	pint (Imp)
l	2.06	pint (US)
gal (Imp)	4.55	l
gal (US)	3.87	l
pint (Imp)	0.57	l
pint (US)	0.48	l

Multiply	by	to obtain
Work:		
kgm	7.25	ftlb
kWh	3.67×10^3	kgm
kJ	0.948	Btu
kcal	3.97	Btu
ftlb	0.138	kgm
Btu	1.054	kJ
Power:		
kgm/sec	7.22	lb ft/sec
kW	1.34	hp
hp	0.746	kW
Nm/sec	0.723	lb ft/sec
lb ft/sec	1.38	kgm/sec
Pressure and stress:		
kg/cm^2	14.2	psi
N/mm^2	139	psi
bar	0.07	psi
psi	14.2	bar

Temperature:
$$°C = 0.56 \times (°F - 32)$$
$$°F = (1.8 \times °C) + 32$$

Speed:		
km/h	0.622	mph
mph	1.609	km/h

Aerodynamik des Fahrrades. Cologne (D): Fachhochschule Köln, 1983.

Barnett, John. *Barnett's Manual.* Brattleboro (USA): Vitesse Press, 1989.

Berto, Frank. *Bicycling Magazine's Complete Guide to Upgrading Your Bicycle.* Emmaus (USA): Rodale Press, 1988.

Brandt, Jobst. *The Bicycle Wheel.* Mountain View (USA): Avocet, 1983.

Clarijs, J. P. and G. J. van Ingen-Schenau (Eds.). *Wielrennen.* Lochum (NL): De Tijdstroom, 1985.

Coles, Clarence W., John Allen and Harold T. Glenn. *Glenn's New Complete Bicycle Manual.* New York (USA): Crown Publishers, 1987.

Cycling. Rome: CONI — Central Sports School — FIAC, 1971.

The Data Book. (publisher unidentified, Japan), 1983.

DeLong, Fred. *DeLong's Guide to Bicycles and Bicycling.* Radnor, (USA): Chilton Books, 1982.

Evans, David E. *The Ingenious Mr. Pedersen.* Gloucester (GB): Alan Sutton, 1978.

Faria, Irving E. and Peter R. Cavanagh. *The Physiology and Biomechanics of Cycling.* New York (USA): John Wiley & Sons, 1987.

De Fiets (catalog to the exhibition). Rotterdam (NL): Museum Boymans-van Beuningen, 1977.

Fifty Years of Schwinn-Built Bicycles. Chicago (USA): Arnold, Schwinn & Company, 1989.

Forester, John. *Effective Cycling.* Cambridge (USA): MIT-Press, 1986.

Hadland, Tony. *The Sturmey-Archer Story.* (self published, GB, location unidentified), 1987.

——. *The Moulton Bicycle.* (self published, GB, location unidentified), 1982.

Hayduk, Douglas. *Bicycle Metallurgy for Cyclists.* Brattleboro (USA): Vitesse Press, 1987.

Konig, Barry (Ed.). *The Proteus Framebuilding Handbook.* College Park, MD (USA): Proteus Press, 1975.

Krausz, John and Vera van der Reis Krausz (Eds.). *The Bicycling Book.* New York (USA): The Dial Press, 1982.

Lessing, Hans-Erhard (Ed.), *Fahrradkultur 1.* Reinbek (D): Rowohlt, 1982.

McCullagh, James C. (Ed.). *Pedal Power.* Emmaus (USA): Rodale Press, 1977.

Below: A page from The Bicycle Wheel *by Jobst Brandt.*

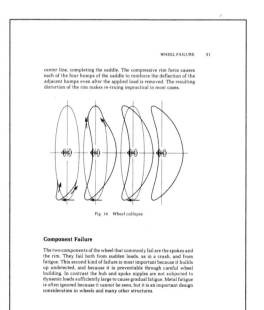

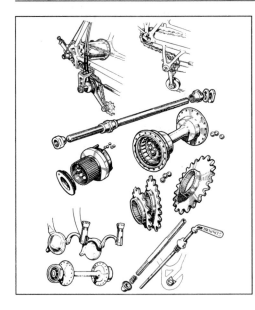

Above: A page from The Data Book

Below: A page from Bicycles and Tricycles *by Archibald Sharp.*

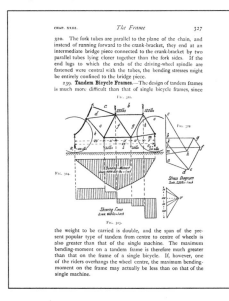

McGurn, James. *On Your Bicycle.* New York (USA): Facts on File, 1987.

Navarro, Ricardo A., Urs Heierli and Victor Beck. *La Bicycleta y Los Triciclos.* St. Gallen (CH): SKAT, 1985.

Oliver, Tony. *Touring Bikes.* Ramsbury (GB): The Crowood Press, 1990.

Rauck, Max B., Gerd Volke and Felix R. Paturi. *Mit dem Fahrrad durch zwei Jahrhunderte.* Aarau (CH): AT Verlag, 1979.

Ritchie, Andrew. *King of the Road.* London (GB): Wildwood House; Berkeley (USA): Ten Speed Press, 1975.

Seray, Jacques. *Deux Roues.* Rodez (F): Éditions du Rouergue, 1988.

Sharp, Archibald. *Bicycles & Tricycles.* London (GB): Longmans, Green, 1896; facsimile reprint: Cambridge (USA): MIT Press, 1977.

Snowling, Steve and Ken Evans. *Bicycle Mechanics.* Huddersfield (GB): Springfield Books, 1986.

Sutherland, Howard, John Porter Hart, John Allen and Ed Colaianni. *Sutherland's Handbook for Bicycle Mechanics.* Berkeley (USA): Sutherland Publications, 1985.

Talbot, Richard P. *Designing and Building Your Own Frameset.* Boston (USA): The Manet Guild, 1985.

Van der Plas, Robert. *The Penguin Bicycle Handbook.* Harmondsworth (GB): Penguin Books, 1983.

——. *Das Fahrrad.* Ravensburg (D): Otto Maier Verlag, 1989.

——. *The Bicycle Repair Book.* San Francisco (USA): Bicycle Books, 1985.

——. *The Mountain Bike Book.* San Francisco (USA): Bicycle Books, 1988.

——. *Cycle Repair, Step by Step.* Huddersfield (GB): Springfield Books, 1988.

Watson, Roderick and Martin Gray. *The Penguin Book of the Bicycle.* Harmondsworth (GB): Penguin Books, 1978.

Whitt, Frank Rowland and David Gordon Wilson. *Bicycling Science.* Cambridge (USA): MIT-Press, 1982.

Winkler, Fritz and Siegfried Rauch. *Fahrradtechnik.* Bielefeld (D): Bielefelder Verlags-Anstalt, 1989.

Wolf, Wilhelm. *Fahrrad und Radfahrer.* Leipzig (D) Otto Spamer, 1890; facsimile reprint: Dortmund (D): Harenberg Kommunikation, 1979.

We issue about four new titles each year. The following list is up to date at the time of going to press. If you want more details, you may order our full-color catalog from the address below or by calling (415) 381-0172.

Title	Author	US Price
The Mountain Bike Book	Rob van der Plas	$9.95
The Bicycle Repair Book	Rob van der Plas	$8.95
The Bicycle Racing Guide	Rob van der Plas	$9.95
The Bicycle Touring Manual	Rob van der Plas	$9.95
Roadside Bicycle Repairs	Rob van der Plas	$4.95
Major Taylor (hardcover)	Andrew Ritchie	$19.95
Bicycling Fuel	Richard Rafoth	$7.95
In High Gear	Samuel Abt	$10.95
Mountain Bike Maintenance	Rob van der Plas	$7.95
The Bicycle Fitness Book	Rob van der Plas	$7.95
The Bicycle Commuting Book	Rob van der Plas	$7.95
The New Bike Book	Jim Langley	$4.95
Tour of the Forest Bike Race (hardcover)	H. E. Thomson	$9.95
Bicycle Technology	Rob van der Plas	$16.95
The Tour de France Up Close (July 1991)	Samuel Abt	$19.95
All Terrain Biking (May 1991)	Jim Zarka	$7.95

We encourage our readers to buy their books at a book store. Our book trade distributor, The Talman Co., can fill any trade order quickly. They have an 800-number (listed in *Books in Print*) that any book shop can use to order our books. In addition, many bicycle and outdoor sport shops carry some of our most popular books.

If your local shop is not willing to order the books you want, you can order directly from us. In that case, please include the price of the book plus postage and handling ($2.50 for the first book, $1.00 for each additional book), as well as sales tax for California mailing addresses. When ordering from Bicycle Books, prepayment or credit card number and expiration date are required. We'll gladly fill your order, but we'd prefer you try the book shop first.

When it comes to buying books, support your local book shop!

To obtain a copy of our current catalog, including full descriptions of all our books, please send your name and address to:
Bicycle Books, Inc.
PO Box 2038
Mill Valley CA 94941
or to the national distributor listed on the back cover if you live in Canada or the UK.